HOW TO FIT A CAR SEAT on a

 CAMEL

and Other Misadventures Traveling with Kids

edited by **Sarah Franklin**

SEAL PRESS

How to Fit a Car Seat on a Camel
And Other Misadventures Traveling with Kids

Published by
Seal Press
A Member of the Perseus Books Group
1700 Fourth Street
Berkeley, California 94710

"Consider Atlanta" by Julia Litton, was previously published on her blog www.julia.typepad.com (Here Be Hippogriffs).

"99 Bottles" by Julie Barton, was previously published on her blog www.alittlepregnant.com.

"Shock and Paw" by C. Lill Ahren was previously published in a shorter version entitled "Safariland Adventure" in the anthology *More Sand in My Bra,* Travelers Tales.

Library of Congress Cataloging-in-Publication Data

How to fit a car seat on a camel : and other misadventures traveling with kids / edited by Sarah Franklin.
   p. cm.
 ISBN-13: 978-1-58005-242-9
 ISBN-10: 1-58005-242-8
 1. Travel. 2. Children--Travel. 3. Family recreation. I. Franklin, Sarah, 1971-
 G151.H677 2008
 910.4--dc22
             2008004013

Cover design by Gia Giasullo
Interior design by Tabitha Lahr
Printed in the U.S.A.
Distributed by Publishers Group West

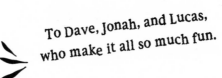

To Dave, Jonah, and Lucas,
who make it all so much fun.

⇒ CONTENTS ⇐

➤ Introduction ≤

Sarah Franklin

Prekids, my husband and I were that cliché of the thirtysomething childless couple, traveling here, there, and everywhere, with just a copy of *The New Yorker* and the latest iPod as accessories. Lest you assume I'm exaggerating our itinerant ways for the sake of a story, here's a list of the trips we made from our home in Seattle the year before our firstborn arrived: Alaska; Hawaii; England and Wales; California; Portland, Oregon; and New York (twice). Oh, and a weeklong road trip to the foothills of the Canadian Rockies, just for good measure.

We traveled by plane, train, and automobile (the "automobile" in question being our "Kids? What kids?" cream convertible Beetle). We journeyed for business and pleasure. We vacationed en masse and à deux. We partook in all activities we could think of, from off-Broadway theater and holistic spa days to snowboarding and surfing. We danced 'til dawn in San Francisco and spent lazy mornings enjoying brunch with the newspaper.

In that last prekids year, with every trip we took we'd look at each other and say, with a mixture of query and reassurance, "We can still do all this with the baby, you know. . . ." Yeah, we were *that* cliché, too: the couple who assumes that our baby, born into a mobile world, will automatically become a mobile baby, fitting neatly into our universe in his/her hipster pouch/sling/backpack, scaling Mount Kilimanjaro with us with nary a peep about altitude sickness.

Ha! Sure, you can travel with a kid. Just don't expect it to be quite the same. In the year after Jonah was born, we held on to our determination to keep on traveling. Okay, so packing for a trip now took a week rather than half an hour, interspersed with algorithm-defying calculations of the precise number of diapers required for a ten-hour plane journey, and just how long a three-hour road trip would *really* take once we'd factored in nursing breaks. *The New Yorker* and the iPods were replaced by *Mr. Brown Can Moo, Can You?* and *Philadelphia Chickens.*

Still, we got out and about—by the time Jonah was a year old, he'd crossed the Atlantic four times, been up to Whistler, B.C., for a week, and taken several weekend minibreaks within Washington State. Not quite the same pace as in the in utero months, but not bad. The destinations themselves, however, were only half the story. As any parent will tell you (and *did* tell us; not that we listened), traveling with a wee one is the time in which the old saying "It's the journey, not the destination, that matters" really comes true. Getting to your destination can be an adventure in and of itself.

Our own experiences of the pre- and postbaby trips made me hungry to hear how others had fared. In yet another cliché of our generation, the individualist in me was keen to find company; surely we weren't the only people for whom the word "vacation" had entirely changed in significance postkids?

The women in this collection answered this question with a resounding "No!", and then some. They proved that not only was I not alone, but that I wasn't even remotely intrepid. Sarah Davies takes the concept of "baby's first flight" to new extremes in her story of flying a two-seater plane across Arizona with her three-month-old as copilot. Elena Aitken braves the high seas in a thirty-nine-foot sailboat with toddler twins, an arrangement that can make any mother shudder in anticipation of all that could go wrong. And Amy Bustraan, in a tale sure to make the most hardened outdoors folk pause, kayaks the rapids with her six-month-old daughter bobbing along in her booster seat.

Sometimes the trips occurred out of necessity rather than careful planning. Julie Barton's tale of "baby's first road trip," involving her premature son, a breast pump with a life of its own, and a freeway full of truckers, is as poignant as it is hilarious. In the same vein, Susan Wolter Nettell tells of taking a six-hundred-plus-mile midwinter train journey from Minnesota to South Dakota with preemie quads, helping her younger sister, the newly overwhelmed mother, bring her babies home. Both of these journeys make for equally touching and hair-raising reading. And as unforeseen road trips go, not many beat Donna Collins Tinsley's story of fleeing Hurricane Frances with a toddler, three teenage daughters, and a motley assortment of pets.

In other cases, trips were not spontaneous events but the result of careful forethought—and still result in outcomes that have us howling in despair and delight. Julia Litton's "Consider Atlanta" will have many readers nodding in rueful recognition with her account of the Thanksgiving trip that almost wasn't, a theme that continues with true Christmas holiday style in Holly Korbey's "Seven Bags, Two Kids, and the Baby Cheeses" and Mary Jane Beaufrand's "Flashdance Snow White."

It seems that there's no end to the variety of situations that can spell disaster when traveling with your beloved offspring. Staying close to home and re-creating the vacations of your own childhood or taking your little darlings to favorite haunts doesn't stave off the mishaps, as Sally Bjornsen, Sabra Ciancelli, and Elizabeth Roca show us. Going abroad just adds a different element of the unexpected to the trip, whether it's in Laos (Willow King), Ecuador (Gabrielle Smith-Dluha), or Niger (Jennifer Margulis). Even a visit to Graceland can be cringe-inducing when one of your party is determined to point out just how dull he finds The King, as Tiffany Fitch's hilarious "All Shook Up" recounts.

Traveling with young children, then, is really an embodiment of the broader life changes that occur when you move from "person" to "parent." Your destination, journey times, suitcase contents, are all determined by the needs of someone other than yourself. Moreover, your own enjoyment of the trip depends on getting these details right in the face of eternal variables. For those of us faintly hoping that travel becomes easier when the wee ones turn into bigger ones and are able to actually appreciate their surroundings and the gift of travel, think again. The sagas related by Dana Standish, Donna Gephart, and Ivy Eisenberg demonstrate all too clearly that preteens and teenagers can be just as "interesting" to travel with as the weenies, even if *Dora the Explorer* has been swapped for the Paris edition of *Vogue*.

So what makes us do it?

In recent years, gas prices notwithstanding, Americans have been traveling more and more. In 2006, 38.3 million people were estimated to have traveled more than fifty miles for Thanksgiving week alone. That's a lot of people traveling with a lot of children. Overseas travel is also on the rise. In 2005, nearly 2.9 million American residents traveled to foreign destinations with their children, according to statistics from the Office of Travel and Tourism Industries. Clearly, despite the pain of packing, despair at the destination, and the obstreperous offspring, travel with our families offers us something valuable that we just can't get at home.

That mysterious something can be found throughout these stories, even among the more hideous details of projectile vomit and frantic potty stops: Traveling, very simply, makes indelible memories that, for better or for worse, are the stuff of family bonding. Think about your own childhood for a moment, and I'll guarantee that you'll start to giggle (or groan) at a long-hidden remembrance of a particularly painful trip or a recurring journey you were forced to make each year, which has now become as integral to your formative years as learning your ABCs.

As our kids grow bigger and more independent, those opportunities to spend quality time with them become fleeting (even if that quality at the time may seem substandard at best!), and we're glad to have had these chances, however cobbled together they were. Stephanie Sylverne, telling of her two-single-mothers-three-kids-and-a-grandfather road trip, touches on the realization that this moment of motherhood will never again be captured or possible—the sense of freedom that comes with spontaneity, and the joys of sharing a twenty-four-hour cross-country car journey and all, with our children. And further afield, on a trip to Germany, J. Anderson Coates articulates the impulse that drives so many of us to make seemingly impossible trips with our young ones; to re-create a memory from our own childhoods; to give to our children what our parents gave to us, be it a sense of wonder, otherness, or simply the feeling of being surrounded by friends and relations for key times in our lives. Certainly this is true of my own family's experience. Trips "home" to the U.K. stopped being merely fun diversions in our hectic urbanite lives and became somehow necessary to the fabric of our family life. Our sense that Jonah needed to know (even at three months) what English countryside looked like and to spend time in his grandparents' homes superceded any horror at the prospect of twenty-one hours of travel time, sixteen hours of jetlag, and ten-thousand-plus miles of travel in a one-week period.

Traveling with kids is undeniably messy, frustrating, and chaotic. But so, too, is life with kids; and if we distill it even further, life itself; and so the memories become a part of our life, and keep us moving forward. As does the sneaking suspicion that once the kids are old enough to be left home and we can travel solo again, we'll have a strange feeling that someone's missing.

All Shook Up

Tiffany Fitch

"I thought Graceland was supposed to be like Disneyland, only funner," Henry, age six, said at the top of his lungs. "It was boring and stupid!"

Tourists decked out in Elvis shirts and caps in the packed trolley broken down near Beale Street, Memphis, turned to stare at us. I wished I could drown in the sweat puddle forming under my rear.

"I want some water," Hannah, age four, howled, although not loud enough to cover Henry, who had perked up under the eyes turned towards him.

"Hate me tender. Hate me true. I hate Elvis. Yes, I do," he sang to his now mildly irritated-looking audience, his entire face a grin, eyes glowing like The King's gold lamé jumpsuit.

"You don't really mean that, honey," I said, loud enough for everyone to hear, lest they think I too was a traitor to the Elvis cause and hang us both as examples from the handholds attached to the ceiling.

"Nope, I really do. He stinks! The only ride that place had was Lisa Marie's crappy swing set and they wouldn't even let me play on it."

Georgie, nine, having recently decided she was too cool for our entire family, scooted down the bench away from us, flipping her hair behind her shoulder.

"That is soooooooooo rude! Pretend you don't know me, okay?"

I ignored them all, daydreaming about running away to Blue Hawaii in a pair of white go-go boots and a mini skirt with a Hunka Hunka Burnin' Love.

"Mama," Nicholas, ten, said, interrupting my reverie by poking me numerous times in the shoulder with his finger. "Isn't it just a *little* strange that the *two* cities with *major* fault lines *both* have trolleys? I find that suspicious."

As if death by Elvis fans' dirty looks wouldn't be bad enough, I thought, looking up at the huge, old buildings destined to tumble down around us at any moment when the Big One hit, *now we have a choice of demises.*

Just the morning before, on our way to Memphis, Nicholas had informed me of the potential for catastrophe.

"Memphis is a time bomb waiting to explode, Mama," he'd said, pushing his glasses up higher on his nose with his finger. "Floods, fault lines, and yellow fever, which is probably lying dormant somewhere."

I wondered for a moment if I should prohibit future viewings of *It Could Happen Tomorrow* and put a parental block on the Discovery Channel. Then I spent the rest of the day planning our funerals while waiting for the ground to shake beneath us. It had been bad enough the night before, waking to Nicholas screaming "Earthquake!!" every single time a guest on our floor shut their door. By the eleventh time, I finally realized we were more likely to crash to our deaths in the Heartbreak Hotel's elevator, which stopped a good six inches from its destination, trembling and shaking with a quick drop before the doors creaked open.

As we waited for the Beale Street trolley to recommence its journey, Nicholas had apparently forgotten my ban on natural disaster talk, telling me every detail of each earthquake in the past twenty years.

"Mama, I'm hot," Henry interrupted us. "Can we go to Disneyland next year?"

I didn't think Memphis was so bad myself. We'd arrived the morning before, meeting up with my mom, grandma, and brother, Oliver, at the Scottish Inn on Elvis Presley Boulevard. We dropped off Nan (who hates Elvis as much as Henry does) at the Heartbreak Hotel and headed out to Graceland, four kids in tow.

Elvis music assaulted us from all sides. People were everywhere, accents and languages spanning the globe, the temperature only four hundred and forty-seven degrees. Perhaps I declared the fact that we'd escaped our first gift shop without making a purchase a sign of good things to come and we moved towards the bus line that would take us to the mansion.

The line was long, wrapping around like an amusement-park-ride queue. Sadly, the wait did not lack in photo opportunities involving annoying Graceland employees with cameras shoving us like cattle to the slaughter up against a wall painted like the Graceland gates, two miles from the actual gates. Once they had you trapped, they snapped pictures before you could suck in your gut, turn your face to the best angle, or even smile.

"I wanted a picture of me alone by the gates," Georgie whined, for the next thirty minutes in line, like a hound dog kicked by a pair of blue suede shoes. "Not with y'all."

Mom crept ahead with Henry and my brother. They caught the bus before us, bringing on another round of complaints from Georgie and tempting me to flee.

I didn't, though, and we squeezed onto the next bus, headphones on ears for the trip across the street to the palace of a King. Mom had already disappeared inside and I gritted my teeth, prepared to go it alone. Nicholas and Hannah bustled ahead and Georgie trailed behind, listening to every moment of the recorded tour. I stayed back with her and prayed I wouldn't find Hannah hiding in the Jungle Room or Nick lounging on the yellow sofa in the TV room.

Five hundred hours later we emerged, skipping the memorabilia entirely, much to Georgie's dismay. The children surged forward, a bulging mass of giggling, pushing, and arguing, to the gravesite. It was a solemn affair, full of quiet tears and millions of camera flashes. Until we arrived.

"Which one is Elvis, Mama?" Hannah asked. "Is that a baby grave? Whose baby is that?"

I made the mistake of answering. So much for a quiet, discreet side comment.

"Poor Elvis, his brother died when he was only a baby and he took too many pills on the potty," Hannah announced to the world.

I scrunched between two now quite angry Germans, snapped a picture, grabbed the children, and ran like hell to the bus line.

Back on the Beale Street trolley, the Graceland fiasco flashed through my mind. "Maybe it was a little bad," I sighed, as the trolley shuddered to life, moving down the track.

Ten minutes later, as we passed the steel Pyramid Arena where the Memphis Grizzlies play and approached our stop, I pulled the cord to signal the driver. Instead of slowing, the trolley seemed to gain speed. I yanked again as she went past our stop, and another and another, halting six long, treeless blocks from where we were parked.

"Disneyland, indeed," the trolley driver huffed under her breath as we trooped past her. I wished I had one of Elvis's scarves to choke her with.

Driving Mozard

Sabra Ciancanelli

"**B**ut, Mom," Solomon says as I strap him in his car seat. "We need room for Mozard."

Shifting the cooler of juice boxes to the top of the tote bag of trains stuffed behind the driver's seat, I push the baggie of Goldfish crackers closer to my four-year-old's car seat.

"Good enough?"

Solomon surveys the cleared space, cocks his head to hear an answer to his left, and nods. "Yeah, Mozard says that's good."

We've done the run-through: made sure the lights and oven are off, the plants watered, and the stacks of cat food neatly piled on the kitchen table for the neighbor. Everything is as it should be; all that's left now is for us to go away.

Nestled in his backwards car seat, my four-month-old, Henry, sucks his binky and squints. My great-grandmother was a Mi'kmaq, and it's as if all her Native American features have been dormant for generations waiting their debut in Henry. Even the delivery nurses commented they'd never seen a newborn with black eyes, dark like coal with nothing to distinguish the pupil from the iris.

Solomon, with his fair skin and hazel eyes, is a replica of my husband. Now and then a glimpse of me bursts in the corners of his smile, but if you look closely, the resemblance vanishes just as magically as it appeared.

Tony grips the wheel. "Ready?"

Solomon hunches over the DVD player balanced on his lap. Sipping my coffee, I sigh. It's eight in the morning, we've been up for three hours, and our road atlas shows the stretch from New York to Cape Cod covering three states.

"You get the *Thomas* DVDs?" I ask.

Tony nods and reverses down the driveway, navigating through the strategically placed rearview mirror. No small feat, since it means peering through a tunnel of Boogie Boards, pillows, suitcases, pails, and shovels, all in the back.

"The baby monitor?"

Another nod.

"Did you put the D-r-a-m-a-m-i-n-e in his j-u-i-c-e?"

Tony furrows his brow. He finishes *The New York Times* crossword almost every day, but deciphering spoken spelled words escapes him.

"Dramamine," I whisper.

"What?" he asks. "Don't want to be on the interstate covered in fermenting apple juice and Goldfish this year? Yeah, it's in his juice."

We descend our country road, leaving behind our white farmhouse with four nervous-looking cats perched in windows.

Solomon focuses intently on the small screen. Getting a DVD player was a difficult decision. "It's like drugging them," a friend of mine said, unaware we had a portable player and planned to use it. "We always played car bingo on long trips," she went on. "Don't people want kids to have memories?" Of course, my friend hadn't said anything we hadn't wrestled with ourselves, and I didn't let on about the player or the Dramamine. Hitting the highway, we speed up. The sun inches over the Catskills, shining glorious rays that beam through the clouds like hope. We've done this trip to Cape Cod for years. Before we had kids, our vacation started the moment the ignition turned. The road filled with stories, Six Degrees of Kevin Bacon, movie trivia, and long, relaxing, silent stretches. We'd stop for lunch at a nice restaurant and stop again right before the Cape for a clam dog and a beer. Somehow, after Solomon, the drive grew thorns, a risk to factor in when deciding how badly we want to see the ocean, to feel the waves on our toes.

Though my siblings and I live within a ten-mile radius of my mother and meet up often, like a cluster of planets in orbit we all go on vacation together. My mom rents a huge house in Wellfleet. My brother and two sisters come with their families and all of our children play on the beach. It sounds sentimental and reminiscent of something you'd see on a Brady Bunch reunion show, but there are fights over the TV, stomped-on sand castles, unhappy Chutes and Ladders losers—you name it. And then there are the adult issues of doing dishes, preparing dinner, and getting parked in. Some days a member of the group has broken into tears. You just hope it's not you or your kid.

This year is Henry's first time to the gathering, and everyone's pretty excited to have a new member of the family. For all of Henry's four months on God's green earth, the one thing he's made pretty clear is that he needs white noise to go to sleep, so we've packed the baby monitor to turn it to the wrong frequency and blast the noise we've named "fuzzy," as in "Henry, you want fuzzy?"

About an hour along the highway Henry whimpers. He shields his eyes from the rising sun. Despite reassurance from the front seat and rattling of toy keys mixed with Solomon's high-pitched tea-kettle scream—his version of "fuzzy"—Henry wails. I tune the radio station to something that doesn't come in and raise the volume as high as it will go. Henry's hysterical cries persist.

Unbuckling my seatbelt, I slip off my flips-flops and contort myself over the console of our Subaru Forester. Wedging my hips in between the car seats, I hold Henry's face in my hands. Henry reaches towards me.

"Mom!" Solomon yells. "You're sitting on Mozard!"

"No, we switched. He's up front with Dad."

Henry's cries pierce the muscles that run the sides of my neck. I once read that a newborn's cries are a perfect example of intelligent design: loud enough to get your attention, fierce enough to wake you from any sleep, yet right on the edge of making you run towards the source instead of away.

"Mozard's under you. You're hurting him."

"There," I inch forward. "Mozard! Go in the front!"

"Okay, he moved," Solomon says. "You hurt him."

I can't remember exactly when Mozard became part of our family. One day Solomon said, "Mom, Mozard wants to know if he can live with us."

"Mozart?" I asked.

"Moz-ARD. He's right there." He pointed to dead space beside him. "He's got green hair and eyes and lives in our tree. He's tired of being alone. Can he live with us?"

I agreed. Since then, Mozard comes and goes as he pleases, joins us for dinner, plays impossible games of hide-and-seek, and races Solomon on his tricycle, though this is his first trip on vacation with us. Henry's face is crimson. His mouth is open in a silent scream. He grips my forearm, his fingertips turning white. Finding his voice, he lets out an ear-piercing shriek. I pull up my shirt, lean as far forward as I can, holding on to the back of the front seat, and offer him my breast. He sucks wildly, his dark brown eyes rolling backwards.

"We can pull over," Tony offers.

"No, keep going." I rest my head on the back of the front-seat head rest. My feet begin to fall asleep.

Solomon pushes the DVD into my shoulder. "Watch *Looney Tunes* with me."

Henry's eyes close.

"Watch with me!" Solomon says.

"Later," I whisper. Solomon beats the DVD player into my arm.

"Stop, or it's off," I whisper through clenched teeth.

We pull over at a turnpike rest area with a gas station and McDonald's. We stretch our legs and order our lunch. In the bright light, surrounded by frantic families also on vacation, we huddle together. Solomon holds his Happy Meal prize, a blue character that looks part bird and part robot. The large, red, unlit light on its chest looks like it should do something. Solomon pinches the button on its back. Nothing happens. He hands it to me. I pinch the button, look at the red unlit bulb, read the one-sentence instruction, and pinch the button again. Solomon sucks his green eyes deep into his head and pouts.

"This is terrible," he says.

I wait in line, eating my cheeseburger and balancing Henry on my hip. My drawn-out explanation to the tired-looking woman behind the counter pays off and we get a new Happy Meal prize free of charge. We open the bird-robot twin, pinch the button, and again the light stays dark, dead red.

"They're broke, Sol," I say. "Junk."

Solomon smiles. Holding his toys, one in each hand, he repeats, "I got two! I got two!"

We go to the bathroom, resolve we're halfway to the Cape, and strap the boys back in their car seats. We fill up with gas, and head back to the highway. Solomon balances his new toys on his knees. He clinks them together, bashing their heads.

"I got two and Henry got none, right?" he says.

The radio is tuned to a station that comes in. An upbeat summer song about love fills the car. I reach over and touch Tony's hand. He smiles.

"Mozard!" Solomon shrieks. "We forgot Mozard!"

"We didn't forget him," I say. "He's right here."

"No! He is not. He's at McDonald's."

Tony looks over at me.

"Go back! Go back!" Solomon screams.

"We're not going back," I say. Henry begins to cry.

Tony gestures to the exit sign. I shake my head. I don't mind stopping for meals, or to go to the bathroom, or even to nurse Henry, but actual, physical backtracking is against every part of the goal.

Solomon whips his head back and forth into a blur. Kicking his feet into the back of Tony's seat, he shouts, "Go back! Go back!"

The exit is five miles away. Caustic screams twist my spinal cord. I fight the urge to open the door and jump. Instead, I roll down the windows, thinking the whirling wind might dissipate the chaos. I look out at the side mirror. The bright sun accentuates the wrinkle between my eyes, the one born by scrunching my face from moments like this. The same friend who remarked about the DVD player once told me I looked different now that I have kids. "Different, how?" I asked. "Well," she said, "don't take this the wrong way, but now you look pissed off most of the time."

Tony pulls off at the exit. We turn left and get back on the highway.

"You know," I say over Solomon's protest, "my father never stopped. Every trip, I was thirsty and nervous, worried I'd have to go to the bathroom."

Realizing we're turned around and are headed back, Solomon whimpers and wipes his mouth. Henry's tear-stained face relaxes. Tony has an angelic glow about him as he puts another notch in the card he's going to show at heaven's gate, and I try to piece together how it is I've managed to snag a husband who not only stops for regular bathroom breaks but turns back for imaginary friends.

Tony pulls up to the entrance of the rest area and stops. Solomon giggles. Tony gets out of the car, opens the door, and ushers in the air.

"Okay?" Tony asks.

Solomon nods and leans forward in the seat, panting. Henry smiles. We drive on.

"Mozard's mad," Solomon proclaims. "He's mad from Mommy sitting on him. That's why he was hiding."

Looney Tunes is on its fifth hour. Solomon yawns but refuses to go to sleep or try a different movie.

"Solomon, play a game with us!" we beg. "Anything you want! Just turn that off."

"Anything?" Solomon asks, grinning wide.

"Anything."

He shuts the player and looks up at the ceiling with glee. "I know! I Spy. I spy with my little eye something green."

Henry begins to cry. We turn the radio-fuzz on high.

"The sign!" I shout, pointing to a highway marker.

"Nope."

"The grass."

"Nope."

"Henry's rattle," I say.

"Nope."

"We give up."

"Mozard's hair!" Solomon says.

Henry quiets and I lower the fuzz.

A half hour into playing I Spy with a boy who sees things that aren't there, we're relieved he's lost interest. "Looney Tunes?" I ask, holding out the DVD player.

We make it over the Bourne Bridge, the gateway to Cape Cod. The air is thick with sea salt, the road lined with soft, white sand. Solomon falls asleep. Henry falls asleep. The map is crumpled at my feet. We toy with the idea of stopping for a celebratory clam dog.

"That wasn't that bad," I say.

Tony lightly hits his cheek. "Are we home yet? Is it over?"

After a silent last hour, we pull into the driveway of the rental house and park beside my siblings' cars. My sister's laughter comes from the back deck. Tony and I glance back at our sleeping sons. I imagine Solomon's little green-haired friend sulking between them. Somewhere deep behind the wrinkle on my forehead, the place where reason resides splits in two as I reconcile what we just went through with the certainty I feel in my bones that these truly are the best years of my life.

Consider Atlanta

Julia Litton

Sometimes holiday travel proceeds so smoothly that you wish you could fly to see your in-laws every day of the year. Sometimes they board your row just as you stroll up to the gate, and sometimes your rambunctious toddler happily counts planes on the tarmac before falling into a deep sleep that lasts until breakfast the following morning. Sometimes the flight attendant brings you a glass of complimentary wine, and sometimes all of the business travelers in rows 6 through 13 spontaneously croon Brahms' Wiegenlied to soothe your screaming baby.

Sometimes, however, you get a Thanksgiving 2006, in which case you are screwed.

For the record, I am fairly certain that one of our wedding vows included a promise to never fly across the country (any country) with the hypothetical fruit of our union during peak travel times. My husband, Steve, does not remember it this way, but I have a clear recollection of swearing that we would never become two of those poor souls we had so often pitied during our seven years of child-free travel. From the safety of the airport bar we would watch the traveling families barrel past: harried, hurried, and weighed down. Their improbably oversized backpacks would spill Cheerios and board books and beeping plastic toys while four hands attempted to juggle the stroller, the carrier, the baby, the car seat, the teddy bear, the sippy cups, and some new little toy just picked up at the gift shop for the price of a used but decent car. Children tumbled along in their parents' wake and appeared in danger of being lost forever, swept away by the surging airport crowd. Those families looked like performers in a tiny circus who have lost their train and been forced to put the whole show on their backs. It seemed so nerve-wracking and exhausting that Steve and I would frequently have to buoy ourselves with another Gin Fizz before grabbing the bag containing only a toothbrush and passports, skipping to our departing flight with three minutes to spare.

F rom the child-free perspective, air travel with anyone under the age of twenty-one looks masochistic under the best of circumstances. Add to this the pressures of flying during the holidays, what with the potential for foul winter weather and overbooked flights and five hundred million families just like yours all trying to go in opposite directions . . .

"No way," I remember saying. "We will resist. We will blaze new paths and forge new traditions. We will restrict our travel to balmy months like May and September and we will only fly on Tuesday afternoons. We will not bring everything we own to entertain a five-month-old baby on a ninety-minute flight. We will not distract the busy steward (who is, after all, just there for our safety) with instructions on how to microwave the child's soy milk for exactly 33 seconds at 75 percent power because he only will drink it hot but not *too* hot. And, most importantly, we will most emphatically *not* travel for Christmas, Thanksgiving, Easter, Flag Day, Jurgi, Michaelmas, or Towel Day." Thus spoke the prechild me.

Steve and I now have one son, Patrick, and he has spent every major holiday since his birth in 2002 lovingly surrounded by extended family despite the fact that we live at least eight hundred miles from our nearest relatives. How did this happen, you wonder? We schlepped him to them. What about my vow, you ask?

"Just *tell* them," I would hiss at my husband as he picked up the phone to discuss another upcoming holiday with his family. "Just *say it*. Say we'll see them the following week. Say we'll come the month before. Be strong. Offer a tempting selection of alternate dates. Just . . ."

"Dad!" my husband would say. "So, um, we were thinking about maybe not flying in for Thanksg— Oh. Oh, sure. Of course. Right! Of course! Great! We're looking forward to it! See you then!"

Five seconds into the call and his father would clear his throat or something, at which moment my husband would fold like an origami crane. Every. Single. Time. And then there we would be again, buying airline tickets with a seasonal markup best calculated by NASA and realizing that there is a very good reason why people travel by the millions on those busy dates: ancestral guilt. Not that I was any better with my side of the family. I never even managed to get past the word "um" before my mother had me promising that we would consider looking at houses for sale in her area during our Christmas visit, a visit, she was certain, that we would not mind extending to a full week this year.

Thus prodded by responsibility and a primal urge to be in the bosoms of our family for the annual guilt-fest, Steve and I reluctantly but definitively joined the circus, a concession that has brought us additional airline miles, an ability to accomplish seemingly impossible changes in the cubic foot that comprises an airplane bathroom, and, of course, the lasting memories of Thanksgiving 2006.

We were feeling pretty good about the trip. The plan was to fly the day before Thanksgiving, nonstop, from our home in St. Paul, Minnesota, to Dulles Airport, just west of Washington, D.C. Total miles in the air: 983. Approximate travel time: just under two hours. Once on the ground, we were to be picked up by Steve's sister and driven another two hours south to Virgina's lovely but remote tidal coast where my husband's parents have a charming vacation home on the water. It was a trip we had made at least a dozen times before with few problems. Most importantly, Patrick was now four. Four is not as adept at flying as, say, forty, but it is eons beyond fourteen months. At four, kids no longer need to have everything from food to diapers to changes of clothes brought onboard for them. They can drink the airplane juice from an airplane cup while eating airplane pretzel twists. They can listen to a story that lasts longer than two minutes. They can color or flip through the Sky Mall catalog. They are not entirely human but they are getting closer.

Our departing flight left on time and I watched as my son happily filled pages of a notebook after there was nothing left to see from the window. I contemplated how much easier it is to travel once the toddler stage has passed and I wondered if I might even be able to read a few chapters of a novel I had in my purse.

"This is cake," I thought.

It must have been at that precise moment—the instant that I moved from feeling complacent to smug—that the pilot got on the loudspeaker to announce that an unspecified mechanical failure would be forcing us to make an emergency landing in Detroit.

Patrick looked up, interested.

"Are we there now?" he asked. "Oh, yay! We're landing!"

Steve and I were less charmed and more wary. Sure, maybe the mechanical failure was just a big misunderstanding or, failing that, maybe the airline had another plane empty and ready to go on this, the busiest travel day of the year. Or maybe elves would fix the problem in a trice while they sang for our enjoyment. Perhaps we would be in the air again with hardly a moment's delay. All things were possible, but we were not feeling sanguine.

Within twenty minutes of the pilot's announcement, we were on the ground in Detroit, rolling past gate after gate after gate. After gate.

"Are they *driving* us to Grandma and Grandpa?" Patrick wondered aloud.

At last we came to a stop in what looked like an unused parking lot. And we waited. They said they would be sending someone to determine if the plane could be fixed quickly or not. We waited. They commended us on our patience. Patrick announced he had to use the bathroom.

Steve and I hesitated. Were we allowed to get up? Were we supposed to . . . ?

"I *really* need to use the bathroom," Patrick repeated with a rising urgency.

"I didn't bring any other clothes for him," I confessed.

Steve picked Patrick up and bolted for the back of the plane.

Then we waited some more.

After about an hour (during which time the child finished the juice we had brought with us and lost all interest in coloring while developing a new passion: kicking the seat in front of him) they started the plane up again and released us to a gate area. They had not yet determined if our plane could be repaired, though, so they strongly cautioned us not to even think about going anywhere more than ten feet from the Jetway. The implication was that the plane would be reboarded with short notice and then we would instantly depart. Anyone foolish enough to be dawdling at a food court when that happened would be walking to Washington as far as they were concerned.

We sat there for another hour. Patrick complained that he was starving and thirsty. I handed over my emergency stash of raisins and a bag of Mini Oreos. We craned our necks as far as we could down the concourse but we could not find a sign of anything but more gates nearby. We thought about leaving to go forage for food but we were terrified to explore any further lest the plane leave without us. "Ho ho ho," I think in hindsight. Steve dozed off. Patrick lay on his back on the airport floor and I tried not to think about how many dirty feet must have stepped on the exact spot where Patrick's head was touching the carpet. A much smaller boy toddled over to Patrick and said, "We going airplane!"

"No we're not," Patrick replied bitterly.

Finally a notice went up saying that the plane would depart but not for another four hours—a mixed blessing. On the one hand we could go in search of food; on the other hand: *four more hours.*

We had a dismal, bagel-based breakfast/lunch and when we returned to our gate the departure time had been pushed back by another hour to five o'clock. I told Steve that this was clearly part of a pilot program, the goal of which was to relocate people to Detroit through gradual acclimation. First it was an hour, then three . . . soon we would forget there was ever a time in which we did not live in Michigan and we would wander away from the airport in search of a realtor. As I enlarged upon this theory to a comatose Steve and Patrick made friends with other Minnesota refugee children, the signage concerning our flight mysteriously disappeared from all monitors. Not only were we no longer departing at 5:00 PM, we had apparently ceased to exist entirely (we later learned that this is the airline's subtle way of letting you know when your flight has been canceled).

We bumbled around for a while, alternately worrying about how we would get out of there and wondering why we would ever want to leave when Detroit has so much to offer, until an agent boarding happy people for a Tampa flight took pity on us and looked up our reservation. This is when we discovered that they had gotten us three shiny new seats on an airplane leaving a mere two hours later. Of course, that plane was flying to Atlanta, not Washington. And our airline could not get us from Atlanta *to* Washington. But they swore they had found some spaces on a different airline leaving Georgia at 10:00 PM so . . . so fuck that, we said, gently.

Gate agents, it turns out, cannot change flight assignments that have been randomly generated by the airline after they accidentally abandon you *en route*. For that sort of clout you need a ticketing agent, and ticketing agents only dwell outside the security lines. So I had to throw away all the water and apple juice and 5.8-ounce bottles of duty-free perfume I had stockpiled during our wait (have you seen the new TSA regulations? with the 3-ounce maximums and the plastic baggies?) and we trudged out to stand in line at ticketing.

Surprisingly, the line for tickets in Detroit was just as long as our original line for tickets had been back in Minnesota. Apparently they must celebrate Thanksgiving in Michigan as well. Who knew? We shuffled through the line a millimeter at a time, encouraging Patrick to keep moving with word, gesture, bribery, and the occasional threat. We finally made it to the front and explained our dilemma: We had purchased tickets to Washington, D.C., and yet they were sending us to Georgia. The agent was sympathetic but we started to discern a certain . . . theme. A recurring motif, as persistent as it was baffling.

"Could they get us into National Airport?" Yes! Well, sort of. Two of us, tomorrow, and the other one could go to Memphis . . . how about connecting through Atlanta?

"But," we pointed out reasonably, "tomorrow is *Thanksgiving*. The whole reason we are traveling in the first place is to spend this *specific* day with our family. You will no doubt find this quaint, but we have a funny little tradition of celebrating the fourth Thursday of November with a large meal. A meal, incidentally, that features turkey and gravy and pie and absolutely no bagels whatsoever. Can you get us to Richmond instead?"

Richmond? Sure. They could connect us to Richmond, on Friday, through Atlanta.

I do not know why the airline was so desperate to have us visit Atlanta on this trip but, my god, they were. Every possible option contained that city in some manner. However, as noted, we did not *want* to go to Atlanta. Nothing against the Big Peach, but we had other plans. So we stayed firm in our refusal and the agent finally put us on a direct flight to Baltimore. It was not ideal but it seemed like the best we could hope for under the circumstances. In retrospect I am glad that I did not notice that she had not given us actual seats for the seriously overbooked Baltimore flight until after we had gone back through security. Because if I had realized at the time that she had permanently changed our reservation to a city four and half hours north of our ultimate destination and had committed us to flying standby, with a little kid and no juice, I might have murdered her. I am not saying I would have, just that I might have.

We crawled back through security. We scurried to our new gate. We forced our way through the swirling eddies of people with our four hands juggling the backpacks and the carry-on and the teddy bear and the thirty-pound boy who had announced he was done with walking, possibly forever. As we passed an airport bar I averted my gaze, lest the ghostly image of my Thanksgivings Past mock me with a Gin Fizz salute.

Eventually we did make it onto the flight to Baltimore, but not before they called the name of every other person in the gate area and I chewed my fingers down to bloody stubs. Needless to say our seats were not together. Needless to say they refused to let me sit in blissful solitude but officiously negotiated some seat changes so that Patrick and I could sit together while my husband mysteriously disappeared towards the back of the plane. What do you do with a four-year-old when you have been traveling for twelve hours longer than expected? He had already read all the books, eaten the snacks, drunk the juice, and colored until he got writer's cramp. I suggested he sleep and when he said he wasn't tired, just *bored*, I offered him all the cash I had left in my wallet if he would just *pretend* to sleep.

Fourteen hours after leaving Minnesota we finally approached our quasidestination. We were still hours from where we needed to be, but hell, at least we weren't about to land in Atlanta. That had to count for something. Just as the plane started its final descent Patrick sat bolt upright and began to turn colors like an oversized chameleon: bright pink and then pale, red and then greenish. I only got as far as, "Do you need to . . ." before he did. Patrick threw up. Emphatically. On himself, on the seat, and on me. Strangely, if anyone in the family had been voted Most Likely to Lose a Bagel on this trip it would most definitely have been me. I once got sick in the bushes after simply breaking a nail. My beloved child, however, inherited his father's less delicate constitution and, apart from a virus and a brief but violent love affair with a tire swing, he had never vomited before. I could not have been more surprised (or less prepared) if he had suddenly turned into a swan. It was as if the gods who had cursed this trip were now starting to throw things at us at random, no matter how illogical. Unfortunately, the meager carry-on that I had so prided myself upon earlier in the journey contained nothing in the way of clean clothes for either of us. I hadn't even brought Kleenex. I did the best I could, though, implementing an emergency wardrobe shift that left me in a camisole and him in a sweater down to his knees. As I shivered I thought about asking to borrow the Armani blazer from the businessman sitting next to us, but catching the look he was giving us, I thought better of it.

Do I need to tell you that we went to Baltimore but our luggage was sent back to Minneapolis? Of course I don't. And that fresh clothes and toothbrushes and pajamas did not find us down in the hollows of Virginia for another three days? No. You can imagine that for yourselves.

It was a little after midnight when we limped into Steve's parents' house. They had waited up and had leftover dinner waiting. I was touched.

Steve's stepmother sat us down as we got there and handed Patrick a plate of lukewarm . . .

"What," Patrick asked, "is that?"

"Moussaka," my mother-in-law said brightly.

"What is moussaka?"

"Eggplant and spiced lamb and goat cheese."

Patrick looked at me. He looked at Steve. He looked at Grandma.

"That is not funny," he said. And he got out of his chair and went to bed (still wearing my sweater) without another word.

"I didn't realize he was such a picky eater," my mother-in-law said, in that tone that mothers-in-law reserve for remarks like that.

Freezing in my camisole, smelling like vomit, exhausted, dying for a drink, being stared down by a congealing eggplant, and my mother-in-law hits one out of the park like that . . . ah, classic. It is these treasured family memories that make the ardors of holiday travel so very worthwhile.

Diapers, Drugs, and Witchcraft

Gabrielle Smith-Dluha

"You're going traveling in the mountains of Ecuador? With your baby?" friends and family asked us in disbelief. "Is it safe?"

"Yes! We've done loads of research," we said.

We were itching to travel; we were flush with student loans—or as flush as student loans can make you—and we had a one-and-a-half-year-old toddler named Jake.

Because of Jake, our university study abroad office had refused us—too much liability. But my husband, Brad, and I were determined to get abroad. At our wedding, we had vowed that marriage and kids would never hold us back from adventure. Besides, we were both passionate about Latin America. We had studied Spanish for so long. How could they deny us?

There was only one thing to do. We created our own study abroad program. My world literature professors agreed to a research project on Andean literature in lieu of my winter term requirements, and Brad had the go-ahead from his Environmental Studies department to study Andean agriculture. In January, we were set to leave for Ecuador for three months—term papers due to our home campus in spring like all the other students.

Once friends and family got used to the idea, they began with a new line of questions—questions that were more taunting than concerned.

"So, are you going to keep on using those cloth diapers while you travel?" They sniggered, hoping to catch us betraying our hard-line environmental stands.

"Yes, of course," we said—oozing the smugness of twentysomething students who know they are saving the world—"We're not going to clog dumps with plastic diapers, like some people we know!"

"What about when you're on the road—in a foreign country?"

"So what? We'll just throw the diapers in a bag and wash them when we can."

"What if there aren't any washing machines in Ecuador?"

"Then we'll wash them in the river!"

But as our departure date drew near, my confidence grew far away. Suddenly, I was afraid for my son. Not only did we use cloth diapers, but we also opposed all vaccination. After reading up during my pregnancy and attending a healthcare workshop offered by our homeopathic doctor, Brad and I had chosen not to vaccinate Jake. Brad and I both felt strongly on the issue. But even safely ensconced in the U.S., I often became mute and weak-kneed in front of medical professionals, never fully knowing if we'd made the right decision.

And now here I was dragging my baby, unvaccinated, to Ecuador! Just days before leaving, I was sure that I'd be endangering him with a slew of third-world diseases. I could think of nothing else. Maybe we should cancel the trip. I couldn't sleep. I looked for a sign to show me what to do.

On a last-minute run to the university library to check out a book on Spanish verbs, I walked into an art exhibit in the library foyer entitled, "Mother in Grief." About fifty small clay figures filled the library foyer depicting a mother in agony over the death of her young child. I stared in horror at the grief-stricken figures cradling the bodies of dead babies.

"Shit. Shit. Shit," I said, walking down the front steps of the library. "This is the sign!"

Straight away, I made an appointment with our homeopathic doctor. In some earlier incarnation, she'd been an MD. I was sure she'd know what was right—maybe some specific last-minute vaccinations. Once in her office, she listened patiently to my hysteria. But in the end, she affirmed that our decision was sound. A round of vaccinations at this point might be traumatic and challenge Jake's long-term health. As long as we stayed out of the Amazon jungle, we'd be fine.

And then her words struck a chord.

"It's really that you're afraid of the unknown," she told me. "Forever; you and your son are going to be walking into the unknown. Trust more."

So, a little shaky, we took the dive. Down the Jetway and into the plane we went—a young married couple, one unvaccinated toddler, and a bulging bag of cloth diapers.

Twenty hours later, in the dark of night, our plane touched ground in Quito, Ecuador. The swirl of the airport engulfed us immediately. Loud, rapid Spanish bounced everywhere. Porters tossed suitcases here and there in some incomprehensible pattern. We saw our bags and stroller being passed from hand to hand.

"Hey! Those are our bags!" Brad shouted as some stranger grabbed our bags with a smile and took off through the crowd.

"Tell him those are our bags. Tell him we'll carry our own bags," Brad called to me, hustling behind the stranger. I was supposed to be the expert in Spanish, but I couldn't manage a single word. Jake clung to my shoulder, his eyes wide. I pushed my way through the crowd, keeping my eyes on Brad's blonde head bobbing above the sea of dark heads.

Then a hand grasped my elbow, making me jump. It was the Ecuadorian businessman who had sat next to me on the plane. He'd been friendly enough during the flight and had offered to give us a ride to our hotel, but there was something about him I hadn't trusted, so I'd politely declined. He continued to insist. We'd secretly planned to escape him in the crowd once off the plane.

Evidently, he'd caught up. Before we knew it, he seized command of our situation. He retrieved our bags and soon had us seated in the back of his comfortable car on the way to our hotel. Jake wiggled on my lap, exhausted, but pressing his fingers against the cold, dark of the window. City lights blurred past and we strained to catch a glimpse of Quito. Trust more, the homeopath had said.

In the musty-smelling hotel room, Brad paced up and down in the space between the twin beds, sure that they'd overcharged us. Jake screamed and ran around on the tile floor and wouldn't lie down. The twenty-plus-hour travel time, including the layover in Costa Rica, had us all off schedule. Jake had hardly slept on the plane. It was near midnight, but it felt more like 2:00 AM because of the change in time zones. All I wanted to do was collapse on the bed, but Jake kept on climbing, chattering, crying, whimpering, shouting, and wiggling in a state of overexhausted toddler mania.

Finally, he fell asleep in my arms after hours of rocking and singing. I lay awake listening to the cars and distant voices floating up from this high Andean city.

"ey," Brad whispered from his twin bed across the room. "Are you asleep?"

"No," I said.

"Can I come over there with you guys? I feel weird here," he said.

"Me too," I said.

Brad crawled into my twin and we all three lay in a tight embrace.

A few days later, we headed south by bus to the colonial town of Cuenca, where we had arranged to stay with a family through the Peace House Foundation back home. Our host family consisted of a small single woman who worked at the bank, her half-indigenous mother, and their little dog.

Their house was nicer than we expected—a two-story Spanish-style home with a small courtyard full of banana trees and bougainvillea. The house was separated from the street by a high white wall with pieces of sharp, broken glass inlaid along the top to discourage burglars. Similar high-walled homes lined the dirt road out front. Only women and children inhabited this middle-class neighborhood on the hill above the city. All the men were long gone, we heard, flipping hamburgers in New York, and known only by the money orders that arrived each month.

We soon settled into an Andean rhythm in our new neighborhood. Rain poured down in the mornings. The sun blazed hot in the afternoons. We took shifts, one of us with Jake, the other engaged in research. We learned to wave down the bus as it slowed and to swing ourselves into the crowd of old women and chickens amid broken seats. And we shared dinners with our host family, heaping our plates with fried bananas, popcorn, beans, and avocados.

As Jake adjusted to the new foods, diaper changes were frequent and messy. People back home would have delighted in seeing us knee-deep in our dirty cloth diapers. They had been right. We had no washer or dryer to make use of. Not even any hot water in the house. And, inexplicably, our neighborhood water lines were shut off from 7:00 AM to 5:00 PM every day. Not a drop of water all day.

Early in the morning, while the water still ran from the faucet, Brad stored water in buckets, as our host mother did, and then heated it on the stove throughout the day. Jake took baths in a small metal tub in the laundry room. Brad and I took turns scrubbing down the colossal pile of diapers with a bar of sticky, brown laundry soap and hung them out in the courtyard to dry among the banana trees.

While we were busy with the diapers, Jake tumbled on the floor with the dog. He watched the goat tethered in the empty lot next door. And bumping along in his stroller on the cobblestones around town, he called out *"Iglesia! Iglesia!"*, insisting that we enter the cool cathedrals and light candles at the altar, as was the local custom.

Jake was fine. My homeopath was right, it seemed.

Famous last words.

One day, two months into our stay, Jake began inexplicably howling and rolling all over our bed. I ran to comfort him. I searched his body for bruises, cuts, or spider bites. I begged him to show me what was wrong. But he only howled all the louder. Brad was out for the afternoon, playing soccer with some new friends. I had no idea what to do. Jake kept on shrieking in pain. He was hot and feverish.

"It's okay. Mama's right here." I said, reaching out my arms to hold him. He kicked me away and thrashed around the bed, screaming.

I'm taking Jake to a doctor, I decided. But where? And how? I imagined carrying Jake's hot, screaming body onto the crowded bus. Oh, why had I trusted? And why hadn't I already found a pediatrician who spoke English? This was it. It was happening. Does he have malaria? Cholera? Leprosy? And where was Brad!? I flashed back to the "Mother in Grief" exhibit and cried.

My host mother opened the door to find out what was going on. When she saw me in tears and Jake out of control, she ran to get her mother, Solena.

Solena was known in Ecuador as a "Chola"—signifying a rich mix of indigenous and Spanish heritage in the Andes. She was short, squat, and broad, with warm brown eyes. She wore a wide, colorful skirt and a straw hat perched high on the back of her head. She giggled easily, made bread in her kitchen every Friday morning, ground chilies by stone, bargained hard at the market with a live chicken squawking upside down in her hand, and could kill and skin a guinea pig with ease. She also fell asleep each night wrapped in her shawl while watching *The Flintstones* in Spanish.

Silently, Solena assessed the situation in our room, then put on her shawl and headed out the front door. Jake still wailed and flung his head against the pillow. In my awkward Spanish I tried to explain to my host mother that I needed a doctor. Right now. She just shook her head no and told me to wait for Solena. Jake howled. I tugged at my hangnail with my teeth, straining out the window to look for Brad, but there was no sign of him anywhere.

Instead, fifteen minutes later, I saw Solena's short figure striding back through the courtyard, her arms overflowing with a bundle of bushy herbs and white lilies. She came into my room, lifted Jake up, and carried him still crying to the kitchen. I hurried behind, my arms dangling.

Standing Jake on the kitchen table, she swished and swatted him all over with the giant herb bouquet, chanting, "*Manchi. Manchi. Manchi. Manchi.*

Manchi"—a mysterious word from the Quichua dialect. I babbled on about the doctor, but neither Solena nor her daughter paid any attention.

Solena lay the herbs down and then squashed little wads of crushed garlic and mud into her palms. Spitting on her hands, she rubbed the strange concoction in small circles on Jake's body, reaching under his shirt to his belly and chest. Jake continued to shriek, but didn't try to get away from her healing hands. She spit on his belly and then began to rub an unbroken egg over his chest. His sobbing slowed and he opened his eyes out of curiosity.

Solena cracked the egg into a glass. She and her daughter peered in and then looked up at each other, nodding their heads.

"Mal ojo," they pronounced together, meaning "bad eye."

They said someone had given Jake the "bad eye" by looking at him with envy or harmful thoughts and thus had stolen his energy. After a hushed discussion, they determined that it was a particular strange man who had been walking down our street the day before. Jake had waved at him.

Mal ojo? I looked at them with skepticism. I looked back at Jake. He sat on the edge of the table, his face now calm and smiling. Maybe there was something to their ancient healing that could touch deep into the unknown.

"Take him upstairs to rest," they said, and Jake climbed into my arms.

Back alone in our room, I rocked him on my lap. Our host mother came in and put a necklace of rosary beads over his head. She rested the cross right over Jake's heart. Jake smiled and fell into a sweet sleep. Brad still wasn't home, but I let myself rest against the bed frame.

Jake woke up back to his normal energetic self, horsing around with the dog. When Brad came back muddy and sweaty from the soccer match, we decided to keep an eye on Jake and find a doctor if needed. But Jake never had that fit again.

"Dios le pague!" I said to Solena later in the evening using the colloquial phrase for thank you used everywhere in Ecuador. When she heard me, Solena sucked in her breath and clapped her hand over my mouth. Translated literally, *"Dios le pague"* means "God will pay you."

"Never, never say that to a healer!" my host mother said.

"Oh, I'm sorry!" I said, not really understanding my transgression. "What can I do to say thank you?"

She whispered instructions in my ear. Obediently, I ran across the street to the shop, which was operated out of a neighbor's kitchen window. I bought two large plastic bottles of Coke and Fanta and brought them back to Solena. She nodded approvingly at my gift, opened up the Coke, and took an appreciative swig.

Shortly afterwards, our study abroad began to wrap up. Winter term had come to an end back home. Our research was complete—term papers frantically written in the last few nights. We bade our host family farewell. The neighbors gathered with gifts and goodbyes. Finally, we headed down the dirt road in a taxi, arms waving out the window.

We spent our final week traveling around northern Ecuador. We visited the lush, folk art village of Otavalo; danced to live Andean music with locals; and slept the last three nights on the floor of a monastery above Quito.

At last we were seated in the middle of the hot Quito airport ready to return home. Jake climbed up on the seat next to me, tugged on my hair, and shouted *"Hola!"* at each passerby. I slumped down and rested one foot on our duffle bag.

We hadn't had time or a place to do laundry in over a week, and it showed. My jeans were grimy where Jake had smashed a fistful of avocado into my thigh.

Bits of rice were stuck onto the back of Brad's fleece sweatshirt from our dinner at a Chinese restaurant. We had only a few clean diapers left, but we didn't care. We were on our way home.

Then I smelled something worse than my own dirty clothes coming from inside Jake's pants. He climbed higher on the seat and pressed his hip into my cheek. I gave in. It had to be done. Heaving myself up from the seat, I grabbed his wiggling body and began to strip down his pants.

Suddenly, the airport loudspeaker called out my name, "Gabrielle Smith, please come immediately to the security office."

I looked up at Brad and felt oddly thrilled: My name had never been called over an airport speaker! I wondered what was up. Jake squirmed to get free of my arms.

"Here, I'll take over," Brad offered. "You go find out what's going on."

As I approached the security office on the other side of the airport waiting area, a group of soldiers with AK-47s slung over their shoulders grabbed my arms.

I looked back at Brad, my heart pounding up into my throat. My lungs contracted. But Brad was on his knees. One hand held a dripping diaper; the other pinned down a naked Jake squirming on the floor. Brad's head was turned and he didn't see me being led by the soldiers through a back door.

I could hear the sound of excited dogs barking coming from behind the wall. The soldiers brought me into the small, decorationless office of the chief of security. Two soldiers stood at the door, fingering their rifles. I was limp with visions of South American torture prisons. Oh, God, here it is. At least they don't want Brad and Jake. I'll tell them anything, everything!

"Do you hear those dogs barking?" he asked me in Spanish, his cold eyes scanning my face.

"*Sí,*" I said in a small voice, trying to look as cooperative as one could possibly look.

"The dogs have found drugs in your bag."

Did some smuggler stuff cocaine into my bag while I was chasing Jake around the airport? Would I waste away in some grim Ecuadorian women's prison for the rest of my life, the U.S. Embassy unable to do a thing?

"But I don't have any drugs!" I protested.

"That's what they all say," he replied.

Oh God, why hadn't I freshened up a little bit? I must look like a druggie with my dirty clothes and mangled, unwashed hair.

Maybe if I work at it, I could give him the *"mal ojo"* and he'll fall writhing on the floor screaming.

"Come with me," said the chief.

I was grabbed by the arms again and led to the room with the barking dogs. Three German shepherds on chains were leaping and barking in a circle around my bag.

"Is this your suitcase?" the chief asked.

I debated lying, but swiftly came to my senses.

"*Sí.*"

The soldiers pulled back the dogs and soothed them.

"Open it up," the chief commanded to one of the soldiers.

He unzipped it to reveal a lumpy plastic bag on top. We all stared at it.

"So, then, what's this?" he asked me.

I looked hard at the bag. Then I began to laugh.

"No, no, no," I said, still laughing. "No drugs! That's a bag of dirty diapers."

I could breathe again.

"Go ahead, look through it," I said. "Be my guest."

The chief peered into the opening of the bag to see the crumpled, sticky diapers. He took a whiff of the week-old stench and yanked back his head.

"So that's what my dogs smelled," he said, coughing.

"See?" I said, shrugging and smiling. "No drugs—just diapers."

The chief's hardened face broke into a smile and we both started laughing.

Twenty hours later, Brad and I, with a sleeping Jake on my shoulder, straggled off the plane, blinking in the bright, sterile San Francisco Airport. What was this strange land? What was this place where everything was so efficient and clean, where every single human had their own car? No guinea-pig roasts? No crowded buses filled with live chickens and goats?

We collapsed that night at Brad's mom's house. We threw a load of diapers into the washer—just snapping on the hot water button and walking away. We were out of clean cloth diapers, so Brad's mom popped down to Safeway and got us some Pampers. We accepted gratefully.

That night, I sang and rocked Jake for hours before he relaxed into sleep. Then I lay awake in one of the twin beds in the guest room, listening to the rumble of the dryer coming from down the hall.

"Hey," Brad whispered from his twin bed. "Are you asleep?"

"No," I said.

"Can I come over there with you guys? I feel weird here," he said.

"Me too," I said.

Brad crawled into my bed and we three all lay in a tight embrace.

The Devil Wears Pull-Ups

Stephanie Sylverne

The passengers in the adjacent Baptist church cargo van were not amused. I'm not ashamed to say that I *was*, though I can definitely see why unruly children making devil ears with their fingers while wearing Pull-Ups on their heads could be offensive to a roaming band of conservative religious devotees in southern Indiana.

We should have known it was a crazy idea—who puts three girls under the age of eight in a minivan to drive halfway across the country? Let alone to attempt a twenty-four-hour road trip with no overnight stops. (Hence the Pull-Ups, for our six-year-old companion with bladder-control issues.) Turns out the vast emptiness of the American Midwest and South is not suitable visual entertainment for small children. But I'm getting slightly ahead of myself.

My friends and I have a tendency to do things that are rather, well, reckless—by some people's standards. So it was without any hesitation that Jennifer and I decided it would be a fabulous adventure to hop in her minivan and drive 1,300 miles from Chicago to her mother's house in Fort Lauderdale for a week. It should be noted that both of us were twentysomething single mothers perilously close to hitting negative digits in what passed—technically—as our bank accounts. That just made the adventure all the more interesting. We would split the gas, drive straight through to avoid motel charges, stay with her mom for free, and buy groceries for the house rather than eat out. The beach costs nothing, and what other entertainment would we need? It was a sweet deal we couldn't resist, even flying by the seat of our pants financially.

Our little excursion really had multiple purposes. Jennifer's stepfather had passed away unexpectedly a few months before, so she wanted to get down to her mother to help put things in order. Somewhere in the midst of the travel preparations, Jennifer's grandfather was added to the entourage. Her grandfather . . . and a month's worth of his luggage and photography equipment. For those of you playing along at home, that's one minivan, one grandpa, two mothers, and three young children. Plus an overflowing cooler, too many blankets and pillows, enough cameras to equip a frenzy of paparazzi, more luggage than a Madonna world tour requires, and no installed CD player. It was radio all the way. Make that fuzzy, static-y, faint, often country-music-only radio. Radio that was too loud for Grandpa no matter how low we turned it. Kids who were too loud for Grandpa no matter how much we shushed them. A car that was too small for all of us no matter how many times we rearranged things.

Truck stops in the middle of the night are intimidating places to be female. Bored truckers stopped mid-chatter when we walked in the gas station as if WE'RE NOT FROM AROUND HERE was tattooed to our foreheads. They called out, "Where ya from?" and "Hey sweetheart!" as I made my way to the washroom. I kept thinking, "Shouldn't I be afraid right now?" and, "My grandmother would be absolutely horrified if she knew that I was here." At the same time, it was perversely daring and even exciting. I was slightly proud to be in a rest stop in the middle of rural Kentucky, as funny as that sounds.

We spent a lot of time in questionable gas stations. If it wasn't one of the kids in urgent need of the bathroom, then it was Grandpa. Eventually, they all fell blissfully asleep and we could finally bring the speedometer over 60 mph without being chastised. The rest of the way was dark and quiet. Jennifer and I cheered at each road sign: WELCOME TO TENNESSEE; WELCOME— WE'RE GLAD GEORGIA'S ON YOUR MIND. And finally: WELCOME TO FLORIDA—THE SUNSHINE STATE.

Despite our jubilation, it was still at least six hours to Fort Lauderdale from the Florida border. Much to our dismay, the girls were awakened by the bright lights of the Florida Turnpike. We made a pit stop there in the early morning hours and loaded our daughters up with food and trinkets in the hopes that they would keep calm or fall back asleep. Unfortunately, they spent most of the rest of the drive whining and fighting over bags of Cheetos and who crossed the imaginary boundary to whose seat. I was beginning to think I had made a huge mistake. Visions of seven days of temper tantrums and hair-pulling flashed before my eyes. I was almost 1,500 miles from home without my own transportation. I started to panic and make emergency plans in my head. If it got too bad, I figured, I could take a Greyhound bus home . . . no, no, too much luggage . . . I could beg my father to get us plane tickets back to Chicago . . . even though I am terrified of flying, maybe it would be worth it if things got that bad. . . .

Thankfully, it never got that bad. We pulled up to the house honking and hooting. The girls fled from the car before we even had time to fully park. "Look, palm trees!! Mom, are these real palm trees in the yard?" Sam asked me. I laughed. "Yes, they are totally real." I heard a screech, then two, then three. "A *lizard*! There's a lizard! Mom, Mom, come here, there's a lizard!" I walked to the side of the house and said, "It's not a lizard. Where is it? Let me see."

"It's right by your foot!"

I ran away squealing while the girls collapsed to the ground in giggles.

It was hot. Heat like I had never experienced. My naturally curly hair, usually straightened, refused to comply. Chicago has notoriously hot summers, but nothing like this! Jenny ended up spending every morning French-braiding all of our hair to keep it under control. I had expected to spend most of our days at the beach, but we couldn't bear the humidity. By the time we wanted to venture out in the afternoon, the daily three o'clock rain showers started. I was worried that the kids were going to get heatstroke from playing tag in the back yard for fifteen minutes.

Ecology wasn't the only thing that differed from home. I had never left the Midwest before, and being in Florida was total culture shock. We may have been in the same country, but it was a completely different world. This was Jeb Bush country and we knew it. Though there is always the occasional "Abortion stops a beating heart" bumper sticker spotted in Chicagoland, I think I counted five or six in the Super Wal-Mart parking lot before I stopped keeping track. Right-wing shows of support were everywhere. I may as well have been on a different planet.

The first time we went to the beach, I thought we'd washed up on the set of MTV's *Spring Break*. Samantha said, "Um, Mommy, why are those girls wearing their underwear?" Try explaining a thong bikini to a kindergartener. As we came into view of the ocean, I said, "Sam, look, it's the ocean!" She said, "It looks like Lake Michigan."

"Lake Michigan doesn't go all the way around the world! Lake Michigan doesn't have whales and sharks!" The minute it came out of my mouth I knew I had made a mistake.

"Sharks?" She looked at me like I had just told her there were monsters under the bed.

"Well. Yes. But they won't bother you unless you go really far out."

Jenny's mom chimed in. "Actually, this is right by where that boy was attacked by a shark recently."

And so Samantha spent her first time at the ocean only allowed to go in up to her knees. Then she saw a crab and decided it was safer to make sand castles instead.

"This is nothing like Lake Michigan," she informed me.

It wasn't long into the week before the girls started to mutiny. I guess the novelty of tropical plants and small amphibians wore off pretty fast. I had planned on a nice, relaxing, easygoing vacation. I didn't anticipate their short attention spans. The swim noodles and pool toys we bought weren't fun anymore, Emily lost her crayons, Lexi spent an inordinate amount of time making KICK ME signs to stick on our backs, Samantha wanted to watch Nickelodeon and no one else did, everyone wanted the last bowl of Cookie Crisp.

One night, we decided to give in to the girls' pleas and take them to the community pool. We got suited up and took a walk down the block. It was still incredibly warm outside, but without the sun, the temperature was pleasant. When we got there, the gate was locked. "Oh, hell no. We came here to swim; we're going to swim," Jenny said.

"It's locked. We're not getting in," I told her.

"The pool lights are on. Maybe they locked it by accident. Lexi, can you climb the fence and unlock the gate?" Jenny asked her daughter.

I was appalled. "No. No. No. We are not letting an eight-year-old break into the pool so we can swim."

"Oh, quiet. It's fine. Let's go. Girls, tell Stephanie we're here to have fun."

"We want to go swimming! We want to go swimming!"

Needless to say, we got into the pool. Every time a car came down the street, we ducked like fugitives. It became a game. Someone yelled, "Car!" and we all hit the ground, stifling our giggles. I was sure that a security guard was going to come by and have us arrested for trespassing. Corrupting minors, even. "I'm not so sure this is the best example to set," I told Jennifer. "Of course it is!" she scoffed at me.

All in all, we survived the week relatively unscathed. The girls fell into a routine, sleeping late, swimming, playing music and dancing in the sunroom at night, watching movies before passing out on an airbed on the living room floor.

It wasn't long before we had to leave. This time, we were going without Grandpa, since he was staying for a few more weeks. This gave us far more space for the girls to spread out in, which meant fewer backseat spats to referee. Crucially for us adults up front, we had full control over the radio volume and the car speed. By the time we got to Indiana, nearly twenty hours into the trip, we were all overtired and slap-happy. We had given up on keeping the kids calm and had long abandoned pulling over for every juice spill and food cleanup, figuring we'd just deal with it all at the end. At some point, one of them got into a bag of Pull-Ups. "Who wears *Pull-Ups*?" Lexi taunted. "Who's the baby?"

"Lexi! Knock it off! That's enough!" Jenny yelled at her elder daughter. Emily sometimes had accidents and she didn't want her to be embarrassed.

Luckily, the teasing was soon abandoned in favor of using the Pull-Up as a hat. A couple minutes later, all three girls erupted in a fit of laughter and I turned around to see them waving at our fellow motorists, all wearing sunglasses and diapers on their heads, and furiously making signs to hold up in the window.

"Do not hold up any signs!" I warned. "What do they say?"

"They say WE HAVE DIAPERS ON OUR HEADS," the girls told me.

I was impressed with their sense of humor, so instead of stopping them, I told them to throw me a diaper. If you can't beat 'em, join 'em. Quickly enough Jennifer and I and our three girls were all wearing diapers on our heads and waving at cars. The kids were stunned. "Look, your mom put one on her head!" "Your mom has one too!" We were already on a roll before the church bus came up to our left side. I briefly considered acting like an adult. In that moment, I turned to see all three of them holding their pointer fingers above their heads to make devil ears and sticking their tongues out at the scandalized members of the Baptist church. Believe me, the van passengers were not pleased, probably even less so with us than the kids.

"Okay, okay, that's enough, come on," I told the girls. We finished our drive a fair bit more subdued, not because we felt guilty or ashamed, but simply because it's hard to top an experience as funny as that.

Without all the unnecessary stops, the drive home took four hours fewer than the drive down. We rejoiced when Chicago radio stations came in again. I marveled at how comforting the sight of the city was as we came in from the Skyway Bridge. When Samantha and I got home, the silence was deafening. Just the two of us again. I missed the constant noise and chatter. It wasn't the most exotic trip, or the most action-packed, but it had a lasting impact nonetheless.

An only child, Samantha learned an invaluable lesson about life with siblings. The girls ate together, played together, negotiated playtime activities, and shared a common sleeping space. They schemed, orchestrated practical jokes, and were subsequently scolded together. In that short amount of time, she experienced what daily life was like with other children her age to contend with. At home, every activity was her choice alone and there was never a lack of quiet. She often told me that she was lonely and bored without a brother or sister to play with; in Florida, she learned there were advantages to being the only kid in the house. The last Popsicle is still there the next day, no one changes the channel, and you don't have to eat the lunch everyone else wants.

Single mothers often find a foster family in their close friends. We lean on each other instead of a partner; we rely on each other for companionship and entertainment. I couldn't offer my daughter much in the way of "family" vacations, but the substitute of traveling with Jenny and her girls was just as rewarding, and perhaps even more fun. I felt guilty when Samantha came home from school and told me about the family vacations her friends were taking over spring break or summer. I was parenting alone and finishing my BA full-time. I had the time and scheduling flexibility, but not the money, for a typical vacation. This was a rare opportunity to create affordable (yet priceless!) lifelong memories. Years later, Samantha still brings up the Pull-Ups incident for a laugh and tells her friends about the first time she saw the ocean.

I could never duplicate the sense of freedom and adventure we had on our hasty road trip. There are black-and-white photos of Lexi, Emily, and Samantha grinning like fools, wearing toddler diapers on their heads; me and Jenny in the front seat, makeupless, tired, her with a messy ponytail, me with a bandana and French braids, laughing. Samantha in her Gap boy-cut bikini at the beach, posing with a palm tree. Me, the last time I wore a bikini, in a huge floppy white hat and white gauchos, barefoot in the sand. And my favorite photo, in color, of

Samantha and me—she's five and I'm twenty-three; she is wearing an orange-and-red halter dress with tropical print, I am wearing a long red skirt and a white tank top, and we're standing on the lawn holding each other tight.

Now Jennifer and I are older, more settled, less flexible. Our girls would probably not enjoy being trapped together in a hot car from sundown to sunup. They are already full-blown tweens who would much rather hang out with their friends than Mom. It is no longer just me and Sam; I am partnered and have another daughter. But that's okay with me, because we'll always have that week in Florida.

The Language of Romance

Cathy Keir

I've always regretted that both my parents were English speakers. How easy it would have been to grow up bilingual if one of them had had the foresight to marry a foreigner. How many career opportunities it would have opened up to be fluent in two or more languages. I could be working in Brussels right now, simultaneously translating all those important Euro edicts for the EU.

It may be too late for me to achieve true multilingual status, but not for my children. Unfortunately, I too have opted for a plain old English-speaking father for them, and the powers that be in the U.K. education system have only just decided it would be a good idea to teach foreign languages to pupils from the age of seven rather than eleven. By the time they start drilling French verbs into the unwilling little brains of British primary school children in 2010, my two will be eleven and nine, far too old to reach native fluency this side of emigration.

My husband and I need to take linguistic action now, before Ben and Hannah reach the "It's too embarrassing to talk with that funny accent" stage. So we decide on a visit to France for the summer. Perhaps if we like it there we can go the whole hog: sell up, move abroad, live like kings on a pauper's wage, and cram a few more European languages into their ethnocentric heads before their learning capacity diminishes with age.

Just how unimpressed they would be with the idea we couldn't have guessed, until we set off across the English Channel to Brittany.

We did it on the cheap, using a ferry company we'd never heard of, which, it became clear, balances its books by charging peanuts and providing endless rows of thinly padded plastic seats instead of proper cabins. The children enjoyed bedding down in sleeping bags between the rows, but Mike and I spent an excruciating night on camping mats in a dingy lounge with twenty or so other people all suffering the same six hours of misery, one of whom had the worst case of sleep apnea I'd ever heard. He sloped off early in the morning, leaving the rest of us to muse on the high-decibel snoring we'd endured, without respite, all night. We decided, too late for the return journey, alas, that cutting back on ferry fares was not worth a night of hell and a subsequent day with our minds wreathed in the fog of sleep deprivation.

The small Breton village we chose was a big hit with the children. Maybe it was the extra week they had off school—we'd snuck them out early to take advantage of the cheaper term-time ferry fares—or maybe it was the rented house with its enormous garden featuring trees and grass, as opposed to our back yard at home, which boasts paving stones and potted plants and is just big enough for a game of Swingball. Whatever the reason for their exhilaration, it gave us hope that in just a few days both kids would be conversing with local villagers and playing Gallic tag between the apple trees.

We started our language familiarity campaign by taking them to the playground in the nearest town, Dol de Bretagne, which was filled with happy, laughing youngsters in immaculate matching gear unsullied by mud or ketchup. Still, kids don't notice things like that, we thought; they'll soon be playing together despite the pristine cleanliness of the indigenous population.

But every time a friendly French child approached, speaking, horror of horrors, French, our two ran to us in confusion. Five-year-old Hannah was appalled, despite two expensive terms of after-school Club Français:

"Mummy, he spoke French to me and even when I spoke to him in English he carried on talking to me in French. I hate him."

A bit of local sightseeing didn't appease their disgust in this unfathomable language. We visited the fairy-tale Combourg Castle, childhood home of Chateaubriand, a man who, as well as having a steak designed for him, seems to have spent a little bit of time in every town in Brittany, perhaps foreseeing how he could help the tourism industry for centuries to come. As we trailed around after the guide, consulting the garbled written English translation and trying to whisper it into our children's suddenly deaf ears, seven-year-old Ben complained loudly, "This is boring. Why is she speaking French all the time? Where are the dungeons?"

It must be said that compared to the multilingual, child-friendly audio guides provided by that glorious British institution, The National Trust, Combourg's lackluster guide was a rather basic attempt to interpret the history of this lovely chateau. The children perked up when they saw the cat, though. Not a living, breathing feline that wound itself around their legs in ingratiating feline fashion, but a skeletal, screeching, mummified cat that had been walled up alive, thousands of years before, to ward off evil spirits. It was discovered during renovations and put on display in a glass case, redolent of the dusty museums of my childhood. It confirmed how different attitudes to historic interpretation are in France, and I worried that animal-loving Hannah would be forever traumatized by the mangy apparition. But she was fascinated and edged ever closer to the thing, not quite believing it was dead.

The one French expression the children did master on holiday, despite themselves and with a perfect French accent, was *"vide grenier."* Its literal meaning, according to the Babel Fish online translator, is "vacuum the attic," but here in Blighty we know it better as the car-boot sale (the U.S. garage sale). We came across them everywhere: on the beach, in ancient village squares, and, a special treat, a specifically child-oriented sale in Cancale, just twenty miles from our house. Ben and Hannah added exponentially to their cache of cheap plastic junk, while their dad became familiar with Brittany's agricultural tools from the last couple of centuries. It seems the Bretons have had enough of the things, so they offload them onto gullible Brits during the holiday season. Mike is now waxing lyrical to anyone who'll listen about a rusty old chisel-type thing that he's been using to gouge crumbly plaster from our walls.

The village bar was only a few paces away from the house we were staying in, and when we got to know some of the regulars, we found there were Dutch, German, English, and Spanish residents as well as the mostly French Saturday afternoon boules team. Great, we thought, the kids will be surrounded by so many different languages they'll have no choice but to absorb something. We took them to a sing-along one evening, at which they sat in stupefied silence listening to Gallic folk songs, French versions of songs they know and, time to take them home, English pub songs belted out by Ronnie and his guitar. And what did they take away from this pan-European musical extravaganza?

"Why couldn't I have two Coca-Colas instead of just one?" complained Hannah.

Ben's comment was typically ethnocentric: "It would have been better if I could have understood all the words." It was probably a blessing he couldn't.

Despite the minor irritation to our children that the people in France persisted in speaking French, we enjoyed the holiday so much that we started considering a move to Brittany. We huddled outside real-estate agents' windows and almost tiptoed into one of their offices, but I saw sense at the last minute and dragged Mike away to the nearest café.

"We could buy a derelict farmhouse and renovate it," he said, breathless at what you can buy for the price of our Victorian terraced house in Devon. "The children would become bilingual, we could grow our own vegetables, walk down the road to the local but international bar . . ."

Ben looked up from the steaming hot chocolate he was spooning into his mouth and said, "I will only move to France if Louis and Silas come with me and if everyone in France speaks English."

So that was that. No chance of his two best friends relocating to the same French village at the same time, and even less chance of every local resident speaking to him solely in English. There was also the small matter of earning a living. We'd be unlikely to find meaningful work in a country whose language we regularly mangle and rarely master.

Then some new French friends invited us, en famille, for a day's fishing. Rural tranquillity with a Gallic twist; what could be more tempting? We envisaged a pleasantly peaceful day in the Baie du Mont Saint Michel while the kids gambolled about at our sides with buckets and spades. What we did not expect was a gruelling three hours of spine-sapping, sand-raking work. Not for the first time we had cause to rue the expression *"vive la différence."*

We soon discovered that the kind of fishing we'd been invited to sample involved nearly an hour's journey at low tide to the farthest reaches of the seemingly infinite sands of Mont-St-Michel Bay, bouncing uncontrollably in a suspension-free trailer pulled by a retching tractor. The driver, our friend and guide, was an elderly but sprightly octogenarian, Monsieur Meslin, whose working life spent hefting sacks of grain up and down ladders had left him bow-legged but wiry and strong.

The children were fizzing with excitement at the thought of travelling in a trailer, kitted out with benches and cushions and towed by a real tractor. The poor, benighted city-dwellers couldn't have anticipated the teeth-rattling drive down pot-holed lanes and across limitless, rolling mudflats that had me wishing I'd worn my minimal-bounce sports bra. They were feeling sick by the time we reached our destination, unable to focus on the constantly jiggling view of sand, sand, and yet more sand.

I eventually realized there'd been a clue in the invitation when Monsieur Meslin asked if we'd like to come with him for a spot of *"pêche à pied."* I'd translated *"pêche"* correctly as fish, but had somehow managed to filter out the giveaway *"à pied."* "On foot," not a mode of transport you'd normally associate with a day's fishing at the seaside.

As the tractor rattled past the flaking wooden poles that stuck out of the sand at regular intervals, I couldn't help wondering if we'd be able to beat the tide back along this route, should something happen to our guide or his aged vehicle. This part of the Brittany coast has the highest tides in Europe, especially in March and September, when locals say the sea comes up at the speed of a galloping horse, covering twenty-five kilometers of undulating sand before it reaches the polders.

On our slow trek across the sand we passed people, keener and younger than our guide, who were walking out to the fishing grounds. One of them made the mistake of asking Monsieur Meslin for a lift. He refused, explaining to us that he didn't know him and didn't want to take the risk of getting him there and back safely. I fixed my gaze more firmly on the wooden posts jutting out from the sculpted sand, and started counting them, just in case.

"La pêche à pied" is a centuries-old tradition in this area, and even in the early 1980s there were still around fifty cockle fishers making a living from the work. They've mostly retired now and there are few, if any, professional seashore fishermen, but the low tides are a magnet for enthusiastic crowds of amateurs who still enjoy supplementing their diet with a day out on the sands, heading for the low-tide mark in hundreds of tractors towing trailers filled with men, women, and children who've been harvesting this free feast all their lives. They gather oysters, mussels, cockles, and in our case, *palourdes*. We didn't know what these were when we arrived on the mudflats, but we knew just what they looked like after three hours of digging for them.

When we jumped out of the trailer, landing ankle-deep in rich, brown mud, we took a rake each, including small ones for Ben and Hannah, and followed our guide to what he judged to be a good spot. We watched as he showed us how to rake the top layer of sand, meticulously searching for these creatures, which look like a darker, larger version of a cockle. There was much excitement when we found our first one, but then disappointment as our guide did the typical French shoulder shrug and said, *"Trop petit, laissez-le"* ("Too small, leave it").

There are strict regulations governing the size of the shellfish you can take, and he told us the authorities often wait at the edge of the beach at low tide to check the tractors' loads.

The weather was bright but blustery, and with only our Neoprene beach shoes and flimsy nylon raincoats, I worried that the children would complain about soggy feet, cold noses, or blistered hands from the unaccustomed raking; but they got stuck in and were overjoyed when they found their own palourdes, rejoicing even more when they got the thumbs-up from Monsieur Meslin:

"*Oui, c'est assez grand, vous pouvez garder celui-la.*" ("Yes, big enough, you can keep that one.")

We soon started spotting the things more easily, and proudly gathered a small pile to throw into the bucket, but when we saw the mountain of sand-encrusted creatures assembled by Monsieur Meslin, our pride turned to shame. What had we been doing? Raking with our eyes shut? It was obviously one of those things that get easier with practice. And I had spent a lot of time twisting my aching back and admiring the endless sand that stretched to a distant Mont-St-Michel, floating on a bed of mist. It was as if we were on another planet, a richly textured, rolling sandscape, swirling its way to the horizon.

I wasn't sorry when our guide said it was time to go, and I was relieved when the tractor started on the first try, as I didn't fancy a long, squelching trudge back to shore. But that still left the question of what to do with the bucket full of palourdes that Monsieur Meslin insisted we should take home with us.

"Moi, je les mange crus" ("I eat them raw") he boasted. I couldn't see Mike, who struggles with crab sandwiches, trying them raw, so I tried to remember the intricacies of Madame Meslin's recipe for *palourdes farcies*. She'd explained it to me as I washed the sand off the children's legs in a bucket in her garden, but all I could remember was that it involved butter, parsley, and garlic. In the end I just cooked them with wine and onions à la Moules Marinières, and made sure all the shells had opened.

And how did we all enjoy our feast of free food that we'd spent three hours collecting? Wait; did I say "we"? Mike tried one, said "Hm, not bad," and refused to eat any more. The children took a gruesome interest in watching the palourdes slowly simmering and crackling open on the stove, but when invited to have a taste, they shrieked, "Yeuch, no thanks. Can we have pizza?"

So it was up to me to plough my way, single-handedly, through an entire bucket of clams, feeling disappointed that the children's first experience of fishing hadn't turned them into instant Francophiles. And as if to emphasize this point, when Ben returned to school in September he refused to continue with after-school Club Français, saying, "It's just drawing and singing, and I don't like either."

We're persisting, though, and even if we don't actually decide to live in France, I'm determined to get the children into one of those brilliant French holiday clubs next time we go; then they'll have to speak the language or starve. It may sound harsh, but total immersion is what's needed. After all, I taught them to swim in the deep end, and that worked.

Mile-high Motherhood

Sarah Davies

The noise-canceling headset did not cancel out the noise of my miniature screaming copilot at an altitude of 10,500 feet. My three-month-old daughter, Emma, was an unwilling second-in-command.

Her infant car seat had attached so nicely to the right front seat of my Mooney TLS single-engine airplane that our loving mother-daughter piloting adventures seemed meant to be. Had Mooney planned for this in the design of their TLS? After all, there are more and more women pilots every day. Surely they sought to accommodate the infants that these women pilots would produce, and undoubtedly wish to travel with. What corporate thoughtfulness, what social insight . . . what was I thinking?

Prebaby, I knew I would never be one of those "traditional moms" who seemed to lose their mind and identity in a whirl of postpartum hormones. I was first and foremost a pilot: A fully instrument-rated, multiengine, commercial and airline transport pilot and instructor. A woman in a man's world. No baby would ever stop me from flying.

Certainly, I thought, the reason most babies and children were such poor travelers was lack of practice. If you feed children hotdogs and chicken strips, they will only tolerate Denny's or McDonald's. Feed a child sushi and brie and you will create a junior gourmet who craves fine international cuisine at the tender age of two.

Similarly, taking my tiny infant on plane trips piloted by me would turn her into a model traveler and junior pilot. I knew that my future two-year-old daughter would sit happily for hours in the Mooney, enjoying foie gras on crusty French bread, while precociously assisting me with transponder and GPS settings.

I had planned for this day from eight and a half months before her birth. I scoured the Internet for little baby pilot headsets. I cut some foam earplugs to baby ear canal size. I bought her a cute little outfit that said "Junior Pilot." I made sure my choice of infant car seat was properly FAA-approved and that it fit snugly and safely in the Mooney while allowing for free movement of the aircraft controls.

My fellow instructors all joked that Emma's first words would be "More right rudder." After all, she had been exposed to airplane engine noise and my insightful instructional commentary for nearly nine months in utero. The FAA allows women pilots to fly during pregnancy for as long as they can safely do so. I took full advantage of this vague and permissive attitude, and flew through my entire pregnancy. So why wouldn't my daughter take to flying as naturally as a baby bird?

I decided that three months seemed a mature enough age for her very first flight on the daylight side of my uterus. She and I arrived at the local airport, excitedly anticipating her debut. The trip would be an effortless one-hour trek over the beautiful volcanic terrain of western New Mexico to visit my mother in Arizona. Mom was not as excited as I was about Emma's first copiloting experience. Apart from the obvious grandmotherly worries at the prospect of her first grandchild hurtling through the sky in a tiny, single-engine plane, my mother also expressed doubts about how easy this expedition would really turn out to be. But I knew best.

Emma sat happily in her car seat, closely studying a small patch of spit-up on her "Junior Pilot" sweatshirt while I hauled the plane out of the hangar and conducted the preflight inspection. She gave me a glorious gummy smile as I strapped her car seat into the copilot's position. I tested the controls. All was well.

In went the ear plugs. Hmm . . . they didn't fit quite as well as I had hoped. I crammed them in a little harder. After all, with the amount of flying we would be doing I had to be very careful to protect Emma's delicate hearing. Emma gave me her first look of disapproval.

I smiled at her reassuringly as I clamped the little blue baby-sized headset onto her bald head. It turned out that Emma did not like headsets, and the wailing began.

I grinned broadly at my tiny copilot and put my headset on. With as much faux enthusiasm as I could muster, I said, "See, Emma, Mama has a headset too!" Louder wailing. Okay, change of plans. Since the flight was only an hour, perhaps we could skip the headset just this one time. The earplugs would simply have to suffice. I removed the offending headset and wiped her tears with my sleeve.

After she had settled down a bit, no longer crying, but not exactly vibrating with excited anticipation as I had hoped, it was time to start the engine. The engine rumbled and came to life and the baby started screaming full timbre. Avionics switch on—*Better get my noise-canceling headset on right now*, I thought. The engine grew quieter as the headset turned on. The baby grew louder as the engine noise dulled.

Well, I thought, they say that noise and vibration soon lull babies to sleep. Besides, since airplane engines are what she heard in the womb; she should soon settle down. We taxied out and were airborne as quickly as I could safely manage.

As we floated miraculously upward into the smooth, fall air, I experienced the thrill of introducing my little one to a world I loved achingly. My daughter, on the other hand, experienced the thrill of screaming while soaring toward the brilliant blue New Mexico sky. She screamed, and screamed, and screamed. A concerned air traffic controller asked me, "What have you got in there? A parrot or a monkey?"

Albuquerque Approach Control handed me off to Albuquerque Center, who had probably been forewarned that they would be dealing with a Mooney full of smuggled exotic pets.

Emma shrieked as we leveled off at 10,500 feet. Once I was out of Albuquerque's busy airspace, level and on course for Show Low, Arizona, my last task was to adjust the throttle and fuel flow settings for cruise flight. With the Cruise Checklist completed, my now decreased workload allowed me to finally return my thoughts to my less-than-thrilled baby pilot. "Perhaps her ears hurt," I pondered, as I desperately shoved a pacifier into her mouth. Emma always hated pacifiers, especially, so it seemed, while airborne. The pacifier shot out of her mouth at high velocity and ricocheted off the transponder, landing somewhere far beneath her seat.

"Hungry" was the next thought that entered my head. Despite our prophylactic preflight feeding, this was an unfortunate possibility. "Is it possible," I asked myself, "to nurse a baby and pilot an airplane at the same time?" The choice I faced was to try it or endure ear-piercing wails for another forty minutes, which would probably scar both Emma and me (not to mention our poor air traffic controller) for life.

In all my many years of training, I had never been briefed on this particular emergency. I was forced to come up with my own Nursing Emergency Checklist:

1. Altitude and heading numbers—VERIFY
2. Heading bug—SET
3. Altitude preselect—SET
4. Autopilot—ON
5. Verify autopilot functioning correctly
6. Shirt and nursing flap on bra—UNBUTTON
7. Nursing pad—REMOVE and secure on yoke in Approach Chart clip for easy retrieval later
8. Screaming baby—REMOVE FROM CAR SEAT
9. Baby position—LATCH ON

So, there we were, gliding through the clear turquoise sky at 10,500 feet above sea level, the two of us enjoying a timeless moment of mother-daughter bonding, and best of all, *silence*! Little did Albuquerque Center realize what was going on inside our little green blip on the radar screen. Emma and I were proving that day that it is possible to pilot an airplane, talk to the controllers, and nurse an infant all at once.

We nursed our way over massive, ancient lava flows that looked like overdone chocolate cake fresh from the oven. We saw miniature antelope, doll-sized octagonal homes that the Navajo call "hogans," and vast plains dotted with little broccoli piñons. We nursed until we could nurse no more and Emma's mom had to become the pilot once again to get us safely back to Earth.

Fortunately, Emma was too busy working on a giant poo to complain much during the landing. Safely back on the ground, we taxied to the parking area and I tied the Mooney up while Emma sat in her car seat with an expression of intense concentration, finishing her business.

Judging by the lack of baby-changing facilities, small airports do not get many mom-pilots with babies flying in for a quick diaper freshen-up. The Mooney's horizontal stabilizer (tail) proved to be an excellent changing table. Did the Mooney company include this dual purpose in their design plan too?

In her diaper, a surprise awaited me (beyond the obvious "natural" one): a tiny earplug. Just one. In all the fuss, it had somehow made its way from her ear to the interior of her diaper. But where was the other one? I checked her ears. Gone.

I never did find the other earplug that I had so lovingly crafted before her birth. Six years later I still wonder where it went. Either it is permanently stuck deep inside her ear canal, festering away to this day, or it worked its way down through a crack in the floor and sits in the landing gear motor, waiting to be discovered by a puzzled mechanic.

Six years of experience and three children have made me reevaluate my opinion of the ease with which one can really travel with kids. I guess Mom was right after all. My children don't like sushi or foie gras, and they don't like airplanes much either. I have learned the hard way that there is a very good reason why one never finds changing tables in small airport bathrooms or Nursing Emergency Checklists in airplane pilot operating handbooks. However, my kids will now eat mushroom crepes . . . can toddler aerobatic lessons be far behind?

International Underwear

Dana Standish

I have never understood the allure of travel. After my two children were born, I understood it even less. Nobody ever believes me when I say I am very happy at home, and do not want to go anywhere or see anything. I have a good friend who is a writer for *National Geographic* magazine. A few times each year she is airlifted to one of the world's exotic and inaccessible places and comes back full of stories of intrigue, derring-do, and ecological disaster averted. I have to take a Xanax just to listen to her tales of stalking the last wild jaguar, stumping for a remaining stand of Portuguese cork forest, or fighting to save endangered parrots. She doesn't believe me when I tell her that I would rather watch water pour out of my kitchen tap than stand at the top of the highest waterfall in the Andes.

Since I do not like to travel under any circumstances, traveling with children seemed especially unappealing. It would be the recreational equivalent of planning an extravagant, blow-the-bank Christmas, shopping for months for the perfect gifts, and staying up late for a week to wrap them, only to have the kids spend the entire day playing with the curling ribbon they tore off the packages. Meanwhile, the miniature-golf sets proved they were under par and the unopened Tickle Me Elmos laughed all the way to Toys "R" Us's bank.

Traveling, like Christmas, was a lot better in theory than in practice. There was no harm in reading travel books or looking at pictures of the Eiffel Tower, as long as one did not seriously contemplate actually leaving home.

So let's just say that I was not elated when my husband announced, three summers ago, that he was going to a four-day conference in Amsterdam, his trip was paid for, and we were all invited to go along. As negotiations proceeded, he threw in a week in Paris, the stinker. In a moment of cheese-inspired weakness I decided to try to be a normal person (an experiment not likely to be repeated) and I said yes.

Traveling in Europe with two teenagers who had never before left the United States proved to be an interesting experience. We were not with a tour or a group, and my husband was at his conference all day, so the three of us bummed around Amsterdam and its environs, traveling by bus, train, bike, and foot. The kids were aware of being Americans, aware of the disdain many Europeans felt for the United States since the advent of the Iraq war, and keen not to be seen as tourists. This meant that they spent an inordinate amount of time distancing themselves from me, the ultimate tourist in their eyes, with my camera around my neck, my Birkenstocks, and my propensity to try out my faltering foreign language skills on innocent bystanders.

As a protest against American imperialism and to keep Kodak and other American corporations from getting even one dime from us, they would not let me take a picture of them in front of anything, even the Anne Frank House. Under threat of my not paying for lunch, they finally agreed to one picture. In it, my son hides inside the hood of his sweatshirt, like a rapper, and my daughter, in an effort to dematerialize, hangs her head so far over her hunched shoulders that she looks like Richard Nixon on the eve of his resignation. As a protest against American imperialism, and in order to distance herself from the United States and from being a tourist, my daughter wore a blue sweatshirt with the word MICHIGAN written in gold three-thousand-point type across the front. As they posed for their one photo, a man leaving the Anne Frank house looked at my daughter's sweatshirt and said, "Detroit Pistons! World champs!"

"It's your fault," my daughter opined. "When you take pictures, everyone knows you're American."

We had many art-related adventures, two of which stand out. The first one involved taking two trains and a bus several hours into the Dutch countryside and getting off at a bus shelter along a highway, near where we'd been told we'd find a museum. We walked for an hour inside a national park, following a tattered map that we'd found in the bottom of my husband's briefcase, until we came to an uncountable fleet of the white bikes that are free for the borrowing in the Netherlands. These bikes lean against trees and fill bike racks wherever you go; you simply take one and ride to your destination and leave the bike for the next person. We mounted the bikes and rode further into the park, not knowing where we were going or what we would find—perhaps Hansel and Gretel's cottage, or perhaps a major European museum; each seemed equally possible. It was one of the few times in my life I remember feeling impervious, as though nothing could hurt me, and being totally happy to be with the two people I loved most in the world, absolutely free. It was better, even, than watching water pour out of my kitchen tap at home. When we got to the museum, we found out that all the van Goghs we had come to see were on loan to the Seattle Art Museum, in our home city, which, of course, we had left three days earlier in order to be exposed to the great art works of Europe.

I also remember looking at some van Goghs that managed to remain in Holland, in a different museum, and thinking how lucky we were to stand in front of such beauty. I had studied these works for years when I was an art student. Seeing them was, for me at least, like seeing a piece of the True Cross.

I learned a very important lesson that day in terms of traveling with children: namely, that rapture is not necessarily a shared experience. As I stood in front of one of van Gogh's self-portraits, transported into another time and place and contemplating artistic sacrifice, my son said to me, "Mom, I've been thinking." I had been hoping to find a piece of art that spoke to him and had been largely striking out all week. I knew that I had finally hit on a painting that would speak to the great loneliness and alienation that is the lifeblood of the teenager, that no one could look into van Gogh's eyes and fail to be moved. I turned to my son, waiting for the signal that he was leaving the self-involvement of the teenager behind and communing with van Gogh's suffering.

"This makes me wonder," he said. "Do we have any bread and cheese? Because I could use a little lunch."

My friend the *National Geographic* writer can pack up and leave on a moment's notice, so happy is she at the prospect of traveling. She frequently carries only an overnight bag for a monthlong trip. For me it is just the opposite. I have an elaborate ritual I've developed that has more steps than the Roman Catholic liturgy and involves about as many props. In addition to my purse, a survival kit unto itself, I travel with two pillows, my portable CD player, enough CDs and extra batteries to survive a quick trip to the Middle East in the event of hijacking, a camera in case I am called upon to identify the hijackers, a few back issues of *People* magazine (so I'll be able to identify the hijackers if they are Paris Hilton or Demi Moore), a toothbrush, an eye pillow, several bottles of water, and enough Power Bars to provide snacks for the Little League World Series.

Some of these props change: the CDs, for instance, or the particular issue of *People*. But I always wear my lucky flying underwear. There is nothing special about them, unless you consider the fact that they have always gotten me safely to my destination, on those rare occasions when I have been forced to leave my kitchen. Our great European experiment almost came to an unfortunate end, therefore, when I lost my lucky flying underwear in a Laundromat outside of Amsterdam and was not able to leave until I had found them. Although my husband and children had been flying with both me and the lucky flying underwear for many years, until this point they had never heard about the reason we had always reached our destination safely. And now, standing on the pavement in front of the laundromat, with minutes to spare before we would miss our flight home, the lucky flying underwear didn't seem to fit organically into the conversation.

It was my own fault for being an arrogant American and leaving my laundry for the woman to tend, as I went out to find a bite to eat. When I returned, someone else's lucky flying underwear was in my washing machine, my underwear was not in my dryer, and I was looking for the number of the American Consulate. I tried to explain the seriousness of the situation to the laundromat woman.

"Those were my lucky underwear," I cried. She looked at me sympathetically.

"You know," I continued, "the ones I need for flying." We did not share a single word of a common language, since she spoke Dutch and I spoke crazy.

She juggled a tiny infant, whom she was bottle-feeding as she moved people's clothes from washer to dryer.

"Here is your underwear," she said as she held up a different pair from my pile.

"But those aren't the right ones," I tried again. "Those aren't the ones I need in order to be able to go home." She looked at me and one eyebrow went up.

"God will look after you," the woman said. "You do not need underwear."

It explained a lot of things about the state of the world to think that God didn't have anything better to do than to keep track of people's foundation garments. There's the whole Middle East situation, for instance. Think how many lost bras that must be worth.

The woman looked at me with understanding. My family waited outside, impatient for me to stuff the laundry into my suitcase so we could leave for the airport. My children pressed their faces against the window of the Laundromat, watching as I opened every dryer all down the line and rooted through other people's clothes, until I found the ratty pair of Carter's that was our ticket home. I was able to don my protective gear and we proceeded to the airport and got home without incident. I didn't even have to do much explaining about the underwear. I think the kids understood, on some deep level, what was going on, and maybe didn't want to hear about it. This is another thing you need to know before you travel with children—that you're not always going to be able to control the things they find out about you or about the world. Sometimes travel expands their perspectives in ways that are best kept under wraps.

Four Babies, Two Sisters, and a Breast Pump

Susan Wolter Nettell

"**M**aybe we could take them home by train."

They, two girls and identical twin boys, currently sleeping and aligned (in birth order) like four peas in a pod on our living room couch, had arrived neatly contained. My sister Lisa had been nineteen weeks pregnant with the quadruplets when she, her husband, Steve, their bed, clothes, and black cat, Ebony, had come to stay with us four months ago. Her doctors in Williston, North Dakota, had sent her to the Minneapolis area to be near medical facilities that could care for high-risk babies.

Brayden, Carter, Keira, and Gracie had been born, in that order, on January 2, small and premature at thirty-two weeks, but healthy. They were all discharged by early February and were now ready for the journey home to North Dakota—a distance of over six hundred and fifty miles, an eleven-hour car trip in the best of circumstances. Our travel plans needed to accommodate feeding four infants every three hours, two at a time: the girls during the first hour, the boys in the second, with one hour free before it started all over. Even if we could beg, borrow, or buy a vehicle that could safely transport four infant car seats, how long would that take us? Snow and icy road conditions were a distinct possibility. And what would we do about the mountain of baby paraphernalia that had accumulated in Minnesota during their stay?

The train idea had bubbled up.

"We could get a bedroom on the train," Lisa had suggested. The idea: Put the babies in their car seats on the lower berth and travel to North Dakota overnight, feeding, burping, and changing diapers as the miles clicked past uninterrupted. Steve would rent a trailer and drive back earlier with the cat, their personal belongings, and the only-slightly-scaled-back replica of the baby aisles at Target. He could quickly set up cribs and meet the train when it arrived in Williston.

At the time it had even sounded reasonably sane.

"Would you come with me and the babies, Suz?" my sister had asked sheepishly.

"Sure." Several years ago I had left corporate finance to stay home with my kids. My husband, Chuck, ten-year-old daughter, Alexa, and seven-year-old son, Zach, would be fine without me for a few days.

The ink had dried on the tickets.

On our morning of departure, snow is falling in big, wet, heavy clumps. Steve loads the cat in the pickup and departs with the packed trailer at 6:00 AM.

Lisa disappears into our dining room turned bedroom. Soon I hear the soft, familiar sound of the Symphony Deluxe Breast Pump.

Whooompha. Whooompha. Whooompha.

My sister Lisa is twenty-nine years old, a pharmacist, and has always been a rational woman. She has never lived under the delusion that she could breast-feed four babies simultaneously. However, she's determined to give her babies the best possible start in life. She pumps during the "off" feeding hour and the babies are fed bottles of breast milk, supplemented with formula as needed.

The snow keeps falling, clogging traffic in the metro area all day. Our train is scheduled to leave at 11:15 PM and arrive in Williston at 11:07 AM the next morning. As evening approaches, we call a 1-800-number and a perky machine tells us the train is running an hour late. We hunker down and wait some more. We finally load the baby vehicle, a large four-wheel-drive SUV loaned to us from a friend of a friend, which has been sufficiently warmed for infants and to heatstroke potential for the adults currently snarling and sweating to properly install and tighten four car seats.

We try to be inconspicuous at the train station, on red alert for a cough or runny nose. My pharmacist sister is acutely aware that RSV, a common respiratory virus, can become serious very quickly in the lungs of premature infants.

"Oh, look at the babies!" a mother squeals as we walk into the waiting room. She urges her son to come look.

Yikes. Lisa's shoulders scrunch defensively.

"Oh, I love babies," another woman exclaims as she runs over to look. A young boy coughs behind us.

Lisa's eyes are wide as she looks down the dark train track.

Someone is sniffling. We pull the babies in closer to us.

"Can I see them? I've never seen quadruplets before."

"*Aaa-choo.*"

The sound of the approaching train is a lifeboat.

Our porter, a young man with a baby face and dark hair, comes to escort us. He has a smile on his face that quirks at the corners. His amusement is a good sign, whether he knew we were coming or not.

"Yes," he tells our party as he looks us over, "everyone can help carry things onto the train." Smart man. We're packing four infant car seats—with infants, a cooler with bottles of frozen breast milk, pillow, quilt, two overnight bags, purses, cameras, breast pump, a couple of plastic hospital bags with empty bottles and brushes, and two diaper bags bulging with clothes, diapers, ointments, pacifiers, bibs, and washcloths. Thankfully Steve took the baby stuff so we could travel "light." Lisa, her college friend Sadie, Chuck, and I each grasp an infant seat and load our other shoulder with straps. Alexa and Zach grab bags and we shuffle to the door in the porter's wake.

"Shoot," Lisa says. The procession stops. The luggage on Lisa's shoulder slides to the ground.

"The strap on the pump case broke." The Symphony Deluxe is compact but heavy.

Lisa reshuffles her load, grabs the handle of the pump, and we start off again.

We navigate the narrow, sharply turned stairs to the second level of the train car, bags bumping the walls, arms straining to hold the car seats up and away from the corners.

We reach the bedroom whose total size, according to the Internet, is 6.5 x 7 feet. Clearly Internet measurements and real-life measurements are different, like human years and dog years. We definitely lost a few feet somewhere in cyberspace. The floor space is smaller than that of most bathrooms. Two berths, one on top of the other, take up one wall of the bedroom. On the other side a sink and vanity make a narrow hallway with the lower berth. A combination shower and toilet compose a small room behind the sink. Chair and miniature fold-down table align the far window.

The bottom berth is folded in an L-shape, a long sofa, where the babies are deposited one-by-one: Carter, Brayden, Gracie, and finally Keira at the window, the birth order lineup abandoned in favor of just getting everyone and everything in the room. Bags are dumped on the floor or pushed in the upper berth as we file in and look around. We can't all fit in the room.

Sadie and Chuck say quick good-byes and go back out in the hall to stand with the porter. Alexa keeps scanning the luggage, babies, and room, but keeps the "Yeah, right" written on her face buttoned behind her lips as she and Zach give me a hug good-bye.

Lisa and I are still standing among the piles of luggage when the train lurches ahead, belching diesel. We stumble and start to giggle.

"Shhhhh!" We are shushed from the bedroom next door. Great. We are in a closet with four babies next to sensitive neighbors.

We uncover the babies, one baby blanket from on top of each, and remove the four blankets that had been carefully rolled and wedged in each car seat to stabilize their small bodies. We search for relatively germ-free corners to pile up the blankets.

Less-used luggage is consigned to the top berth. Diapers and baby bags go on the floor. We now understand why "capacity for two suitcases" was written on the room description on the website.

The porter is back and introduces himself as Chris.

"Wow," he says, looking at the line of babies. "I've never seen anything like this." He shakes his head. "Wow."

"Babies usually like trains." Chris says as he helps us put the cargo net up across the luggage in the top bunk. "The constant swaying seems to relax them."

Could we (and our neighbors) be so lucky?

"Can I get you anything?" he asks.

"I'd really like a can of pop," Lisa requests. "Keep me going through the night."

Chris looks sheepish. "Can't. Everything's closed at this hour."

"What?" A hint of desperation edges her voice.

"You could've purchased pop at the train depot," Chris tells her.

Oh yeah, like she's going to abandon her babies in the germ cesspool and browse the concessions at the railway station.

"I was waiting to get one until after I got on the train."

"Sorry." Chris is now backing out of the room. "We'll have complimentary coffee and juice early in the morning. Right outside your door."

"I don't drink coffee. Is there *anything* available now?"

"I'll see what I can do." His voice is apologetic, his face doubtful. "What kind would you like?"

"I'll take anything with caffeine."

Keira cries out, but when we turn she's still sleeping. We've been alerted; our time is limited. Tiny Keira was born the smallest of the quads at 2 lbs 9 oz, but with a spark that is not dependant on size. We get two bottles from the cooler and start running water in the sink. We soon learn maximum temperature is tepid. Lisa picks up Keira, gently talking to her about the excitement of her first train ride. I run more water, trying to coax it hot. Gracie's eyes are now open too.

I wash my hands and disinfect them with alcohol foam that stings as it seeps into the cracks that have developed across my knuckles from repeated hand washing. I lift Gracie, my hands spanning her back and my fingertips bracing her head. Settling cross-legged on the floor, I cuddle her small six-pound body in my left arm. She drinks her bottle with small, dainty sucks, visible in the rhythm of her cheeks. Gracie lay on top during the pregnancy, next to her mother's heart, and above the fray of her active brothers and spunky sister. She's still watching and processing all that goes on around her, solemly studying my face with big, unblinking eyes.

Lisa takes the chair with Keira, bad knees her one lingering physical memento of several months of bed rest.

Dirty diapers quickly become an issue. In front of the combination shower/toilet door, we turn a precious square of floor space into the diaper changing area. We lay down blankets (a couple of layers) and strategically position the box of wipes.

The girls finish their bottles. We chart the amount they drank to ensure a trend isn't overlooked in the shuffle of four babies. Condition of their diapers is also noted. The charts tell us what we already know; Carter is long overdue a bowel movement.

Carter delivers while drinking his bottle. He's an easygoing baby, the quiet hero at the bottom of the pile in utero, his head the cork that held everyone back until they were large and developed enough to be born. The tiny diaper packs a pungent potency in our small space and we quickly toss it in a white garbage bag that boasts "flexible strength" and a "fresh scent that eliminates odors." We twist the bag shut, crack open the door to the combination shower/toilet, and chuck the whole thing inside.

Brayden is the leading-edge, first baby: first one born, first to gain weight and strength, first one home. He's sporting a black Sharpie dot on one fingernail, his dad afraid we might get him confused with his identical twin brother. He drinks his bottle quickly and immediately falls back to sleep.

The world outside the window is dark, farming country mostly. We make an occasional stop, a single bright light on the brick wall of the depot highlighting the name of the town.

Whooompha. Whooompha. Whooompha.

Lisa pumps while I chart the boys. We're starving. We have formula and frozen breast milk, but if it doesn't go in a bottle—nothing. No can of pop has magically appeared either. Apparently we should have been much more mindful of the vending machines at the depot. The train has provided complimentary packages of dried fruit and nuts and warm water bottles. We try to identify the chunks of chewy fruit by the listed ingredients.

At 3:30 AM, a little over a third of the journey behind us, all is quiet and Lisa leans the chair seat back, trying to get comfortable. I shove things around to make room on the floor in front of the berth, diaper bags at my head, breast pump at my feet. The area is narrow, about a body width, but it allows me to stretch out. I lie on the room's two pillows, trying to disassociate my distaste of walking barefoot in hotel rooms from my current situation.

Sleep is immediate.

When we wake around 5:00 AM we are stopped in Grand Forks, North Dakota. We prepare bottles. While the girls drink, we wonder why the train still isn't moving. The stop is scheduled to be short and the quads have 1:00 PM doctor appointments in Williston.

Brayden grunts as he wakes up. Carter is busy filling his diaper, apparently dealing with pent-up supply. I slide out the door to find the nearby coffee pot. Lisa gets orange juice.

While we're feeding the boys our porter stops by. Our train has been sidetracked, waiting for a freight train to pass. Apparently there's only one track out of Grand Forks and it's owned by the freight company. Chris isn't sure when we'll get going again. He shrugs. Hopefully soon. Soon as defined by whom, I wonder—a boxcar of wheat or two sisters with four preemie babies?

"Can I bring you some breakfast?" Chris asks. He hands us a menu and we order.

We're in the off-feeding hour and we quickly brush our teeth by the miniscule sink. The fresh-scent garbage bag is becoming overwhelmed. Lisa escapes down the hall to find a bathroom that doesn't host a bag of acrid, urine-soaked diapers.

Chris returns with our breakfast, omelets and fried potatoes. We are on one of the last trains in America that still cook food instead microwaving it. The food tastes fabulous; whether from our famished state or the chef's efforts it's hard to tell. Our hour is quickly passing and we shovel it in with the heartiness of freight handlers. Still no word on when we might leave Grand Forks. The eastbound passenger train is now waiting here as well.

Whooompha. Whooompha. Whooompha.

"We're never going to make their doctor appointments," Lisa says, her tone tight. "It's Friday. My babies are preemies. They need to be checked and weighed." A new mother's desperate grasp for control punctuates each sentence. "This has to work out."

I slip a pacifier back into Gracie's mouth and look out the train window. The wind is blowing across the prairie, fresh snow scouring the dirty ice and snow covering the ground at the train station. I don't know when we will leave, but we are in this train car for however long it takes.

"I'll call Steve," Lisa says. She punches numbers into her cell phone. "He can call the doctor's office when they open and try to get us in later."

Around 8:00 AM we start feeding girls again. We hear something and look out the window. A freight train passes. We look at each other. A few minutes later the eastbound passenger train goes through. We feel the slow roll forward of the train as we are burping the girls. I check my watch; we are leaving Grand Forks over three hours late.

Steve calls back while Brayden and Carter are finishing their bottles. He talked to the clinic. When we get to Williston, we'll go straight over and they'll fit us in.

The train's sway rocks the babies to sleep.

Lisa sits on the floor, her legs stretched out, purple sweatshirt rumpled, and shoulder-length blond hair laminated against her head. Her shoulders droop. She's probably slept only three to four interrupted hours a day since the babies were discharged.

"I can't bear the thought of pumping." Tears pool along the bottom rims of her eyes. "I can't imagine ever sleeping again." Her words stumble over each other. "Even if someone else feeds the babies, I still have to pump. I'll never sleep. Never."

"Why don't you sleep now?" I suggest. Through constant worry and two months of hospital bed rest, my sister kept it together. Lack of sleep is the string that unravels her.

"I need to take care of my babies," her words slur.

"Your babies are sleeping," I remind her. "Now is a good time for you to sleep too. I'll watch them."

"You shouldn't have to watch them. They're my babies." Lisa's eyelids slowly slide down over her eyes. "And I need to pump." Her eyelids pop back up, only to slip down again.

"Pump later," I say. "I'll call you if I need you."

Lisa crumples over on the floor next to the berth. She's asleep immediately, her mouth open and her face mashed into the pillow on the floor.

Lisa is my baby sister, fourteen years younger than I. Standing, I check the quads. Brayden's small fist feels sufficiently warm. Carter is slumped to one side, but not so much it is worth the risk of waking him. I remember baby Lisa Jo sitting in a bouncy seat, her blue eyes already analyzing the world. My heart melted a long time ago. Now it tightens in sadness at the thought of her many sleepless nights ahead. Keira awakens and I sniff suspiciously. This train is relaxing a lot of things.

The train pulls into Minot, North Dakota. The conductor announces that passengers can get out and stretch their legs. Lisa stirs and sits up.

"Gracie is still sleeping," I tell her. "Do you want to run into the station?"

Lisa looks out the window. "Yeah. Maybe I'll get a can of pop and wake up."

When Lisa gets back, plastic soda bottle in hand, she looks more awake and energized. She selects a clean outfit for Keira while I give Keira a quick bath with a washcloth. No way are we presenting babies smelling of sour milk to the doctor in Williston. We have a new mother's pride at stake.

Whooompha. Whooompha. Whooompha.

Lisa pumps as I feed Gracie, who decides to deposit her own stinky diaper. Carter is awake and looking for his bottle, but we tease him along using his pacifier and talking to him, our faces up close.

The train chugs by our brother's farm, signaling one and a half hours to go. Oil wells pumping on the prairie flash by our window. I start feeding Carter. Lisa is repacking. Another dirty diaper. The chug and sway of the train seems to be finding secret reserves in Carter.

"Shit." Lisa jumps to her feet. Our table is the size of a handkerchief, cluttered with bottles, baby vitamins, and breast pump supplies. In the chaos we've managed to tip over the coveted bottle of soda and it pours down between the wall and the lower berth.

We pass the small farm town of Ray, about thirty-five miles from Williston. I try to quickly finish Carter's bottle. Maybe every last drop isn't critical. Gracie cries. Lisa takes care of her while I wash and change Carter.

I start on Brayden. Lisa starts slinging dirty bottles and dirty clothes into a bag. Packing rules have suddenly become much looser.

Finally Brayden is fed, changed, cleaned, and back in his car seat. We scramble around trying to find all the baby blankets.

We approach the outskirts of Williston. We roll and stuff support blankets around the babies. They are starting to get hot. So are we. The train is slowing. The last blankets go on as we slow and jerk to a stop, brakes squealing, at the Williston train station.

Lisa grabs a baby and heads out the door while I check under the bed and in the shower. Chris helps us carry out luggage. Lisa's back and takes two babies. I'm the last to leave, a baby in one hand and the flexible strength garbage bag of dirty diapers in the other.

"Can I help you with that?" Chris asks.

"Sure." I hand him the white bag. "This can go in the garbage. It's dirty diapers."

Chris's hands go up in surrender and he backs off.

I navigate the diapers and last baby off the train.

After the clinic we take the babies to their home for the first time. The momentousness of the occasion is lost in the scramble to get bottles warmed and babies fed. My legs feel like jelly, whether from lack of sleep or the movement of the train I'm not sure. There are many hands to help now, but I still feed a baby, my heart not ready to let go. Lisa disappears into her bedroom.

Whooompha. Whooompha. Whooompha.

Got Milk?

Sally Bjornsen

My son throws up. Okay, if you're a parent you're thinking, "Big deal, all kids hurl now and then." But I would wager that you haven't seen projectile vomotosis until you've witnessed my little guy blow like Mount Vesuvius. We should have named the kid Ralph or Chuck instead of Cameron. In his four and a half years, he has spewed white curdled goop in our car no fewer than fifty times. On one particularly memorable trip to Grandma's house, he erupted in his Buzz Lightyear action figure's helmet, filling it to the rim with scrambled eggs and ham. Thanks to Buzz's head gear, there was no major damage to the car interior that day.

Cameron's spewfests have debuted in the car on the freeway, in the car on a ferry, in the car on a bridge, and in the car in the parking lot at IKEA. Lest you spot a theme here and are thinking "So stop taking him on long car journeys," let me put your mind at rest. My baby's puking performances aren't just reserved for vehicular entertainment: He has even vomited at the dinner table with our minister sitting directly across from him. Our good-humored holy man, bringing a whole new meaning to "there but for the grace of God," assured me that Jesus probably barfed as a youngster too.

Cameron's propensity to puke has made me rethink my preteen obsession with a favorite gag, the fake puddle of barf. You know the one: the sink-stopper-sized patch of bile-colored rubber embedded with chunks of faux vegetables and chewed-up Cheerios. My brother and I spent the summer of our fifth- and sixth-grade year hurling that thing out onto the sidewalk while unsuspecting neighbors gingerly stepped around or over it, grossed out by the sight of our clever prank. Who knew that one day our childhood high jinks would be repaid with the real stuff embedded into the upholstery of my car and my clothes? It doesn't take the Dalai Lama to confirm that that's karma.

My son does not have a serious disease or some three-syllable chronic intestinal yeast allergy that causes him to explode at the mere mention of gluten. No, my son is perfectly healthy, a veritable four-and-a-half-year-old in a seven-year-old's body. He's just a big, strapping, happy kid who just happens to puke—a lot—especially when we take to the road, and notably when the trip includes Goldfish crackers and dairy products.

Last Christmas vacation, my husband, Mark, and I got the bright idea to take two of our three kids skiing for the day. Our local mountain is a relatively short, straight drive, two hours and some change from Seattle, all depending on weather conditions, potty stops, and the never-ending road construction due to the overbuilding of Starbucks drive-thrus. We Seattleites would not survive without our coffee. Our boys, Cameron and eleven-year-old Kalen, were anxious for the trip, egging each other on with threats to catch "radical, earth-defying air." I liked Cameron's optimism, but the fact that he'd never really been on skis before made catching anything but the rope tow hard to imagine.

We woke at the crack of dawn, gathered our skis, boots, poles, jackets, scarves, overalls, hats, long underwear, goggles, and of course, Rabitee,

Cameron's weathered stuffed bunny, which was beginning to look more like a dirty, dead possum than a cuddly plaything, and headed out the door—in the drizzling rain. Both Mark and I were optimistic that rain in the lowlands could only mean great powder on the slopes.

I didn't have vomiting on the brain that morning when we drove out of our wet neighborhood in the thirty-three-degree weather. At four and a half, Cameron seemed to have turned the corner on projectability. It had been a few months since we had had any incidents; as a preventative measure we had officially sworn off road milk, which seemed to have done the trick. This trip I was more concerned about Cameron's pus-oozing ear infection that just wouldn't go away. Although his ear looked gross, it didn't seem to be cramping his style. He was as active and happy as ever and barely noticed the amber-colored substance dripping from his ear. Our pediatrician had guaranteed me the day before that a third round of antibiotics was sure to wipe out the infection and put him on the road to recovery.

The voyage started out well. We made our requisite Starbucks stop like everyone else heading to the mountain, and ordered our tall, skinny latte, no foam, and double Americano, with room for cream. We passed through the valley in record time. Let me clarify, the valley isn't much of a valley anymore, it's more like sea of strip malls, complete with tanning booths, Subway sandwich shops, grocery stores, nail salons, and stop lights at every intersection. The trip was going smoothly, like the Partridge Family on tour, until I remembered that Cameron needed to take his medicine.

"How are you feeling, my baby?" I asked him over my shoulder, straining my neck to peek inside his ear.

"I'm good. Can I ski all day, Mommy? Until it's really dark?"

"Well, we'll see. We need to find out what the plan is with your lesson."

"Will I get big air, Mommy? Just like Kalen?"

"I'm sure you will, honey. How does your ear feel?"

"It's fine. It's just a little drippy."

Cameron had his infection for so long that I had gotten used to the waxy drool that occasionally pooled up in his ear or dripped from his lobe. But the teachers in the "little tot" ski program might just be plain grossed out if not alarmed. And so I did what a good mother would do: I dug out the bottle of horse-sized pills and asked, "Please, honey, take your medicine."

"No, Mommy. I hate that medicine."

"You'll feel better, I promise. Skiing will be so much fun when you feel better."

"No I don't want any," He said rearing his head, closing his eyes and covering his mouth.

"Come on, honey, pleeeeezzzzzze."

"No!"

Okay, nice Mommy hadn't worked. Time for mean Mommy.

"If you don't take your medicine you can't go skiing," I threatened. At that he opened his eyes and took his hand away from his mouth.

"Do you have milk?" he asked sheepishly, knowing full well that milk was off limits in the car.

"No, baby, you need to swallow your medicine without milk today. Remember our new rule, no milk in the car."

"Then I am not taking it and you can't make me." His hand went back to his mouth and once again he closed his eyes.

My husband, who likes to pretend he's Bono while he's driving, was belting out *Where the Streets Have No Name* and drumming on the dash while I negotiated a deal in our son's antibiotic strike. Kalen was behind Cameron in the back seat, headphones on and rockin' out to Yes (an "old school" band he had recently discovered in his dad's stack of CDs). Like father, like son: classic rock obscuring any awareness of family drama, completely oblivious to the fact that Cameron and I were at a standoff.

Cameron sat stiffly in his car seat, shaking his head with his lips and eyes pursed shut. I could see that no antibiotic would touch this kid's lips until I could produce a chaser of organic 2-percent. And so, reluctantly and hidden from view of the distracted rock stars in the front and back seats, I dug inside my backpack and like a magician produced a pink sippy cup full of milk, stashed there earlier for unspecified "emergencies." Then, as if I were reaching into the back seat for a tissue, I discreetly slipped the cup to the little guy, unnoticed. Cameron gave me a knowing look that said, "Thanks, Mom, I won't tell a soul." Mark had no idea that I had broken our parenting pact of "no milk in the car ever." Like a frat boy to a beer bong, Cameron swallowed the two purple tablets, chasing them down with the entire sippy cup of milk. When he was done he passed the cup back to me quietly.

I breathed a sigh of relief a few minutes later when I turned around to see that Cameron was as happy as a lark, unfazed by the eight ounces of dairy. *He must be over* it, I said to myself. Within an hour we would be on the slopes. I could rest, take a little cat nap, and prepare for a day of carving turns.

I briefly dozed off. Suddenly I was Picabo Street racing down the mountain, wind in my hair, gliding through the gates, taking in the cheer of the crowds and basking in the glow of Olympic stardom when I was startled awake. "Oh shit!" I heard my husband say, looking in the rearview mirror. "Oh shit. I think he's going to blow."

I turned around to see my sweet little partner in crime release a little burpish hiccup. His tiny nose scrunched up and his lips puckered as if he had suddenly bitten into a lemon. Then with a bit of a pause he reared his head against the car seat and he began spewing rancid, curdled milk. His head spun like a lawn sprinkler moving in a syncopated circular motion from one side of the car to another, hitting nearly every surface and human being in sight with what looked like wet, antibiotic-infused cookie dough.

"Oh my god, that is sick. Daaaadddddddd!!!!" Kalen yelled from behind the parka that was doubling as a shield. "He threw up all over my CD player. It's so gross. Stop him. Oh my god, Daaaaaadddd. Stop the car."

Cameron began to cry.

"Oh, fuck!" said Mark, turning to see the disaster in the back seat and wiping vomit from his ear.

"Mark, watch your mouth. That's not how we talk around here," I scolded, glancing at the boys to make sure they hadn't registered the F-word.

"Well then, shit," he said pulling into the nearest gas station.

Cameron began to yell, "My bunny, my bunny. Rabitee!" I turned to see that Rabitee, the stuffed rabbit that had been his best friend since birth, the one that looked like a diseased marsupial rather than a cuddly Easter Bunny, was covered from his velvet ears to his cotton tail in disgusting puke. Cameron held Rabitee up by one ear and began to flail him around the back seat trying to shake puke from his dirty, worn polyester coat. The toy rabbit spun in the air, creating an aftershock of barf.

"Put that down," yelled Kalen, who was now hunkered down in the back seat like a solider anticipating an air strike. "That's disgusting."

Mark wheeled into the nearest parking spot and immediately moved into action like an EMT at a gory accident site. He pulled Cameron out of his car seat and ripped his shirt off. The cold drizzle that had been with us since we left Seattle had suddenly turned into a torrential downpour. "I'm cold," cried

Cameron. I ran around the car to pull off his pants and cover him up in my parka. Kalen was on the other side of the car, coat over his head, gagging and threatening to do a knee-jerk vomit himself. Mark continued to work his way through the car, pulling all the clothes, toys, and gear that were coated in Cameron's blended breakfast from the back seat. Nothing had been spared. Mittens, hats, parkas, water bottles, car seat, cup holder, and CDs were all coated in the thick runny substance. It smelled like an old shoe stuffed with aged Parmesan and a baby diaper.

"Are we still going skiing?" Kalen asked no one in particular. Both boys stood in the middle of the wet parking lot surrounded by our soiled clothes, car seat, and stuffed bunny watching Mark and me curse, scurry, and clean.

"Yes, we're still going skiing," Mark barked.

With that he picked up Rabitee and several pieces of vomit-soaked apparel items and shoved them into the trash bin.

"Rabiteee!!!" Cameron screamed. "You killed my little Rabiteee!!! Mommy, help! Daddy threw Rabitee in the trash!"

I ran to the trash can and looked inside. At the bottom of the greasy trash bin among oil cans, candy wrappers, cigarette butts, lottery tickets, water bottles, window rags, and some of our prized Patagonia pieces lay Rabitee . . . dead. It went through my head that this could be a watershed moment in my son's life. The one that turns him from normal boy to stuffed rabbit–obsessed weirdo. Flash forward to the future: a Furrie convention at the Atlantic City Hilton. Cameron, in his late twenties, dressed up in a hairy, white rabbit suit alongside other people dressed in stuffed-animal getups trying to find their inner Thumpers and Bambies. With that thought I looked over my shoulder at my whimpering son dressed in a ragtag outfit, mourning the death of Rabitee.

"Oh, baby, it's okay," I said, making my way over to Cameron and wrapping my arms around his shivering body. "Rabitee is dead. He's going to go to pet heaven to live with Cloudy," I explained. Cloudy, our family cat, had passed away last summer, so pet heaven was fresh in his mind and a logical next step for Rabitee.

"But, Mommy, that's my Rabitee," he continued as I plied him back into his soiled car seat.

"We'll get you another Rabitee, baby. Don't worry."

"Today? Can we get a new Rabitee today? Huh, Mommy?"

"Yes, we'll get you a new Rabitee either today or tomorrow. Now sit still." I said.

Finally we were sealed back in the car and on the road up to the mountain.

"Are we still going skiing, Mommy?" Cameron asked, a little confused, having missed the earlier exchange during his focus on Rabitee. I was pleased to see that he had moved on to something less furry.

"Yes, baby, we're still going skiing."

"The car really smells yucky, Mommy."

"You'll get used to it," Mark piped in. "Pretty soon you won't even smell a thing."

"Yeah, right," said Kalen, still speaking from under his jacket.

We rode in silence for a few minutes. All of us were weary from what seemed like a full day's adventure, and it was only 7:30 AM. Even the rock stars had been temporarily abandoned for the time being as we each pondered the day ahead. Then from the back seat Cameron asked sheepishly, "Mommy, I'm thirsty. Can I have some milk?"

Captain Safety Out the Window

Jennifer Margulis

I f my husband were a superhero, he'd be known as Captain Safety. Captain Safety is always proactive. Helmets are mandatory, sun hats and sunscreen nonnegotiable. Life jackets must be worn on the water at all times. Captain Safety carries a flashlight on his key chain, a Swiss Army knife in his pocket, and he never leaves the house without water and a map. And he is especially vigilant when it comes to any danger that could face his children.

Now imagine this man deciding to travel to Africa.

More specifically, I somehow managed to convince Captain Safety, the same man who worries about his offspring getting hit by cars when walking in our safe and pedestrian-friendly hometown of Ashland, Oregon, to travel with our three children—ages seven, five, and two—to Niger, West Africa. If you've never heard of Niger, you're not alone. When I say we are going to Niger, most people look at me quizzically. "You mean Nigeria?" they ask, unaware that Niger (pronounced KNEE-JHAIR) is actually a separate country, a place which for two years in a row has been deemed the poorest and least-developed country in the world by the United Nations. Landlocked, Niger has one of the biggest landmasses in Africa and one of the smallest populations.

I had spent time living in Niger thirteen years previously, and adored it. But James, a.k.a. Captain Safety, had never been anywhere farther than Canada when we first met. He had trouble imaging how anyone could possibly want to visit West Africa, let alone live there. We had only moved to Niger for a year. I had a Fulbright Fellowship and was teaching 19th-century American literature at the University in Niamey (Abdou Moumouni University). We took many day trips to explore while we lived there. To prepare for our trip he started reading everything he could about the country.

"Did you know 1.2 million people die from malaria every year?" he came into my office to ask me one night.

"Hmm," I said, without looking up from the computer.

"And did you know that in addition to malaria, there are huge epidemics of typhoid fever, rabies, measles, schistosomiasis, meningitis—it's in what's called the 'meningococcal belt,' for Christ's sake—amoeba, giardia, dengue fever, and hepatitis every year?!"

I looked up this time. "It sounds so much worse than it is," I said, trying to allay his fears without dismissing them altogether. "You'll see once we get there—it's not like people are dying on the streets of dengue fever. We'll be in the capital. We'll be okay."

James frowned, his brow so furrowed you could see every worry line, like cracks in dried mud. "I just don't want anything to happen to the kids," he said, laying his head on my shoulder.

We went for our physicals the next morning. "Malaria is a problem, and you want to avoid it," the clinic doctor told us, almost as an afterthought. We had been in his office for two and a half hours and he had just finished writing twenty-three prescriptions for different emergency medication that might not be available in Niger. Among the stack of illegible white paper he handed me were prescriptions for malaria medication, at $5.00 a pill, at a pill per person per day dosage, none of which our insurance would pay for. "Make sure you cover up," he advised, almost cavalierly pausing for a minute by the open door. "Don't go out from dusk to dawn. Sleep under a mosquito net. You know—all the standard stuff."

Captain Safety approved and visibly relaxed. It sounded straightforward enough at the time. Good, sensible advice from a good, sensible doctor about how to avoid mosquito bites and reduce the threat of malaria. From his air-conditioned sparklingly clean office in southern Oregon, the mosquito problem and the myriad other health and safety concerns all seemed more than manageable.

Two months later, on a hot day in early September, our plane touched down on Nigerian soil. As we walked across the tarmac seven-year-old Vespérine started complaining. "I'm sweating so much it's running down my back, Mommy," she cried. The air was hot and humid, the heat so thick you could actually see it. I was accosted by the familiar smells of cooking oil, hot air, and sand, and a flood of happy memories coming back to me. An embassy van picked us up and Captain Safety jumped into the vehicle to secure the seats.

We waited. And waited. And waited.

James fiddled with the car seats for what seemed like forever. Too polite to raise his eyebrows, my new boss made small talk, glancing from time to time at the car to see what was taking so long. Captain Safety triple-tested the seats for security, added a locking clip to one belt just to be extra safe, and finally announced that we were ready to go.

"Nobody's wearing helmets," James said, as a driver on a moped swerved in front of our car.

"Mommy, I see a man carrying a table of carrots on his head!" cried five-year-old Athena.

Only the main roads in Niamey are paved. The rest of the labyrinthine streets are dusty orange sand. Camels galumph along without balking at the cars and trucks that screech past. Young boys whip donkeys pulling carts with bales of hay stacked eight feet high. Mopeds race cars and bicycles, as white taxis loaded with passengers buzz by past like angry albino hornets.

"People drive like maniacs here," James muttered to me. "It's worse than Italy."

"Look at the camel! That man is riding on a camel," Vespérine pointed. A dark-skinned man with a white turban wrapped around his face, obscuring all but his glasses, sat with his legs crossed in front of him on a muzzled camel, a rope attached to the muzzle in one hand and a short stick in the other. In addition to his rider the camel was loaded down with plastic buckets on each side of the saddle.

"That's a long way to fall," James said.

By the next day our two-year-old son, Etani, had twenty-seven mosquito bites. His older sisters counted them. Even though we were sleeping under nets, spraying the rooms, plugging in an antimosquito device at bedtime, and using two different kinds of mosquito repellent—one natural and one full of DEET—the mosquitoes managed to eat us alive. The doctor's sage words ("Avoidance is the best prophylaxis") echoed in my ears like a sick joke. Nigerian mosquitoes, it turned out, were stealthy, fast, and skinny. Unstoppable.

Not unlike Nigerian taxi drivers. The first taxi we rode in had a huge crack in the windshield. A scratched CD hung from the driver's rearview mirror as a decoration, and on the dashboard was a fake flower in a plastic vase and a prayer rug. There was a sticker proclaiming the greatness of Osama bin Laden on the driver's side door and several other Islamic propaganda stickers ("God loves a good Muslim" and "Don't doubt God's greatness") We realized too late, after we were all squeezed into the cab, which already had two other passengers in it, that the taxi only had one working seatbelt, in the front. It was so covered with dust that when I pulled it out to buckle Etani and me in, it left filthy streaks on our clothes. Captain Safety would not have been happy. Luckily, he wasn't there.

But after awhile we got used to the odors and the trash heaps and the careening cars. We hugged the side of the sidewalkless roads and held the kids' hands tightly as we walked. We avoided taxis as much as we could and closed our eyes getting into the ones that we did take, pretending not to see the spiderweb cracks in the windshields and the missing rearview mirrors. Captain Safety relaxed. Well, actually, Captain Safety took a headlong dive out the open window, disappearing from view. He had to. It was either that or board the next plane back to America, which none of us (well, none of us except James) was keen on doing.

One blue-skied day we went on a camel ride along the Niger River and then took a pirogue back, looking for hippos as we glided through the sparkling water. Captain Safety—he hadn't really disappeared completely—insisted that we wear our bicycle helmets on the camels, though he himself donned a broad khaki sun hat and tied his helmet to the camel saddle. I rode with Etani, who gripped my arms so tightly he left bruises. The camel ambled unevenly through the low shrub, her splayed feet steady on the sand.

"When are we going to get there, Mommy?" Etani asked. Our saddle was listing so far to the right I imagined we'd thud to the ground below at any moment. The camel man noticed and clucked to his beige beast, who stopped immediately. He had her lie down and we dismounted so he could better attach the saddle. We got back on. I heard the camel men laughing—I had unconsciously squeezed my eyes tightly shut as the camel stood up again, straightening first her back legs and thrusting us so far forward I thought we'd be catapulted off. Then, just as I felt us falling, she balanced herself by straightening her hind legs and standing all the way up.

"Madame a peur," the turbaned camel men chuckled. *"Elle ferme les yeux!"* Too right. My eyes were clamped shut; looking would only have terrified me more.

It was a peaceful day, and not too hot. From camel-eye view, I could see the sparkling river to the south and the majestic dunes of orange sand to the north. Everything was still and quiet, as it must have been at the beginning of the world. It was a relief to be away from the bustle of Niamey. In the bush alongside the river there were no screeching taxis or careening mopeds, only an occasional grazing donkey or a woman carrying a bundle of sticks on her head.

"I hated it!" Athena cried as soon as we dismounted in Boubon, a small village on the river known for its lively pottery and animal markets.

"Me too!" Etani shouted gleefully as he backed away from his camel.

"I'm sore," Vespérine said, walking stiff-legged away. Etani fed his camel a crab apple and the three children watched, riveted as the animal, which had to have its muzzle taken off to eat, swallowed the fruit in two big chomps.

A group of village children followed us laughing and pointing as we walked to the Niger River where a wooden pirogue was waiting. Two young men, one at the bow and the other at the stern, paddled the boat. We glided along the water, listening to the call of birds and the slapping sound of the paddles as they sliced into the river. The guide tapped on the front of the canoe to warn hippos of our approach so they wouldn't upturn the boat. We passed three gray-haired, straw-hatted fishermen in a dugout canoe who were holding strings in the water, waiting silently for fish. The one with a gray beard and a hole in his yellow pants smiled broadly at us, his white teeth sparkling in the sun. He told the guide in Zarma that there was a hippo down the river so we paddled off in the direction he pointed.

And so there was. Blowing water through its enormous nostrils, an adult hippo swam near the shore opposite our pirogue. The children, who had been restless moments before, shouted and pointed. Etani tried to stand up and nearly tipped over the canoe. We took a million photographs of the fat beast, the water glistening off its dark brown skin.

A few days later my husband, children, and I watched a slide show on our computer of the pictures we had taken of that day, the most exciting one we had spent in Niger: James in his styling shades and wide-brimmed sun hat; tousle-haired Athena gliding down the Niger wrapped in her special blankie—the green quilt Auntie Lolo made for her when she was born; Vespérine in the lavender butterfly baseball cap that matched the pants she was wearing (of course), a gap-toothed grin on her face; and two-year-old Etani scowling at the camera, the wind blowing his hair to one side. James looked at the photos with a pained expression on his face, his teeth clenched.

"What's wrong?" I asked.

"I can't believe we let them go in that boat without lifejackets," he said, cringing. "What were we thinking? It's so unsafe!"

Perhaps West Africa hadn't changed Captain Safety as much as I thought. He hadn't gone headlong out the window after all.

"Next time we'll bring life jackets," I promised. And the next time we did.

New York Plus One

Madelyn Rosenberg

6:07 AM. Saturday morning. Brooklyn, New York.

There are certain times when it's okay to see 6:07 AM in New York on a weekend. Say you awaken from a dream in which you and Joey Ramone are splitting a pizza in the back room at CBGB on Bowery. You open your eyes and see those digits on the clock. You remember, suddenly, that Joey is dead—CBGB, too. But you also remember that there's nothing pressing you into either reality or full wakefulness. You roll over. Another three hours of sleep remain, which is plenty of time for you and Joey to share another slice.

Or say you're coming home from a night out in the city, a night that started at a coffee shop on Ludlow, peaked at the Knitting Factory, and ended with a long walk across the Brooklyn Bridge and a meal at a restaurant frequented by Pakistani cab drivers. You roll back into your brother's apartment and see it on the clock—6:07—and you're aware of the magic of night, of the sleight of hand that has turned it into morning.

I have lived and dreamed in times like these. But now, my husband and I learn, times have changed. There is a new way to see 6:07 on a Saturday morning. We are viewing it at the behest of our baby, our spawn, the fifteen-month-old boy we have sworn will be able to fall asleep in a pile of coats, will eschew Barney for free jazz, and will snub grilled cheese in favor of Chicken Tikka Masala.

Our beloved offspring's brown eyes are wide open, amused to find his parents sprawled out on the futon, our fists boxer-tight, fighting off the dawn. He is standing in the Pack 'n Play near our bed, reaching, reaching, for my husband's ear. "Play," he says.

"Mmmmph." My husband grabs a pillow and pulls it over his head. Thwarted, our son turns to me.

"Milk," he says.

"In a minute."

"Juice. Juice. *Juice*."

I anticipate the wail, the ever-ready siren, and bolt upright before it comes out and awakens my brother, his girlfriend, the cats, and the fussy gentlemen who live in the apartment below and who are decidedly NOT awake at 6:07.

I pad into the kitchen and pour the juice into a sippy cup just as my son climbs out of the Pack 'n Play, grabs a hat box that is filled with my brother's poker chips, and pours them all over the floor. Below us, the fussy gentlemen are certain of an April hailstorm.

I look out of the window. The sky is gray, all right, but it isn't hailing. It's raining.

Even so, it's obvious that we can't stay put, in this apartment where my son is plucking steel wool out of a mouse hole and pondering whether the kitty litter isn't really some sort of indoor sandbox.

I pull on my sweatshirt and my husband pulls on his. We head outside, into the morning rain.

6:22 AM. The park near the subway station is empty. The homeless have found a place to sleep indoors, but it seems those of us who are visiting this city with children have no place to finish out the night. The bagel shop will be open soon, an inside destination at least. For now, it's the park with its slide, with its swing, with its rain. In a few hours we'll return to the apartment, our noses dripping, our shirts soaked, our hosts awake.

"It's not so bad out," we'll say. "It's not as bad as it looks."

Noon: The Staten Island Ferry is the poor-man's circle line. We are on it because kids like boats. My brother and his girlfriend are on it because it is now a respectable hour to be moving about the city. The rain has stopped and the sun is out. It's a successful voyage, but it's over in twenty minutes. We ferry back to Manhattan. "Again," our son says, and we think about it, really we do. But we are not at his mercy. Yet.

1 PM. New York stomachs seem to operate on a two-hour delay, so at lunchtime no one in our entourage is hungry, save the fifteen-month-old who wants to eat *Now Now Now Now*. We forego any attempt at building a proper food pyramid and lovingly shove Cheerios into his mouth on the slow walk up Wall Street. He gets a piece of bagel in front of the stock exchange, where he is a little afraid of the bull. But he loves watching the security guards shove boxes of pizza and rice and General Tso's Chicken onto the conveyor belt that leads into the stock exchange. He watches as the food runs through the metal detector, preparing for a journey into the world of high finance. He likes watching this *a lot*. He may keep watching all afternoon, in fact, but my brother's girlfriend is getting bored. She is giving me a look that says that since she is a girlfriend and not an aunt—not officially, not yet—about five more minutes of this is all she can stand. We move on.

2 PM. Cheerios supply exhausted. Parents exhausted. Toddler nowhere near exhausted. We go into an annex of the Strand, our favorite New York bookstore. My brother and his girlfriend browse, leisurely—remember browsing?—while I sit in the corner with my son and read *The Very Hungry Caterpillar*. The caterpillar gets fed. My son compares this to his own predicament and senses a great injustice. His protest is too loud for the bookstore so I take him outside. My husband, my hunter and gatherer, forages in a nearby shop and returns with an Italian ice. We eat it on a bench as the rain returns.

3:30 PM. My brother's friend has suggested an alehouse on Front Street, which appears to be frequented by the closest thing New York has to pirates. The beer is served in Styrofoam cups. Bras hang from the ceiling. My son, being no stranger to bras, is intrigued by the red one. He watches it swing, back and forth in rhythm with the ceiling fan. He falls asleep before the clams ever make it to our table.

6 PM. The long, heavy rain keeps us in Jeremy's through happy hour. There's no sign that it's letting up, so we throw a blanket over the stroller and make our way back onto Front Street, back toward the subway. We discuss dinner plans. Dining in New York is a highlight of our trips, but the chance that our son will sleep peacefully through another restaurant is remote at best. My brother suggests a trip to the grocery store instead. His decision-making is slow. Fish or beef? Broccoli or asparagus? My husband races the stroller through the crowded aisles and my son laughs as they avoid a crash with a woman who is examining a dozen eggs too closely.

7:15 PM. On the subway again. A Korean man sings sweetly about Jesus. My son sings the ABCs.

7:45 PM. My sweatshirt is wet. My jeans are sticking to my skin. We stumble out of the subway and pass an outdoor bistro on the corner of Smith and Union. The rain has stopped, the seats are dry and, by chance, our friends are there, gathered at a table under twinkling lights. Their hair is slicked into sophistication and they are dressed in the uniform of City People: black pants, tight button-up shirts. They radiate the beauty, the freshness of the unencumbered.

"Hey, come on," they say. "Sit with us."

But my hair frizzes. My feet hurt. My son cries. I am swamp-green with jealousy and I cannot answer them because I fear I will cry myself.

Someday, perhaps, they will have children too, but right now I feel like I've settled the West alone. I have a brief daydream of my son sitting quietly in my lap after I've changed into City Pants, tamed the frizz, ordered a beer. But no. Not tonight. I walk back to the apartment with my little boy, who plays with poker chips while my brother fixes dinner. This time, I am the one who falls asleep in the pile of coats.

I stay there until morning and awaken early to wide brown eyes, open and amused.

Seven Bags, Two Kids, and the Baby Cheeses

Holly Korbey

5:15 AM, December 22, JFK International Airport.
American Airlines domestic departure drop-off.

It's dark. We arrive at the airport: bright, precocious three-year-old Holden; sunny, sleepy two-month-old Zane; and pale, tired Mommy. Exhausted Daddy's driving, and it's pouring the biggest, grayest drops of rain, like someone with a bucket right over our heads. There are taxicabs and cars triple-parked around the bend and into infinity, ignoring all driving rules, and appearing to actively attempt running over pedestrians. Unable to get anywhere near the terminal doors, we begin a slow crawl to a spot across the street from the terminal building.

"Daddy, why is it raining?" Holden says.

"Because God's laughing at Mommy so hard, he's crying."

"Why's God laughing at Mommy?"

"For taking the two of you on an airplane two days before Christmas."

Holden pauses. The previous explanation clearly accepted, he moves on. "Daddy, can you tell me the Christmas story again, please?"

"Mommy will tell you once you get inside the airport."

"Mommy, was Mary going to have a baby?"

"That's right, sweetie."

"And they were going to Beflehem?"

"Yep."

"Why were they going to Beflehem?"

"To pay their taxes."

"What's God?"

Daddy rolls his eyes.

My husband's not sure how he feels about us talking about Jesus and God and the Real Story of Christmas. It's complicated. We're not particularly religious people. He gave up God a few years back when he discovered guilt. And booze. For myself, I consider myself *spiritual*. I do believe very strongly in a nongender, universal giving Spirit, and everything Oprah does. And yoga. And coffee shops.

I used to be religious. In fact, maybe that's a euphemism. Growing up in the Bible Belt, I sang in our born-again church with my family's band. I shed my religion years ago, when I moved to New York City, and became one in the throng of agnostic, "spiritual" liberals.

But kids do curious things to your beliefs, pulling you back to your most primal values. To my surprise, I discovered that I felt Holden needed to know the facts of the Christmas story. Santa Claus, my upbringing had taught me, was not really why Christmas happened, and even as an apathetic Brooklyn *spiritual person*, I felt hollow inside leaving Holden in the lurch without the details of the Real Story. Knowing Holden, the world's most curious child, he'd find out anyway, and then grill me for the next fifteen years about why I hadn't told him.

"God is a spirit."

"What's a spirit?"

"Ah—"

My husband is giving me the *cut it off* signal, the one where you take your index finger and slice it across your neck. Fortunately, the three-year-old's goldfish-like attention span came to my rescue before I waded in too deep for salvation.

"Daddy, when are you coming to Grandma's?"

"On Christmas Eve. Sunday. In two days, honey."

"Why?"

"Because I have to work."

"Why?"

"Because I need to make money to take care of you guys."

"Why?"

"Because we live in a capitalist society."

"Why?"

"Because Mommy wanted to live near her sister in New York."

"Say goodbye to Daddy," I say brightly.

Holden says goodbye, and we jump out of the car and into the rain. Holden grasps my hand, taking time to jump in every single puddle in our path, while I'm yelling at him like a football coach in an inspirational movie, barking orders at him, giving him tough love to try to get him to hurry it up. It doesn't matter, though, because by the time we reach the door of the terminal, we're all three completely soaked through our carefully chosen travel-fleece outfits. Big, wet drops are dripping from Zane's tiny nose onto my pants. Holden's hair is stuck to his head in tangly clumps. I get us through the automatic doors, then say, "Okay, turn around and wave at Daddy!"

"Why?"

"Because we won't see him for a couple of days."

"Why?"

"Because he's got to work before he comes to Grandma's."

"Why?"

"Because he needs to work to make money."

"Why?"

"Because that's Daddy's job."

"Why?"

"Because he's lucky."

Holden seems satisfied with that answer. We wave madly through the terminal window, and then turn ourselves toward the ticket line.

5:55 AM. JFK Airport. Ticket line. Baby still sleeping.

It's not yet 6 AM, but everyone in line is already mad, wet, and confused. I think about Mary, the first stressed-out holiday traveler, super-pregnant on that donkey. She had it worse than this, for sure. We take our place at the end of the line.

"And Mary had the Baby Cheeses in the barn, didn't she?"

"Yep, she sure did."

"What animals were there, Mommy?"

"Let's see, there were sheep and pigs."

"And *horses!* And *cows!*"

"Yep, horses and cows."

"And *mice!* And *roaches!*" Peals and peals of little-bell laughs at his joke, the kind of laugh you want to trap in a jar like a firefly, poke holes in the top, and keep for as long as it will last.

"Can I stop holding your hand now, Mommy?"

"Only if you stay right by me."

"Why?"

"Because there are a lot of people here and I don't want you to get lost."

"What's get lost?"

"I don't want to turn around and have you gone."

"Why?"

"Because you're my baby and I want you to stay with me."

"I'm not the baby! I'm a big boy!"

"That's a good point."

"When will we get on the airplane?"

"After we go through this line. And then another line. Later."

"How later?"

"In two hours."

"What's two hours?"

"Look up at that clock."

"What clock?"

"The one by the pizza place."

"What pizza place?"

"The one over there. See it? With the red lights?"

"Pizza!! Can I have pizza?"

"Not right this minute."

"Can I have it after the line?"

"We'll see."

"Can I have it now?"

"No."

"Can we walk over and get some now?"

"No."

"Can you tell me the Christmas story again, please?"

"Not right at this moment, honey."

"When do we get on the airplane?"

"In two hours."

"Why?"

6:45 AM. Security line, JFK International Airport. Baby wakes up hungry.

kay, Holden, now listen to me. Zane's crying and we need to get through this line."

"Why's Zane crying? Mommy, you need to *feed* him."

"I know, I know."

"Mommy, does he have a poopy diaper?"

"Why?"

"Because you've got yellow all over your shirt."

"Shit!"

"No, your shirt, Mommy."

"Okay, now listen Holden. We have to take off your shoes and your jacket."

"Can I take off my socks?"

"Nope, just your shoes."

"Can I show them my Spiderman undies?"

"Nope, just your shoes and your jacket."

"Can you tell me the Christmas story now, Mommy? I want to hear about Baby Cheeses!!"

"Soon. Soon."

I squat down to undress Holden, while the BabyBjörn squeezed up to my chest, pressing against my ribs. I can barely reach Holden's shoes, and as I pull one off, he loses his balance and falls. Zane is wailing in my ear, starving and covered with poop, and there are fifteen people ahead of us in line.

"Okay, Holden, now listen. When it's our turn, you're going to walk through that magic door up there."

"Why is it magic?"

"Because, when you go through it, then magically, you can get on the airplane."

"Can you walk with me?"

"No, hon, you have to go by yourself."

"Can you hold my hand while I go through the magic door?"

"I can't; you need to go by yourself."

"Can I walk by myself to the airplane?"

"No, we have to hold hands."

"Can we hold hands now?"

"No, you have to go by yourself."

My head starts to pound from Zane's painful sobbing, a hunger cry so loud and penetrating that it feels like it's being piped directly into my eardrum. I also sense the familiar laser beams of disgust penetrating my skin from every angle as the angry, childless mob of the security line impatiently waits and watches me struggle to get my lace-ups off with a crying baby strapped to my chest like a bomb and a three-year-old with diarrhea of the mouth who now has his pants pulled down, for security purposes, in tow. I blanch with shame and low blood sugar as I clutch the wall for a moment; I've forgotten to eat a thing before we left the house.

Finally, it's our turn. "Okay, now Holden, I want you to run through the magic security door, okay?"

"Run?"

"Run. Show me how fast you can run through it."

Holden lets go of my hand, and just as instructed, runs through the security door.

Without pausing or looking back, he then blows past all the security guards, past the conveyor belts of bags, coats, and purses, and into the terminal. I lose sight of him instantly in a sea of people. "Somebody please catch that boy!!" I scream. But no one can hear me because of Zane's insane screaming. Or nobody cares.

"*Please somebody catch that little boy!*" I run through the security door, past all the security guards (who just stand there), past the conveyor belt, abandoning our carry-on (and Holden's shoes) still in the security line. My heart jumps straight through my ribs and into my throat, and I cannot breathe. Zane's head is bouncing all over the place. I turn my head frantically left and right. Finally I spot Holden two hundred feet down the terminal corridor, still running, as fast as he can go.

"*Holden!!! Stop!*"

He keeps running, giving no sign of having heard me.

"*Holden! Stop this instant!*" I'm beginning to panic; the thought of losing him is taking over my brain, causing my calves to ache and my arms to shake.

He begins to round the corner of the hallway, toward the baggage claim escalator, down an unknown passageway full of travelers I'll never get to in time.

"*You stop right now or there will be no Christmas story, young man. Do you hear me?? We will never discuss Baby Jesus or Mary or her donkey or the roaches now or ever if you don't turn around and come to Mommy rigggghhht noooooow!*"

Zane stops crying. He looks up at me, genuinely concerned.

Holden stops slowly, like he's run out of gas, putt, putt, putt, until finally, he comes to a complete stop.

"Turn around. And get back here now."

He turns to face me, head hanging low, and walks slowly down the hallway back to me. I look down at my sock feet; I notice my knees visibly quivering in fear.

"Don't you ever do that again! You always, always stay with Mommy. Always. Do you understand?"

"Yes, Mommy. I'm sorry. You don't want to lose me."

"I don't ever want to *lose* you. Ever."

"Because I'm special?"

"Because you're the most special thing in the whole world. In the *whole world*," I choke. Holden puts his little hand on my shoulder. I cringe at how perceptive he is for three, how he knows how spooked I got that I almost lost him.

"I love you, Mommy."

"I love you, too."

"I'm sorry I made you a bad mood."

"That's okay."

"Can you tell me the Christmas story now?"

7:30 AM. JFK bathroom. Poop cleanup.

"Can you tell me the Christmas story *now*, Mommy?"

"In just a few minutes; as soon as I clean Zane up and clean me up, then we'll get on the airplane and I'll tell you the Christmas story."

"The three kings came to see Baby Cheeses, didn't they?"

"Yep."

"Did they ride on camels?"

"They did. They came because they saw the star in the sky."

"Why was the star there?"

"God put the star right over the barn, shining right over the barn, so the kings knew how to find the Baby Jesus."

"Who's God?"

"It's complicated."

"But who is he?"

"He's a friend of Jesus. Like his Grandpa."

"Why?"

"Why is he Jesus' friend?"

"No, why did he put the star over the barn? How did he do that?"

"It's complicated. I'm not sure. You know, Holden, I'm not sure of the answer to that one. Why did he put the star over the barn? I'm not sure. I'll get back to you on that one, honey. I promise."

Ugh. I picture Holden in a dorm room many years in the future, drinking beer and sobbing to an unwitting roommate about how I didn't tell him about God, I didn't even tell him there was a God. I didn't tell him at all. He didn't know about God, he never even *heard* of God until he got to college. Once when he was about three, he'd bawl, he had asked, who is God? And his mother had said, quite persuasively, that she'd have to get back to him. That's the last he heard about it.

"So, why did they have to sleep in the barn?"

"They went to every hotel in town, but they were all full."

"Why?"

"Everyone had to go to Bethlehem to pay their taxes."

I just don't know what to say in the face of the constant why's. I don't know how much to tell him. The quandary, of course, has to do with me rather than with Holden: I believe in God, but I don't believe enough to do anything about it, I guess. That's embarrassing.

It occurs to me in a lightbulb flash that maybe I'd like to believe the Christmas story was true, like I used to. I'd love to tell the story, the one with so many details that I remember so clearly, with passion, with *conviction*, the kind that would let him know that this is what I Believe, capital B, and it's okay for you to believe it, too.

But I can't do that.

I scrub the poop off the front of my gray fleece pullover with two thousand wet wipes. Zane has been wailing and hungry for so long he's exhausted and unhungry. As soon as I snap up his clean onesie, he closes his eyes and falls asleep on the changing table.

8:30 AM. Seats 30A and 30B, awaiting takeoff.
Destination: Evansville, Indiana.

"I need to go *wee-wee!!!!*"

"Okay, just hang on a minute."

"But the potty's *right there!*"

"I know, I know, but we can't get out of our seats until we take off."

"But I have to go really *bad. Really, really bad.*"

I hit the call button for the flight attendant.

"We have a wee-wee emergency. Is there any way he can go?"

"No, ma'am, we're next in line to take off. Can you hold it for a few minutes, little buddy?"

"I don't think I can hold it. I have to go really bad."

"I'm sorry. Holden, you're going to have to wait. Let's hold it just a few minutes."

"Sorry."

"There's no way he can go?" She glances around warily. She sees a cleanup in her future.

"The captain's not going to let me. We're about to take off, miss." My neck is tight, like it's about to snap.

"Okay. We'll hold it."

I need a distraction technique.

"Holden, do you want to hear the Christmas story?"

"Yes!"

"Well, Mary and Joseph had to go to Bethlehem when Mary was very, very pregnant. She looked like Mommy did right before she had Zane."

"She had a very fat tummy. Baby Cheeses was in there."

"That's right. And she didn't ride a subway or a taxi or a car, because they didn't have those. She had to ride on a donkey." Holden puts his hand over his mouth, rolls his eyes back in his head, and giggles. "So, they get to the hotel, but there's no room in the hotel. The innkeeper, the guy who runs the hotel, says that if they want, they can stay—where?"

"In the *barn!* With the animals!"

"Yep. It's called a stable. So, Joseph makes a bed for Mary in the hay. And that night, she has the Baby Jesus."

"And the three kings come on *camels!* And they bring him *presents!*"

"That's right, they bring him Christmas presents."

"Why did they want to come see him so bad?"

"What?"

"Why did the kings want to see him so bad? Was he a special boy, like me?"

Oh, Spirit, oh Spirit of Oprah and fair-trade coffee, please guide me, please help me to say something—at the very least—decent. And if you're feeling generous, Spirit, let me say something brilliant, something *enlightening.*

But I'll take decent.

"He was a special boy. A very special boy. And God . . ."

"Jesus's Grandpa?"

"Um, yep. God, you see, he had magic powers, and put a star over the stable so the three kings could find Jesus. God wanted everyone to know Jesus."

"Why?"

"Because God knew his . . . Jesus was a very, very special boy. A very kind boy. Jesus grew up to be a very nice guy, even to people who didn't like him."

"Am I nice? Am I nice like Jesus?"

"Yes, you are, hon."

We didn't even realize that the plane had taken off. Holden and I look out the window at the gray clouds whizzing by as we climb up and up, into the sky. Then, the misty clouds separate, and we see the sun. "The sun! The sun! Mommy, the sun!"

Zane wakes up and begins to cry. Holden sucks his thumb with one hand, then reaches over and pets Zane's newborn curls with the other. "It's okay, Zaney. Look at the sun! It's okay, Zaney. It's okay."

I want to fossilize this Christmas trip forever in my mind: the one where Holden, still a baby himself, reaches over to comfort his baby brother, in an airplane, with the sun shining in the window, on our way to celebrate a holiday—and we're just not sure what we're supposed to be celebrating, and who we're celebrating it for.

"Where does Santa Claus live?"

Saved by Santa! My voice goes up two octaves. *"In the North Pole!!"*

"Can we sing Rudolph?"

We sing the whole song, even the verse. I start thanking God, Oprah, yoga, anyone who's listening, that we got off the subject. Now we can just have fun.

After the initial ascent is over, we hear the mysterious *bing*, and suddenly, the flight attendant appears.

"Ready to use the restroom, young man?"

"Yes, I need to go *really bad.*"

"And where are you flying for Christmas, big brother?" she says to Holden.

"To Indiana," he replies. "To pay my taxes."

Road Trip Through Adolescence

Donna Gephart

"I hate you!" shouted my eleven-year-old son, Andrew. He needn't have shouted. He was sitting across the kitchen table from me. "I can't stand your rules. I can't stand living here. I can't stand you!" Andrew exploded from the table and barricaded himself in his room before I could say anything.

What, in fact, could I say? Whatever words I chose were always the wrong ones. Whatever I did proved exasperating to my son, who was beginning his rocky journey through adolescence. How would I bridge the chasm growing between us?

I glanced over at our nine-year-old son, happily reading a comic book on the couch. I knew he, too, would soon navigate this challenging stage of life.

Later that night, I knocked on Andrew's door. "How would you like to go on a road trip this summer?" I asked. "Just you and me."

He raised an eyebrow. "Sounds cool. I guess."

When I mentioned the idea to my husband, of Andrew and I alone on the road together for a week—he, too, raised an eyebrow. "Sounds crazy!"

As our departure date neared, I found myself bolting awake in the middle of the night, heart thumping. What if our car broke down? What if some creep bothered us at a rest stop? What if Andrew and I couldn't stand one another's company for a day, let alone a week?

On June 25, I dropped our nine-year-old son off with relatives while my husband remained home to work. Then Andrew and I climbed into our rented car and headed north. Andrew brought one duffel bag and his favorite stuffed animal. I lugged a suitcase and a large dose of apprehension.

"How many hours is this part of the drive?" Andrew asked, chomping on a wad of gum.

"About five," I said, bracing myself for the litany of complaints that usually followed anything I said.

"Okay." He opened our map and examined the route. "Hey, I like sitting in the front seat."

I stared in surprise. What was that unfamiliar thing on Andrew's face? A smile!

After five peaceful hours on the road, Andrew helped me navigate the crowded streets of Boston. Once parked at the marina, I hesitantly approached the boat where we'd spend the night. Would Andrew or I plunge into the murky water of the Boston Harbor? My son read the fear in my eyes and grabbed my hand. He helped me make the leap from dock to boat. A new world order: Previously, I had always been the one to take his hand.

That night, after a late dinner, Andrew insisted I join him for Bugs Bunny cartoons.

My son clearly had one foot in adulthood and one in childhood. Could he make the leap without stumbling? Could I?

From Boston, we headed to Bar Harbor, Maine, for four days in a rustic farmhouse—no TV, no video games, and no access to friends.

At Acadia National Park, Andrew took off across the rocky terrain. At first hesitant, feeling his way and checking his balance, he soon learned he could run across the formations. "Come on, Mom!"

I couldn't keep up with him. He was all wind and grace. Was this the same boy who tripped over his own feet?

The next day, we ventured on a hike around Jordan Pond. At 3.3 miles, it was a short hike for me, but excruciatingly long for Andrew. His complaints began immediately. "How far is this? My legs are killing me!" I tried to distract him with suggestions of skipping rocks while I memorized breathtaking mountains and the shimmering lake. It didn't work. If the terrain wasn't composed of craggy rocks to bound across, Andrew wasn't interested.

When I stopped to look at a frog, Andrew, impatient to be finished, sprinted ahead. I rushed to catch up, but couldn't find him. Don't panic, I told myself. "Did you see a boy in a red jacket?" I asked every person who passed. "Oh, yes. Up ahead. He's fine," they'd answer.

But was I?

Finally, I saw Andrew's face.

"I was afraid to come back," he said. "I knew you'd yell at me."

"You are never to separate from me again! Do you understand?"

"See," he said. "You're yelling." I felt such relief from seeing him that I laughed at his comment. We finished the trail together, racing one another over logs.

At the end, we treated ourselves to blueberry crisp and root beer at Jordan Pond House restaurant. As Andrew sipped his soda, I noticed the fine hairs of a moustache above his lip. I pretended I was wiping something off his cheek, but examined the area to be sure it wasn't dirt. (It wasn't.)

Late that evening, I took a wrong turn out of the park that led us onto winding, unfamiliar roads. Panic rose in my throat. How would I find the way in the dark?

Suddenly, a song blasted from the car's speakers. Andrew grinned. He'd put in his *Grease* CD and insisted we sing together. So we belted out "Greased Lightning" and "Summer Nights." Before we knew it, the farmhouse came into view.

"Sorry about getting us lost," I said, ruffling Andrew's hair.

"Don't be," he said. "That was fun!"

During our last day at Acadia, Andrew and I struck a compromise: He would allow me one morning hike, and after that, I would let him spend as much time as he wanted climbing over the rocks.

Mindful of Andrew's complaints the other day, I deliberately chose a nonstrenuous hike. Andrew made no such concession when it came to his part of the day's activities.

Even though the muscles in my legs were tired from hiking, I made a valiant effort to keep up, scrambling in terror over the twenty-foot-high outcroppings of rock.

"I was born to do this!" Andrew called, raising his arms in triumph.

When my son leapt effortlessly over a small chasm, I stopped. My legs turned to water. He was so close to the edge. I wanted to scream for him to come back.

Instead, I lowered myself onto a rock and watched Andrew glide and leap across the rocks with his arms spread wide.

The days of hiking trails and climbing rocks and eating blueberry crisp ended too soon. Before we knew it, we were on the road, heading back to pick up my younger son, who had no doubt spent the week being doted upon by relatives.

Andrew sat in the copilot seat with maps, directions, and doughnuts at the ready. He glanced up from a novel, clearly not taking the navigation duties too seriously. "You need help with directions?"

I patted his knee. "I'm fine. Keep reading."

"Okay. But I'm here if you need me."

I noticed his lanky legs curled beneath him and his lips moving gently with the words he was reading. Soon he'd begin middle school. I realized that if Andrew handled the rocky landscape of adolescence with the same grace that he handled the rocky landscape at Acadia, he'd be just fine.

And so would I.

Shock and Paw

C. Lill Ahrens

A thunderous rumbling and harsh Korean harangue scared me awake. Soldiers? Tanks? North Korea invading Seoul?! I bolted from the sleeping mat and, heart pounding, cracked open the frosted-glass window and peered out. The sudden reek of fish brought me around like smelling salts, and I laughed at myself. No invasion; it was a traveling fishmonger. Down in the empty alley, he stood in the back of an unmufflered pickup, boot-deep in fish, announcing his presence to the neighborhood through an electronic megaphone. In the first light of dawn, the fish gleamed like polished knives.

I had been in Seoul four months, but my culture shock was getting worse, not better, exacerbated by frequent cultural surprises that felt like practical jokes. Though I still had a sense of humor about life here, these little blindsidings were having a cumulative effect on my nerves. Compounding the problem had been four solid months of indelicate headlines in the expatriate newspaper, such as, NORTH KOREAN TROOPS MASSING AT THE BORDER. Our little family lived on the very northern edge of Seoul, only thirty miles from "The Border," also known as the Demilitarized Zone, or DMZ.

I didn't know how much more shock I could absorb.

I closed the window so I could take deep breaths to slow my thudding heart. Feeling sheepish, I crawled back under the covers next to Paul, who, like our three-year-old in the next room, somehow slept undisturbed.

I wanted more sleep before our boy, Spencer, awoke. I needed my cat for a soothing fix of fur and purr, but she was back in Colorado with the house sitter. All I could do was focus on deep breathing and the day ahead. It was Thursday, "playgroup day," when I could hang out with some English-speaking women, three young moms from Paris, Berlin, and Amarillo, who I'd met at an expatriate tea downtown. The two-hour bus trip to see them each Thursday was worth it. Having lived in Seoul for years, they were fully adjusted to life here, and, generous and sympathetic, they did their best to help adjust *me*. The global corporations their husbands worked for provided them with luxurious homes, servants, and nannies who watched our kids while we relaxed. As my husband's fledgling company could barely provide us with a small apartment, a kitchen table, three wooden chairs, and two sleeping mats, a day with my expatriate friends was like a day at a five-star spa.

Today promised to be an extra-special treat. The expats had decided that what I needed was a good dose of familiarity. So after Spencer and I met them downtown this morning, we'd be transported via chauffeured-car convoy to my friends' favorite amusement park in Seoul. They said it was like Disneyland but smaller and without the long lines.

The park proved to be just the tonic I needed. We twirled in teacups. We boated past animatronic dolls who were dressed in folk costumes—the USA dolls in football uniforms and skimpy cheerleader outfits—while the song "It's a Small World After All" played in English over and over and over and over. I found this oddly soothing.

Then it was lunchtime. The three nannies took our tots to one picnic table while we four moms sat at another. We ate gourmet sack lunches prepared by the expats' cooks and delivered to our table by the chauffeurs.

Pleasantly stuffed, I sighed, "Now this is a life I think I could adjust to." We laughed, and to keep it rolling, I told them how I'd mistaken a fishmonger for a North Korean invasion.

They stopped laughing.

"*Ja,*" Hildie said darkly. "You vould be having dat vorry—being new here. But invasion vould not be likely, *liebchen.* For decades dey talking and talking attack vid never der attack."

"But the newspaper—"

"We ignore ze rattling of sabers, mon amie," Monique patted my nail-bitten hand with her plump little scarlet-tipped one.

"But darlin's," drawled Wanda, "are those air raid drills a pain in the butt or what? Traffic stops. Ya gotta git outta yer car . . ."

"*Oui, oui,*" said Monique. "I do not see why I must get out when my chauffeur he gets out of ze car already." Her little arms flew out in consternation, "But he *makes* me!"

"Air raid drills?" I asked.

"You having no air raid sirens vhere you live?" Hildie asked in surprise.

I shook my head.

"Hell, Hildie," said Wanda, "Lill's neighborhood is so close to the DMZ, North Korea can drop-kick missiles into it. Air raid sirens wouldn't do 'er any damn good."

My stomach dropped.

"*Vanda!*" scolded Hildie.

"Oops, sorry y'all." Wanda whipped out her lipstick as if her lips needed freshening after their lapse in tact.

"That's okay, Wanda." *Thank you for my next nightmare.*

"Lunch over, ladies!" Hildie cut through the embarrassed silence. "Lill, vhat you need is someting vould take your mind off your vorries. I know joost *der* ting! *Der* Safariland Adventure!"

"*Oui, oui!* Ze Safariland she is our most favorite ride!"

"Like Adventureland?" I said. "Super! Spencer loves that mechanical hippo."

Wanda grinned, "Then let's git a move on, y'all."

Ten minutes later our playgroup was first in line by the side of a wide asphalt path, across from a high wooden fence, awaiting the arrival of a safari vehicle. Hildie's nanny handed Spencer to me and I folded him in my arms. He smelled like moist towelettes.

At the sound of an approaching engine, the kids in line behind us shouted gleefully in Korean, and Wanda's little boy Travis hollered, "It's comin', y'all!"

But around the corner came a vehicle that looked nothing like a safari ride. It was an ordinary city bus, painted plain white, and must have just been washed because water trickled down the sides. Around the outside hung small white paper bags, one near the top of each window. The bus grumbled to a stop in front of us. The door squeaked open.

"You and Spencer git on first," offered Wanda.

"Und sit on der left," said Hildie.

"The left she is ze best view," added Monique.

"Thanks!"

Spencer pulled me into the seat directly behind the driver. Wanda and Travis sat behind us, and the rest of our group behind them. The bus stank of stale cigarette smoke and sweat. I reached around Spencer to open the window but it had no latch. The last seats filled. The door squeaked shut and the bus jerked into motion. High wooden gates swept open before us, revealing a spacious savanna.

"Hey, Mom!" Spencer pointed eagerly out the windshield. "Look!"

"Ooh *wow*, sweetie!" Up ahead, on a raised wooden platform next to the road, lazed a pride of six, real live lionesses. They lounged like bathing beauties on a sun deck. Some lay on their backs, thighs spread wide, their soft, furry tummies turned up to the sun. They groomed each other with affectionate, lingering tongues.

"Aren't they beautiful, Spencer? Like big pussy cats." As a kid I'd loved the book *Born Free*, about Elsa, the tame African lioness who sucked the author's thumb and purred, even when full grown.

The bus slowed. The lions' ears twitched at the sound of downshifting gears. Stretching languidly, they pushed themselves up to their haunches, yawned, and watched as we approached. The driver pulled alongside, about eight feet out from the platform, and turned off the engine. Spencer knelt on the seat and pressed his nose to the window. I skooched up close and wrapped my arms around him. We were eye-to-eye with the lions. Aside from their teddy-bear ears they looked so much like our cat—tawny fur, golden eyes, pink bristly tongues . . . I heard purring.

Or was it a growl?

ROAAAAAAAAAAAAAAR! The entire pride lunged at the bus, slammed into it, and dropped to the ground. Everyone screamed—except Spencer, his nose still pressed to the glass. Roaring and snarling, the lions leapt up at the windows. I tried to pull Spencer onto my lap but he held fast to the sill. Wanda and Travis screeched with laughter as a lion swiped at their window, then with slathering jaws crushed the little white paper bag against their window, smearing the glass with drool, grease, and blood.

The bags contained chunks of *raw meat*! The bus was *baited*. I kept screaming. And laughing. And we all kept screaming and laughing, except for Spencer, frozen in place, his face still glued to the glass.

I shouted over the pandemonium, "It's okay, sweetie! They aren't after us. It's like watching *The Lion King*."

KRUNK!

"Yikes!" I ducked and looked up. The ceiling had dented in right above us. Lion on the *roof*. With claws like meat hooks, one massive paw reached down outside our closed window right in front of Spencer's face. It swiped at but missed the bag on our window. Another lion stretched up from below, snarling and snapping at the lion above us, dodging, slashing. The lower lion snatched the bag and devoured it in the grass, bloody butcher paper and all.

The driver tapped ashes into the dashboard ashtray, stuck the cigarette in his teeth, and started the engine. The lion on the roof sprang back to the platform, her tail lashing in disappointment. She'd have to wait for the next ride.

The bus pulled away with a few bags on the right side miraculously still intact.

Spencer peeled his face from the window and stared over my shoulder at the receding lions. I hugged him tight. "Was that scary, sweetie?"

He pressed his nose to mine, looking cross-eyed, and exhaled, "Yeeeaah!" He grinned, then sat on my lap facing front, ready for whatever else life had in store.

Whomp!

"Eep!" I yipped. Wanda had clapped me on the shoulders from behind.

"Wasn't that fun, darlin'?"

"We did not vant to tell you beforehand!" called Hildie behind her. "It vould spoil der surprise!"

Wanda shook my shoulders, her bracelets rattling my eardrums. "So? What didja think? Did it take yer mind offa North Korea?"

Heart pounding, I laughed. "That it did."

"But didja *like* it?"

"I *loved* it!" I said in all truthfulness. But strangely, I was also feeling a bit faint. My hands tingled. I'd been hyperventilating without realizing it. I needed my own little white bag to breathe into.

"Y'all would never get this ride in America," Wanda drawled behind me. "Not even in *Texas.*"

Bloody, greasy, and drooly, our bus passed through a tall chainlink gate, headed, I surmised, for the Safariland vehicle wash. I had a feeling the bus was white for the ease and economy of painting over claw marks.

BANG!

"Aaaaa!" My lone scream sliced through the happy chatter. The ceiling had popped back into shape. I breathed into my cupped hands.

"Hey, Mom!"

"Ack!" I flinched. "Sweetie, *please* don't startle me like that."

"Look!" He was pointing out the windshield.

Up ahead, on a platform on the right side of the road, lazed an ambush of tigers.

The Backbone of the World

Jennifer Graf Groneberg

Tom points to the topographic map spread open across the kitchen counter and says, "Here. This is where we'll go in." He moves his finger along a low, flat valley thirty miles from the Canadian border, in the North Fork area of Glacier National Park. I peer at the map, repeating the names I read. Columbia Falls. Polebridge. Bowman Lake. Akokala. I look at the thin dotted line that marks the trail. Our eighteen-month-old son, Carter, will be with us. I sigh at the weight of it all, both the decision, and what we'll be carrying if we go ahead with the trip. Carter weighs twenty-eight pounds, and the backpack to carry him in weighs six. I could take that much, plus my sleeping bag, but Tom would have to carry everything else—the tent, our cooking gear, food, water.

"It's too much," I say aloud. "Isn't there another trip we could try?"

Tom, as if he hasn't heard me, opens the hiker's guide and reads the description of the trip. "A moderate hike through pristine alpine forests with spectacular scenery." He's trying to tempt me. "Profusion of wildflowers in late summer," he adds.

Not for the first time, I wonder why we do these things—the pushing, the uncertainty. When we were younger, I'd wanted the adventure. In fact, it was part of my pledge to Tom—I didn't care if our life together was easy, I just didn't want it to be boring. But since we'd become parents, adventure was less appealing to me, or rather, more complicated. We had a son to worry about now.

Deciding the small things, such as what to bring on a camping trip, pulled me away from the broader uncertainty of our lives. Our home, a dryland wheat-and-cattle ranch on the sagebrush flats of eastern Montana, wasn't ours anymore—it belonged to a neighboring family. It had been Tom's and my dream to move to the country and try to make a go of it, but four years of bitter winters and summers when the rains never came had turned the wheat to nothing more than grasshoppers and dust; the cows, thin and gaunt-eyed.

Still, the time we'd spent there felt more real and more alive than any other place I'd known. Despite the struggle, I'd begun to put down roots, and just as I realized that, life as we knew it was about to change. Our things would all be sold at a farm liquidation auction: my kitchen table, the hand-stitched quilts from the beds; the set of crystal we got as a wedding gift, never even used. I'd told Tom, "I can't bear the sight of those things; they're too much part of this life that failed. Sell them all."

On the day of the auction, I was six hundred miles away across a mountain range, in the region of Montana the Blackfeet call "The Backbone of the World." This was where Tom and I had gotten married in a morning ceremony on the banks of a lake, and it felt right returning to our beginnings, as if we could go back and somehow retrace our steps and everything would become clear. We would see it and say, "Aha! *This* is where it all went wrong."

I spent my time unpacking what we had saved into our new place, a house that didn't quite feel like ours. We had books, but no bookshelves. A computer, but no desk. A green couch and an overstuffed chair, but no end tables and not enough lamps. I settled Carter's room first, which was easiest. I put his crib against a wall near the window and organized his toys, mostly hand-me-downs from my aunt and uncle who lived in Colorado. Even as I was pulling things out of boxes, miles away at the farm, others boxes were filling up. The image was too much for me to manage without tears, and I willed it out of my mind.

The camping trip was supposed to be a reward, a way to mark the end of the liquidation and the beginning of our new lives. So I spent my days caring for Carter and planning our hike, letting my mind drift to the wild places, mountains and clear streams and lakes so smooth they look as if they're made of glass.

My camping list included the Kelty pack for Carter, our sleeping bags, and two tents. Diapers, wipes, plastic baggies for the diapers and wipes. Instant coffee and Tang. Freeze-dried meals. Ramen noodles. Tortellini with a small packet of sauce. Plates that doubled as pot lids. Cups that collapsed down into thin discs. I weighed and considered everything, which soothed me. The problems in our life that led us here—four years of drought, a summer lightning fire that burned the hay, a brutal, record-breaking winter—were so large and unmanageable, so far beyond my control. Packing these small things felt easy, free. A deck of cards, a lightweight set of plastic dominoes. Three matchbox cars, a small bag of crayons and one coloring book.

Bowman Lake was our first night's destination. I could see it in my mind's eye, a cold, clear glacial lake. We'd drive the three hours to the trailhead, set up a base camp, and stay the night. The next morning, we'd hike up to Akokala, a remote, backcountry lake, with the little tent and enough supplies for one night. The next day, we'd hike back down to the base camp, spend another night, then head home. We'd talk about these plans over the phone, Tom in the eastern part of the state wrapping up the final details of our old life, me in the West, trying to begin anew.

When the day of the trip arrives, we head north. The scenery unties me like a knot. Douglas fir trees and ponderosa pines; wide, lazy rivers; a busy, noisy stream. Fields of lupine and paintbrush and yarrow. Listening to classical music on the tape player, Carter asleep in his car seat, all our gear packed neatly in the back. We drive through a ghost forest, burned gray and charred in a fire, but recovering now, slowly. I felt like the trees—light and scrubbed bare, but still standing.

We continue on, until the driving turns unpleasant. A washboard road wakes Carter. He's hungry, but there's no place to pull off, and there's no time to stop. We have another thirty miles to go, and then we have to set up camp. Worry descends like night; what are we doing? What were we thinking?

I give Carter a few M&M's and rub his leg, the only part of him I can reach from my seat. We drive into the night. At the campsite, I quickly set up the tent. Tom starts a fire and gets the water boiling. Nearby, I hear the nighttime sounds of other campers—the clang of pots and dishes, low talking, laughter. I toss a handful of tortellini in the pot of boiling water, and it immediately smells delicious. Tom sets another pot on to boil water for us to drink later. When the noodles are done, I drain them and toss in the Parmesan cheese. Carter eats with his fingers, wearing the tortellini like rings, nibbling at them. I open a can of pears, cut off a hunk of cheese, and we share an apple for dessert, passing it among the three of us. Carter sits in the cup of my lap, and we watch the moonrise over the lake.

I wake to the sound of rain hitting the tent in the darkness. Carter is curled into me in our shared sleeping bag. Tom is still asleep. I listen to the pit-pit-pit of the water, and the slow and easy breathing of my boys, my whole world reduced to the square footage of the tent, everything I care about contained in this small, manageable space.

Morning comes and the rain continues, a light mist. It's not uncommon. It's not enough to deter Tom; I don't even ask. We begin our day, dressing Carter in a snowsuit. Tom ducks out into the gray light and starts the fire to boil water for coffee, Tang, and our instant oatmeal with cinnamon sugar.

After, we grab our hiking gear from the car, already packed. I strap Carter into the Kelty pack and hoist him onto my back. Tom carries everything else: our smaller tent, food, water, extra pots and pans. We head up the trail.

The mist hangs with us all morning, hovering between rain and fog. I'd hoped the sun would come out and burn off the clouds, but no. We keep hiking, past a patch of cow parsnip, bent and trampled. For a moment, I wonder what could have caused this; then I think elk, or deer, or even bear, bedded down for the night. We walk through a field of thimbleberries, which are pretty but not very good for eating. The trail descends, and we follow it. Down and down, lower and lower. Here, among the dampness of the ferns and mossy logs, the trees are so big you can't even see the sky.

The trail takes another turn, and we begin climbing. All the while, we've been singing silly made-up songs, or "Now I Know My ABCs," or a hopscotch chant I remember from childhood, "Miss Mary Mack-Mack-Mack, All Dressed in Black-Black-Black." When we run out of options, Tom teaches me the words to a German beer drinking song, *"Lass Im Boot Das Schaukeln Sein."*

By now, my feet are sore and my legs ache. It doesn't bother me; it feels good to have a pain that I understand. Still, I begin wondering how long until we get reach our destination. We need to find a place to rest and have lunch, but the trees are thick on either side. There's nothing but the trail in front of us. Off to our left, deep in the darkest part of the woods, I think I hear the howl of a wolf. We stop singing. A shiver runs through my body.

We keep hiking.

The trail bends around a ridge, and I think, surely we'll see something ahead, some flat, grassy spot. But no, the trail descends again, down to a creek with a makeshift bridge crossing it. There was no bridge on our maps. Where are we?

There's no singing, no happy banter. We are mostly quiet. The only sound is from the nearby stream, which is thick with mosquitoes. Carter is hungry and cross. We drop our packs and set up temporary shelter, spreading a tarp. I pull out the jerky and cheese and a bar of chocolate with almonds. Just as I'm sitting down, it begins to rain hard. Tom and I scurry to put things away, to pack up Carter, to get moving again. But where are we going?

Tom takes the map from its Ziploc bag, the rain pelting it and us until we're soaked. I can't see anything; neither can Tom. It's impossible to know where we are.

If I'd been a child and this were my family, the parents would have begun arguing. They'd take their frustration, and their disappointment, and their fear, and blame each other, erupting into a fight. If Tom were the child, our situation would have been seen as a chance to teach perseverance and determination. If it were Tom's family, they would have forged ahead, no matter what.

Tom and I look at each other. He's wearing a maroon baseball hat, water dripping off the brim. His parka is soaked through. The backpack, dripping wet. All our plans, everything, undone. It is a defining moment. Which way will we go?

"I'm sorry," I say, and I'm talking about more than the hike.

"Me too," he says. "I never meant for any of it to happen."

"I know," I say. "It's not your fault."

"But it is," he says.

"No, it's not. It's just life. Sometimes things happen," I say, reaching out to touch his face, his wet cheeks.

"I love you," he says.

"I love you too."

Without another word, we turn around and begin retracing our steps. The clouds have closed in, and the trail is hidden in mist and fog. The large leaves of the cow parsnip hold water like plates; as I brush past them, water dumps down my legs. My shoes squish when I walk. Carter falls asleep in the pack. I'm so tired, and now my thighs have begun cramping up. Tom reaches back and takes my hand. "Just keep going. You can do it," he says. "We can make it. It'll be okay." I appreciate his kindness and his gentleness. This is the man I will spend the rest of my life with. And Carter, our beautiful boy.

I can't see the path through the rain. My shoes squish, squish, squish, and I concentrate on simply putting one foot in front of the other. The only sound is the chattering of my teeth, which I can't control. Eventually, the rain slows to a drizzle until finally, it stops. As we continue walking, a sadness sets in. Despite all the trouble, I don't want to go back. The new house, with its mismatched furniture, its creaks and groans in the night, its unfamiliar smell, doesn't feel like home yet, and we have no other place to go.

Out of the fog, I see the campsite in the distance, hugged by low clouds. Wisps of smoke rise from the campfires. There are tarps spread between trees, makeshift porches. The sight feels familiar and I'm overcome with happiness. Home is where we are now. Home is the three of us, together.

Splish, Splash, We're in First Class

Sarah Franklin

As the breast milk ricocheted off the lovingly polished badge of our first-class purser and splashed into the proffered glass of Veuve Clicquot, I realized quite how inured to embarrassment I'd become since starting to travel with our three-month-old. Rather than wondering how I could exit a moving plane at thirty thousand feet, or requesting another cashmere blanket to hide underneath, I found myself musing on just what fancy name could be given to the brand-new cocktail my son and I had just invented. "Lactation Luxury"? "Mommy's Marvel"? "Bubbles and Boobs"? I'm not sure this particular tipple is likely to make it onto the in-flight menu any time soon, but surely it deserves its own nomenclature.

Of course, the question should be what possessed me to occupy the first-class cabin of the Seattle-to-London flight with a three-month-old, and it's not an unreasonable one.

Entrance to the Holy Chamber of Flight, the First-Class Cabin, had always evaded even such a fan of the free upgrade as myself. And, of course, by becoming so unobtainable, the experience had gained an even bigger desirability. Even while ensconced in a (free) business-class seat, rather than enjoying the seven kinds of champagne and the forty-five movies on offer, I would spend my time imagining just how much *better* the flight would be if I were a couple of rows forward. Forget the free champagne; there was probably an onboard winery up there. To say nothing of soothing massage, free mani-pedis, and a Booker Prize–winning author to lull me to sleep with my very own bedtime story.

Even on our honeymoon, an eight-leg extravaganza of aerospace for which my husband had oh-so-sensibly used air miles for business-class seats, first-class upgrades weren't forthcoming. The smiles of blissed-out newlyweds, it seems, aren't enough to enter the Sacred Chamber. You need a secret code.

The secret code, it turned out, was a pint-sized, klaxon-voiced three-month-old. Flying back to Britain for a family wedding while Jonah was still tiny struck us as overwhelming in many, many ways. Still, our concerns (How will we manage to visit our forty-five nearest and dearest in a three-week trip? How will our reflux-prone teeny sleep in a variety of loaner Pack 'n Plays? What on earth will I wear to the wedding that's halfway funky but won't let slip an errant boob when doing the Chicken Dance?) were outweighed by one glorious fact. By a fabulous twist of fate, the only tickets available on our corporate air miles were in first class. So not only would we finally get to see what's behind the damask curtain separating the silver-spoon crowd from the plebeians but we'd have more space and convenience for our tiny child. Bliss!

Our first indication that first-class travel was different from any other kind of upgrade occurred at check-in. Peering around our mountain of luggage, the baby strapped on the top for safekeeping, we beamed hopefully at the check-in agent and asked for two adjacent seats, both for baby-wrangling and to avoid disturbing anyone who'd actually shelled out the $15,000 per seat that we had bagged for free.

"Certainly, Madam," said the agent, and seemed to mean it. Whizz, click, whirr: two tickets popped out of the machine.

Already a little overamped at the prospect of a trip home, I instantly spotted a problem on the tickets.

"Um . . . these aren't actually next to each other," I said, about to launch once again into my tortured explanation of why, exactly, it would benefit all concerned not to split us up. "These are for seats 1A and 1K. We were hoping for 1A and 1B. Do you think we could try again?"

The check-in agent shot me a pitying look, airline code for "Well, it's obvious *you're* traveling on a freebie, you peasant."

"These *are* adjacent seats, Madam," she replied. Did I detect a slight hint of sarcasm around the "madam"? Surely not.

"You're in the very front of the plane, and your seats are the only two in the row. The "A" and the "K" merely denote what the seat numbers would be if you were back in economy" (*where you belong*, you could almost hear her thinking).

Okaaaay then. We essentially had the entire width of the plane to ourselves, with about six feet of aisle space between us for ease of bringing the stroller all the way up the plane.

As it turned out, we also had an entire closet to ourselves, not to mention padded leather full-size beds, a choice of car seat or bassinet for Jonah, and a couple of pre-takeoff rounds of blinis and caviar. I was mentally calculating how many organs we'd have to sell to make traveling first class a habit rather than a fluke when Dave discovered the pajamas. Freshly pressed, organic-weave cotton pajamas for our flying comfort. Taking advantage of the cavernous bathroom, we changed into them straight away, much to the consternation of our fellow passengers who, far classier than we, clearly thought we were a little over-enthusiastic for the caliber of person one normally hopes to encounter in first class. The looks we were getting for being pajama-clad at 7:00 PM were nothing, however, compared with the sniffs and sidelong glances that Jonah was attracting. Happily ensconced in my seat, pulling magazines out of the rack and scattering them around our four-acre designated space, he seemed quite content to me. However, I could tell that this wasn't a crowd that would be delighted by his predilection to wake up every four hours with a perfectly pitched yell I had come to recognize as his way of demanding MILK! NOW, DAMMIT!, and the subsequent love of chattering at me for a couple of hours about just how delicious the milk had been.

Ah, well. Whether or not our copassengers felt we belonged, we were having a ball—the pajamas were as luxurious to wear as they'd looked. So that Jonah didn't feel left out, we changed him into pajamas too—alas, no mini-sized airline ones with the flight insignia, but an exclusive, pastel blue, French ensemble sent to us by unbelievably tasteful London friends. It was the maiden voyage for the pajamas, as well as for Jonah, and all too soon we discovered that pastel blue isn't the best color for concealing a blowout in the diaper department. And that the scent of caviar doesn't do an awful lot to counteract the stench of a full-scale diaper disaster. At least at this point, several hours into the flight, people had stopped staring at Jonah and taken to ignoring us altogether.

In anticipation of the need to entertain an infant for the better part of twelve hours, we'd packed an array of extravagant toys and more books than at Borders. Needless to say, none of this impressed Jonah, whose standards were clearly being raised by his surroundings. With a glance that said "Look, Mum! Here's the best thing *ever*!", he pulled from the magazine rack a laminated plastic sheet of disembarkation instructions in seven languages. Another look from our pint-sized passenger, this one clearly signaling, "And hear the fantastic crinkle-crinkle-CRACK noise the sheet makes when I whack it against the seat!"

In an attempt to deter Jonah from performing his best impression of the flight techs in *Top Gun*, waving said laminated sheet above his head as if summoning in the fighter jets (and thus achieving maximum crackle from the card), I removed the card and, before Jonah could object to the disappearance of such an enticing toy, plonked him down on the spare acre of floor space between Dave's full-length bed and mine (Dave, being both sensible and not possessed of lactation devices, had by this point snuggled down under the three-hundred-thread-count covers provided by the airline and was away with the fairies). Jonah, delighted by the new surface to explore, gurgled and beamed up at me as if to say, "This flying lark's a bit of all right, isn't it, Mum?"

Before he'd even had a chance to inspect the logo on the five-inch-deep plush carpet, however, a flight attendant magically appeared, swishing down the mile of aisle towards us. His name badge announced that he should be referred to as Giles, and was fluent in French and Mandarin should English not be to my liking.

"Pick that *up!*" he hissed at me, clearly keen not to wake the (paying) passengers and be faced with having to actually serve anyone.

I checked to see what we'd dropped. A quick inventory of our worldly goods came up with precisely zilch. The diaper bag was fully stocked, the seventeen books were neatly stacked in our in-flight bookcase, the thrilling piece of laminate was stashed back next to the sick bag. Both boobs were neatly encased.

"Pick what up?"

"*That!*" Giles hissed again, jerking his chin floorwards, his face turning a delicate shade of puce that clashed with the liveried uniform. Following his gaze, my eyes alighted upon my beloved firstborn.

"The baby?" I clarified. "But he's quiet and happy down there, and he's not in anyone's way, since we're right at the front of the plane." Jonah, as if in confirmation, grinned gummily up at Giles, who remained unmoved.

"Regulations are regulations," he pontificated. "Can you *imagine* what would happen in economy if we let the . . . *children* roam unfettered?" He flinched at even uttering the word "children," shuddering at the thought of said feral beings charging the plane like wildebeests. "No child must touch the floor for the duration of the flight—it's the rule. At least adults know better."

My mind boggled so much at this that I entirely forgot to do his bidding and left Jonah on the floor, where he proceeded to merrily slobber on Giles's calf-leather size 9s. "What if they need to use the bathroom?" I asked. "What if someone needs to get past them to another seat? What about boarding the plane in the first place?"

"Well, clearly we'd rather they didn't," said the charming, family-friendly steward of the skies.

Sighing, I scooped up Jonah from his position half-buried in the carpet. Indignant at being relegated to my knees, Jonah deemed it time for a quick game of "Let's see just how loudly I can shriek and how many people's sleep I can disturb simultaneously." Giles's complexion deepened from the delicate puce to a decidedly indelicate violet and he raised an eyebrow in disdain. Stifling the urge to smother him with a used diaper, I raised, not an eyebrow, but a goodly chunk of my pajama top and presented the miracle child with the magic boob. Instant calm.

Silence reinstated, Giles nodded curtly and returned to the fully outfitted kitchen, bigger than the one in our Seattle apartment. A series of pops and clinks announced the imminent arrival of champagne and, presumably, more blinis—clearly this was to be a high-class, high-altitude midnight feast. Either that or by proferring champagne when two-thirds of the cabin was asleep, the crew got to keep the open bottle for themselves, I speculated.

Lulled quickly into a doze by the gently nursing infant in my nap, I was startled awake by a rattle. Looking up, I saw Giles glaring down. "I suppose *you* won't want champagne," he sneered, daring me to contradict him and out myself as Britney-in-waiting. As I prepared to take a glass for myself *and* one for Jonah, just to show him, Jonah realized something interesting was going on in the outside world and popped off the boob to investigate for himself. As any current or former lactator will know, the garden-variety boob doesn't have on-and-off switches; it's more of a power hose than a faucet. And babies, the little suckers, don't generally give you a signal that they're about to disengage (although maybe this is something that could be remedied with baby sign language—teaching the wee ones to tap three times gently as advance warning to make ready with the breast pad).

Jonah bounced off just as Giles bent down with the tray. *Swoosh!* went the milk. A good trajectory, even by normal standards, I observed, reaching a distance of at least three feet. *Ping!* went the badge. *Splaash!* went the milk as it dove into the champagne.

Shrugging, I looked up at the open-mouthed Giles, who was clearly struggling to reconcile what had just happened with anything he'd ever read in his flight-training books.

"Madam!" he sputtered eventually. "Here in first class, we do *not* permit passengers to mix their own cocktails!"

Not a bad response, all things considered.

To Grandmother's House We Go

Katharine D. Morgan

L ike all loving parents, my husband, Dennis, and I always wanted what was best for our children. Our definition of the best? Well, it wasn't going to be a cruise around the Caribbean or a trek across Europe. These adventures were not in the stars (or budget) for our family of five. There was only one way for us to journey . . . over the river and through the woods, traveling thousands of miles to Grandma's (and Grandpa's) house! But not by horse and sleigh, mind you. For every trip we packed our economy station wagon to the brim with suitcases, three kids, and two adults. We strapped bikes to the back of our four-cylinder flivver and topped it with a Burley (a child's cart pulled behind a bicycle). We definitely weren't thinking aerodynamics, but we were prepared for all eventualities and ready for the open road!

Each family holiday left us with a legacy of memories. We ran out of gas, had flat tires, and lost keys. Our tales are many, our memories innumerable, but reminiscing about one specific trip always brings our family to tears of laughter (and maybe a little embarrassment for our son; sorry, Matthew).

We were heading east. New Hampshire was our destination. We entered Ohio, paid our toll, and proceeded, traveling at sixty-five miles per hour.

Problem was, Ohio's speed limit was fifty-five miles per hour. Less than a quarter mile into the Buckeye State, the welcoming tollbooth still in sight, we were pulled over by Ohio's finest. As the officer approached our car, six-year-old Matthew got his first bloody nose—caused by the sight of the police, or just coincidence? Needless to say, he freaked out. As he screamed, I plucked Kleenex from a box, reached over the seat, and grabbed his nose. Our children always preferred their father's gentle approach to bodily care, and this was no exception. Matthew wanted nothing to do with me. His cries escalated and Dennis came to his rescue. As we both knelt across the car, Dennis helping Matthew, me on standby, Matthew screaming, blood everywhere, a callow police officer peered into our car. (I swear he looked young enough to be in the back seat with our children.) Seeing our chaos, he looked to me for answers.

"Hi!" I tried to sound optimistic, but I'm afraid I came off more sarcastic. "We're just having one of those fun family vacations."

He profusely apologized for stopping us, and gave my husband a warning about the speed difference. As if by magic, Matthew's nosebleed stopped almost instantly, and we were on our way again.

We made it through Ohio without further incident, slept over in Pennsylvania, and woke the next day refreshed and ready to reach our destination. Today's agenda was New York State, complete with captivating countryside and, unfortunately, construction. I was the navigator. Dennis drove. And we could not find our exit off I-80. How could we have missed it? Was the sign down due to the roadwork? Did I look away for too long to pour water for the kids, get one of them a cracker, settle a dispute, or hold a hand?

We had no clue where we were headed. Just as we realized we had somehow merged onto I-95, we saw this spectacular bridge ahead. It wasn't your ordinary bridge; it was a bridge of significance. Having recently visited New York City on a business trip, Dennis felt his heart sink. "It's the George Washington Bridge!" We were heading into the heart of New York City.

We were in bumper-to-bumper traffic, not an exit in sight. As a matter of fact, it seemed traffic was only merging onto the highway. No one was getting off. At one point, Dennis tried to give another driver a break and let her in ahead of us. She showed her gratitude with a hand gesture I'd rather my kids hadn't seen.

"Why did she show Dad her finger?" asked ten-year-old Amy.

As I figured out how to reply, Matthew saved me by crying, "I have to go to the bathroom!"

"You'll have to wait. We can't get off the road." I sympathized.

"But I have to go *now!*"

"Do you see a bathroom? You have to wait."

"I can't hold it!"

"And I can't create a bathroom in the middle of a New York City highway!"

"Or can I?" I noticed the water cooler at my feet.

Matthew reiterated, "I can't hold it!"

I did what any mother would do when faced with the possibility of a saturated car seat. I rolled down my window, threw the water out of the cooler (too bad it couldn't have cooled off the hand-gesturing lady) and handed it back to Matthew. He stood up in the seat and used the cooler as a makeshift urinal. (I know. I didn't like the no-seat-belt thing either! But the poor boy had to go. And besides, we weren't moving.)

"Keep your back to the girls, Matthew," I instructed.

Amy screamed, "He's going to splatter!" But her anxiety eased and her concern turned to laughter when she realized that this would be great ammo the next time she wanted him to do something for her.

Matthew did what had to be done and we eventually figured out how to head north, adding just a couple hours to the trip. But hey, what's a little extra time in the car when we were having such fun? Besides, we were elated to be out of New York City. As for the cooler, it became recycling.

Raising kids, you always hear, "Enjoy! Someday you'll miss this." Who do they think they were kidding? Seriously, did "they" enjoy driving down the road listening to the shrill pitch of siblings yelling, "He touched me!", "I have to go to the bathroom," "Are we there yet?", and "I'm hungry!"? Call me crazy. Call me insensitive. But I specifically remember looking at Dennis after several hours on the road and saying, "I'll *never* miss this!"

And truthfully, I don't. What I do miss are the kids. With Amy and Matthew off to college, Breanna now sits alone in our back seat. Dennis drives. I read, write, or crochet. Bre does homework or plays movies on her DVD player.

She dreaded her first road trip without siblings. "What am I going to do?"

"Enjoy the peace and quiet," I thought.

But the fact is, she'd rather have her brother and sister along for the ride.

I'm reminded of Joni Mitchell singing "Big Yellow Taxi" (or if you're younger than I, you'll think it was the Counting Crows, but regardless . . .), "Don't it always seem to go that you don't know what you've got til it's gone." I knew what I had then. I know what I have now. A thankful heart that remembers the good, laughs at the chaos, and celebrates the uncertain adventures of traveling the open road with family.

Double Trouble on the High Seas

Elena Aitken

An audible gasp went up from the table as soon as the words came out of my mouth. Life-sustaining mugs of hot coffee sat unattended, mouths hung open, and the shrieks and squeals of twenty small children playing in the background became a distant buzz. As I looked around the table at the women in my playgroup—my friends, my peers—I viewed expression upon expression of disbelief and horror. I had just announced that my husband and I would be taking our eighteen-month-old twins on a two-week sailing vacation to Antigua.

Although the women in my playgroup—all, like me, mothers of twins—thought I had completely lost my mind, I eagerly anticipated our Caribbean vacation with my parents on their thirty-nine-foot Beneteau Cruiser. I was counting the days until I would be lounging in the hot sun, sipping piña coladas, watching my toddlers play happily in the sand nearby. While my girlfriends' reactions had given me some reason to doubt my vacation fantasies, I pushed those doubts out of my mind and got on with the gargantuan task of packing for our adventure on the high seas.

Because there isn't much room on a thirty-nine-foot sailboat, we were allowed to take only two duffel bags among the four of us. I packed more than that in my diaper bag when I went to the store! How was I supposed to fit enough clothes for two adults and two small children for two weeks into only *two* bags? Never mind the diapers, wipes, sunscreen, storybooks, dolls, trucks, swimsuits, and lotions that I would need. And that's just a two-day supply. Never let it be said that kids travel lightly.

After arranging and rearranging, I somehow managed to streamline our possessions and squeeze them into two bulging bags, which we hauled through the airport while juggling two very sleepy children. A word to the wise: Even though children under two fly for free, you pay a very steep price for that free flight. Having a twenty-five-pound child bouncing on your already numb legs, which have been folded into an impossibly small space for a five-hour flight, is a new form of torture. Perhaps the only thing worse is the burning pain that emanates from your bladder when you are forced to "hold it" for two hours just as the bouncing child finally falls asleep on your numb legs. Spring for the extra ticket!

After a twenty-four-hour layover and another four-hour flight with our over-tired, bored children and no room to move, we finally reached our destination, the international airport, nestled between the pristine beaches on the island of Antigua. Exhausted, my husband and I thrust our children at their eagerly awaiting grandparents. If I didn't need a vacation before, I sure needed one now! Bring on the piña coladas!

However, if I had thought I was going to be able to kick back and unwind with a cold drink right away, I was sadly mistaken. We still needed to transport our two wiggling little children, our two heaving duffel bags, and four adults in a rather small dinghy to the boat anchored in the middle of the harbor.

I carefully explained to the twins the importance of boat safety and the necessity of wearing a "boat coat" in the dinghy, instructions that went completely unheard with the excitement over all the boats. After carefully helping the children off the dock and into the waiting dinghy, we were off. We zipped through the harbor to our destination, *Sailbad the Sinner*, our thirty-nine-foot floating home for the next two weeks.

A thirty-nine-foot boat is an extremely small living space for two very active toddlers; imagine taking your entire home and squeezing it into a space that is roughly the size of the average living room. Although I had been on the boat years earlier, I now looked around through the eyes of a young mother, and for the first time I was worried. Maybe my girlfriends at playgroup had been on to something. Maybe taking my toddlers on a small sailboat wasn't a very smart idea.

The living quarters below deck consisted of one very small room that served as the galley kitchen, sitting area, dining area, and navigation area, all within about ninety square feet. Sleeping arrangements involved the three even smaller bunks leading off the main salon. Above deck, the only living space was the cockpit, a small square area consisting of two benches on either side of a small table. There was little room to walk, and the area that was available had coils of ropes, winches, and all sorts of other perils lying about.

My job as a mother is to examine new areas for anything that could pose a hazard for my children. The entire boat was a floating time bomb. Not sure what I had gotten myself into, I put on a brave smile, mentally prepared myself for a nervous breakdown, and headed above deck to look for that piña colada and prepare for our first sail.

The amazing thing about small children is that they are remarkably adaptable. By the end of the first day on the boat, they had assimilated completely to boat life. As a crew, we only experienced one narrow escape when my son ventured out on the ship deck. He was having a great time swinging on the lifeline over the ocean waves before Daddy caught him and hauled him back into the cockpit. We sacrificed a few sippy cups to King Neptune along the way, rigged up a practical, if not very stylish safety gate out of an old lounge chair, and learned that the toddlers had better luck operating the depth gauge than the captain of the ship.

Dingy, beach, ocean, and sailboat were all new words quickly added to the children's budding vocabulary. I don't know why I ever worried about packing clothes since the kids quickly abandoned them, along with their diapers, as they ran bare-bottomed along the beach and played in the surf. For two weeks we sailed up and down the length of the island, dropping anchor in a new bay or harbor every day, and setting off for shore to explore new beaches and villages. My daughter had her hair braided by a local woman, and they danced to steel-drum bands in the beach villages. My husband and I had the remarkable opportunity to look through our children's eyes as they saw all of these things for the first time, and through them, we experienced the magic of the Caribbean as well.

When the time came to say goodbye and board the airplane back to the cold reality of a February winter in Canada and everyday life, nobody wanted to say goodbye. After all of my worrying, I was now ready to move my family to a boat in the Caribbean permanently.

Unlike on all of my previous holidays, I returned from this trip needing another one. Sailing with small children is an exciting adventure but not for the faint hearted. A few days later as I looked around the table back at playgroup, I still looked into the faces of disbelief and horror, but I think I also saw some wonder and admiration in some of the faces of my friends. But then again, maybe I just needed to get some rest!

Mosquitoes Be Damned

Veronica Chater

To camp, or not to camp? To uphold a family tradition, or to hurl its carcass into the oblivion of the past? To hammer a ritual solidly in place, or to knock it down like a house of cards?

I ask you. Is it such a terrible thing to allow a tradition to die? I mean, if going out into nature for three days with an unsociable husband, three young kids, and twentysomething relatives and friends doesn't appeal, is it a crime to just not do it?

In my family, tradition is a powerful force. And one of its traditions is the family summer campout. Every year I ponder this campout with lip-biting deliberation, my head in my hands, my eyes zipped shut with indecision while I consider the painful consequences of attending, and the even more painful consequences of declining the invitation.

My mom and her ten siblings look forward to the event all year like children anticipating Christmas (Dad giddily looks forward to the peace and quiet of our four-day absence). Sometime around February someone will say the "camping" word, and set off a conflagration of debates. Soon after, the phones start ringing. Where should we go this summer? To the mountains or sea? How many campsites should we book? Should we organize a menu?

Who'll bring the canoe? The fishing rods? The camp stove? I try to catch the bug of excitement, but for some reason all I can think about are the negative aspects: How will I keep track of my toddler twins? Will our tent accommodate a crib? How will I wash the cloth diapers? What about snakes? Bugs? First aid? My four-year-old's asthma?

My mom and siblings are adamant. Don't worry about the kids, they say. We all have kids. Everyone will pitch in. Come on! It's camping. You'll have a great time no matter what.

Their message is clear: To fail to continue a family tradition is to be guilty of a breach of contract—or child abuse.

In theory, I love camping. In my late teens we went to Bodega Dunes or Big Basin. Mom made eggs, home fries, and bacon in the morning on the camp stove while I made toast and coffee on the grill over an open flame, and we all sat around on our beach chairs and watched the activity of the birds and chipmunks, and listened to the sounds of the sea rustling through the trees from the distant shore. Later, when John and I got married, we made a point of camping together often. One summer it was the Sierra Foothills beside an icy cold lake. Another it was Mendocino County under a cloak of wet fog, surrounded by fields of spiky porcupine grasses that stung our bare legs as we marched through them. We've camped in the thermal gloom of the Sequoia Redwoods, in the rippling yellow dunes of Death Valley, and in the craggy volcanic wonderland of Mount Lassen. I've always loved the close-to-nature feeling I get from camping, and I don't mind the little inconveniences. When necessary, I seem to be able to whittle my body's requirements down to a few occasional animal proceedings, and the rest is just hiking, fishing, and stabbing the campfire into the late hours of darkness.

But camping with kids is an entirely different experience from camping without them. Camping with kids, I'm here to tell you, is not camping.

Last summer was no exception. My sister Mary, official taskmaster, organizer, and cheerleader, chose the campground. "You'll love it," she chirped through the phone. "It's only a four-hour drive for you, and it's super family-friendly. Perfect for kids." If I hadn't erased the name of the place from my memory bank I'd mention it right here, but I can't for the life of me recall the family-friendly place only four hours away. I do remember the reservoir being too small to justify its appearance on my California map, and that as we followed the signposts Daniel, my four-year-old, kept asking, "When are we going to get to Broccoli Lamp?" (Brockley Camp? Brocklay Ramp?). But except for those meaningless little tidbits I come up blank.

It's symptomatic. From the first moment of our arrival at the campground, John and I seemed lost in a kind of stupor. Maybe it was because the place was hotter than the sunny side of Mercury. Maybe it was because the four-hour drive had somehow stretched out to five and a half. Maybe it was the trauma of organizing all the stuff and packing it—playpen, high chairs, bottles, formula, baby backpacks, a borrowed porta-crib, ice, food, warm clothing, beach towels, Advil—and then worrying that we'd forgotten something.

By the time we pulled into Broccoli Lamp (or whatever the place was called) our Vanagon stunk from burning asbestos, one-year-old twins Cameron and Kyle were both pink-faced from crying and covered in banana slime, Daniel was asleep with vomit on his shirt, and John was in a bad mood because I'd misread a possible shortcut on the map, causing the extra hour-plus. Sensing fresh meat, gluttonous mosquitoes fat from campers in nearby lots hummed in through the van windows by the dozens. Before I could roll up the windows, three mosquitoes went to work on Cameron's forehead and two drove their suckers into Kyle's neck.

Oh, well. At least we're here, I thought. But where was here? As we sat numbly in our seats, the engine clicking as its fever cooled, we surveyed our lodgings in a hypnotic trance.

Our site, Lot 80, was (as a realtor might say) all potential: a dirt driveway pockmarked with bottle caps, old cigarette lighters, and an imbedded condom, and a barbecue pit topped by a rusty grate heaped with cinders, chicken bones, and broken bottles. To the side, chained to the ground, weathered by sun, stabbed with a fork, carved by knives, and spray-painted with the names of a million departed campers, a picnic bench cringed with hurt pride, and behind that a few embarrassed trees wished they were elsewhere.

Lots 81, 82, 83, and 84, which were reserved for the rest of my family, were still empty. At any moment, the four dirt driveways with their enchained park benches would be crawling with twenty-seven relatives and friends with nothing but fun on their minds. (There were three birthdays to celebrate, John's and my sixth wedding anniversary, my niece's high school graduation, and my brother Danny's return from a trip to India.) In the meantime, there was no lack of company. As far as the eye could see were people. Big people, small people, fat people, skinny people, old people, young people, disabled people, teenagers, babies. The people were busy. Extraordinarily busy. They talked, laughed, sang, smoked, cooked, ate, danced, threw footballs, set up tents, rolled out awnings, unfolded lawn chairs, built gazebos, assembled camping stoves, and blew up every manner of flotation device imaginable. Where did all these people come from? Did somebody turn a city upside down and shake it over the campground? I hadn't seen so many people in one place since I'd attended a Rolling Stones concert at what used to be Candlestick Park back in the eighties.

"Wow," John said simply. "Popular place."

Okay, I thought. It's not exactly camping the old-fashioned way, in peace and quiet and solitude. Fair enough. No point in sniveling about it. Enjoy it for what it is. And with that categorically positive thought I took a few deep breaths, acquired a Zenlike acceptance of the inevitable, and forthwith helped my dispirited and laconic husband to unpack our gear. What else could I do?

An hour later, our five-man tent was erect (a fluorescent yellow dome that so effectively absorbed the heat that our sleeping-bag zippers threatened to melt), the porta-crib was assembled inside, and the peanut butter and jelly sandwiches were hardening to toast on the table. In addition, our twins were swollen with mosquito bites, sunburned, and completely and utterly clothed in fine red dirt, and Daniel was over in Lot 85 playing with his new friend, a barefooted, mosquito-bitten ten-year-old who was shouting, "I'm going to kill you, ninja boy!"

When Zenlike acceptance of the inevitable fails, I usually start laughing uncontrollably, and did so then. Not so amused, John looked pained, as if a hard-boiled egg were lodged in his throat, and I could hear the first stages of his asthma creating a whistle when he exhaled.

I stifled my giggles. "Why don't we eat first, and then go down to the reservoir and cool off?" I said.

John agreed that a cool dip would be welcome, and went to rescue Daniel from his ninja executioner. Then, after eating our dehydrated sandwiches, we each loaded a twin on our backs and hiked down to the reservoir, a walk of about ten minutes along a wide, sun-drenched dirt road fringed with fine bits of trash and those ubiquitous bottle caps. I still had high hopes and they rested on the success of the reservoir . . . a sandy beach, a shallow shore, partial shade, clean water, and all would be well.

But as we rounded the crest of a dirt hill, sweating like field hands from the heat, I lapsed into hysterical laughter again at the sight of the waterfront. John turned to me, smiling. "By George, it's Club Med," he said.

The shore did have sand, but it was hard to locate it beneath the riotous spectrum of turquoise, quince, hibiscus, and tangerine swimsuits teeming under the white glare of the incandescent sky. It was like the whole of humanity had gathered on the head of a pin and we'd arrived too late to claim a piece of it.

"You stay here," I said. "I'll check it out."

Okay, just a three-foot strip of water for the kids to splash in. That's all I need, I thought, as I high-stepped with my twenty-eight-pound passenger over the multitude of oiled limbs to the softly undulating surf. There, the truth laughed at me with serrated teeth. Ha! Ha! Ha! I dare you to let your babies swim in here! Where the water's edge met the sand, a ridge of mossy rocks descended sharply into murky darkness. The only swimming to be done was forty feet out, where twenty or so people dove from a floating platform.

"What do you think?" John yelled at me over the bodies. He was grimacing and gritting his teeth because Cameron was pulling out handfuls of his hair as he tried to extract himself from the backpack to get at the water. When John read the look of doubt on my face, he turned back, and without even an explanation to poor Daniel, we hiked the dusty road back to our dirt driveway and functional art picnic bench.

"It's too hot! Why can't I swim?" Daniel pleaded in his especially plaintive voice. "Stop! I want to go back! It's not fair! Why can't I play in the water?"

Arriving at Lot 80, Cameron, being the sort of child who can't tolerate a missed nap, reached his limit and began screaming and thrashing wildly in his backpack. On the ground, he rolled in the dirt like an animal giving himself a dust bath, and ended up in some blackberry vines, his tender, sunburned thighs finely scratched by thorns. Meanwhile, Kyle got a lip-bleed from chewing on a bottle cap, and Daniel raced from campsite to campsite in search of his ninja buddy yelling, "Hey, kid! Where are you?"

Sitting at the picnic bench with the twins kicking and squirming on our laps, John and I stared at each other, depressed and confused over what to do next. "What if we . . . " I'd say, then sink back into thought. "Suppose we . . ." "Maybe if . . . "

His buddy nowhere to be found, Daniel began whacking a stick against a tree saying, "Kill! Kill! Kill!" A rottweiler galloped over to him, hoping to get a shot at the stick, an arm, anything. Images of Daniel's limp body in a pool of blood, his jugular torn out, filled my head.

"Daniel!" I shouted. "Give the nice doggy the stick and come back here!"

John sighed. "What do you want to do?"

I smiled weakly. "Drink something strong."

Just then, my mother's overloaded Chrysler rolled grittily up the path, steam spitting through the apertures of its hood as she waved ecstatically out the window. "Hi! I got lost and drove an hour out of my way, but thank God I'm here!" Behind her a trail of autos, trucks and RVs loaded with my siblings and their friends and packed to the gills with food and outdoor gear created a dust storm that seemed to lift the entire floor of the campground into the air and lay it carefully over our heads, shoulders, plates, utensils, cups, clothes, food, and shoes like an enormous reddish-brown blanket.

There is no insult quite as unpardonable as that of a guest leaving a party too soon. The look on my mother's face told me that I was not behaving the way she'd raised me to behave. But that didn't stop John and me from strapping the boys into their car seats and throwing our stuff into the van with both hands as fast as we could grab it. We didn't even bother to make a good excuse.

"Sorry! Got to go!" we blustered. "The babies . . . Water . . . Daniel . . . Ninja boy . . . Scary dog . . . Blood . . ."

My family tried to make sense of what we were saying and nearly chased us down the road (we would have laid rubber if we could). But within minutes we were on the freeway, the windows open for the wind we knew would drive the mosquitoes out and for the fresh air that we felt we'd been deprived of for a year. I knew we had just desecrated the Most Holy Traditional Family Campout and at the same time earned a reputation of first-class snobs, but during the three-hour drive home (going twice the speed downhill, following road signs to the Bay Area) I didn't care.

"I'll make up for it next year," I promised myself, and I meant it.

But now it's that time of year again. The sites at a Calaveras County campground were reserved and paid for in March, the list of essential campers is at a fixed twenty-six (subject to expansion), and, God help us, John and I and the kids are a critical organ of the camping body. If we fail again, camping morale will drop, a pox will descend on the tradition, the camping body will fall ill, grow anemic, and finally wither away for lack of a full-body commitment.

Someone once said, "A precedent embalms a principle."

I have just pounded my fist on the table. By God, I will camp! Filth and mosquitoes be damned, I will not be responsible for depriving my kids of a tradition! Nothing will come between me and my duty as a parent!

There. I've done it. I've made the decision to camp. Sure, I'll probably dread it for months. Then, when the time comes, I'll over-pack, and we'll get lost and John will blame me, and the kids will get covered in dirt and bug bites, and I won't sleep well, and I'll wish I hadn't come, and I'll tell myself I'm not enjoying myself one bit. . . . Except that I'll be enjoying some of it. Like maybe those moments around the campfire when the kids are staring wide-eyed at the flames as their marshmallows ripen to brown. I might enjoy that. And maybe when my brother Nick hides in the bushes and lets out one of his convincing wolf howls and sends all the kids screaming to their tents. I might enjoy that, too. And maybe when John wakes the kids at dawn and takes them down to the lake to fish for trout and they come back beaming and full of stories of the-one-that-got-away. I might get a real kick out of that. And then there will come the time when the kids are all grown up and have such fond memories of our family campouts that they will start a camping tradition of their own with their families and invite me along. And I know I will like that.

99 Bottles

Julie Barton

I f you are an adult who enjoys a road trip, it is 742 picturesque miles from San Jose, California, to Manzanita, Oregon. Grassy hills give way to scrubland, which yields in turn to mountains furred with pine forests, and finally to the windblasted rocks of the Pacific Coast. On the southern end of the route, you will recall Steinbeck and the hope and despair of his unforgettable American dreamers. On the northern section, you'll think of Lewis and Clark's exploration of the breathtaking Columbia River Gorge, marveling at the vision and endurance that drove a fledgling nation westward.

But if you are a toddler, the trip is 3,917,760 excruciating feet of mind-boggling blurry scenery. And if you are eighteen-month-old Charlie, you will spend approximately 3,917,750 of those feet plucking at the straps of your car seat, thrashing in impotent rage, keening, "Pickckck! Upp! Pickckck! Upp! *Peeeeeease.*" Of the ten feet that remain, three will be spent sleeping, and seven will be devoted to massaging plugs of overripe banana into the upholstery of the rental car.

Only too late did I really understand how much this trip would ask of Charlie, whose only job responsibilities at the time were lurching around, exploring new terrain, and mouthing every filthy new object he stumbled across. Even four hours a day in the car was too much. Requiring him to sit still, to stay strapped in his seat for a third of his waking hours, felt, in the end, uncomfortably close to cruelty. The thrashing, plucking, and keening seemed almost justified at times. And when you make allowances for the fact that Charlie's meals consisted largely of cookies and lukewarm water from a none-too-clean plastic sippy cup, that he was away from everything familiar, and that MapQuest's twisted version of the geographical truth turned his mother into a shrieking bitch who stopped giving a shit about Steinbeck about three hundred miles ago, overall he did well.

Sure, he briefly lost himself in frenzied biting when I started to buckle him in one day, but who wants to leave a petting zoo? If you're an adult, you can lodge a reasonable protest: "There were goats, I tell you, *goats*—lovely velvet-lipped, pink-tongued, palm-licking goats." If you are a toddler, your options are limited, especially if you've already wasted your banana on the aforementioned reupholstering.

Charlie's no stranger to road trips. His first was six weeks after his birth, and still a month short of his due date. He came early and unexpectedly while we were visiting my husband's family at Thanksgiving. I'd had a complicated pregnancy overall, but Paul and I had been given the go-ahead to travel by my obstetrician, so it was without any real warning that I became ill and found myself in the hospital on the Saturday after the holiday. I was sick enough that a doctor I'd never met glanced at my lab work, said, "We need to take the baby," and whisked me off for a C-section. A few cuts, ten clamps, and several stitches later, I was a mother, 270 miles from home, ten weeks before I'd expected to be.

With good weather and a remorseless disregard for posted speed limits, you can drive the stretch of interstate from that hospital to our house in four hours. This trip took forty-three days just to get started. Charlie would rally, seeming ready to make the long trip home, and then there would be a setback, buying him another week in the hospital. We would pack our bags and check out of our ratty residential hotel, ready to imprison our son in his car seat for the very first time, then trudge back into the same room only a few hours later, sad and discouraged again.

But on the forty-third day, we were finally on the road. Five-pound Charlie was immobilized in his car seat, making the occasional adorable sucking motion in his sleep, a newborn's witty take on "Are we there yet?" (Stroking his forehead with a tentative thumb was my own clever twist on, "No, and if you ask again I'm going to turn this car around and there'll be no trip to Disney World.") Paul was in the driver's seat, coasting along at a terror-stricken thirty-five miles per hour, so tense I could hear the hair on the back of his neck prickle to strictest attention every time a car moved within two hundred feet of ours. I was in the back seat, staring intently at Charlie to make sure he didn't suddenly stop breathing or vomit or unbuckle his car seat or flip off a passing state trooper or anything—in short, being a brand-new parent—and occasionally exposing myself to passing truckers. And not for the giddy rush of it, either. The thrill was simply a fringe benefit.

Like many babies who've come early, Charlie left the hospital without having mastered breastfeeding. In his earliest days he hadn't yet developed the sucking reflex. Once he had, it still expended more energy to breastfeed than he could safely spare; nursing was so challenging that he fell asleep before taking in all the calories he needed. And later on, he'd grown comfortably accustomed to bottle-feeding, inclined to glare mistrustfully at my bosom every time I unbuttoned my shirt. When for all these reasons I couldn't deliver mother's milk to him straight from the source, I took on a sidekick: an electric double breast pump. It came in a fake-leather shoulder bag—presumably putting the "style" in Pump In Style—emitted an upsetting asthmatic gasp with every pull, and could suck the very patina off the coppery tits of the Statue of Liberty herself. For the next six months, my Medela and I would be an inseparable team, pumping every few hours, car trips included, thanks to its handy twelve-volt vehicle adaptor.

For the long drive home, I'd packed up my pumping apparatus and donned a zip-front sweater to allow easy access. I made sure there was a warm blanket within reach so that I could cloak myself modestly as I pumped. I unzipped my sweater, unclipped the lanolin-stained cups of my nursing bra, conscientiously rebuckled my seat belt across my naked rack, and hitched myself to the pump.

But the blanket wouldn't stay up on its own, and I couldn't spare a hand to hold it. Even when I adjusted the suction setting to "limitless black hole," I couldn't manage the pump with a single hand; I needed to hold the funnel-shaped plastic cones and collection bottles in place. I tried another tack, arranging the blanket around myself without using my hands. Naturally this involved my mouth. I repeatedly grabbed the edge of the blanket with my lips and tried to tug it into place. All this maneuvering achieved was to give me a mouthful of fleecy lint, not unlike what you might expect after going down on a Muppet.

When you're intimately attached to a wheezing piece of machinery and flying down the highway—well, all right, crawling, at a still-fearful forty-five—your options are somewhat limited. Finally I gave up on the troublesome convention of modesty and let the blanket go, trying to shake off my discomfort by chanting to myself, *I'm feeding my baby. I'm feeding my baby. Thank you, O motorized suck-o-mat!* But just to be safe, when we were within visual range of a truck, I kept my eyes forward, my spine rigid, and my chin high, regally ignoring any slack-jawed stares I might have inspired.

To combat the embarrassment, I imagined Queen Victoria passing through the streets of London in an open barouche, infrequently offering her subjects a stiff-armed wave. I like to believe I'd have saluted the truckers similarly if I could have let go of the cones. Nevertheless, as Paul safely steered us clear of curious state troopers and incredulous road crews, I was every inch the naked-breasted, funnel-nippled, fuzzy-tongued monarch—a real live dairy queen.

Incredibly, Charlie slept on, through my awkward backseat fumbling, the noisy laboring of the pump, and the rollicking choruses of "Ninety-nine Bottles of Beer on the Wall" that I sang in time to the Medela's wheezing just to irritate Paul. As we pulled into the garage, it was hard to believe we'd made it. Made it at all, with Charlie having been so early and so sick. Made it without careering into a highway embankment, so nervous and spooked were we by our sudden sole custody of a baby who felt so fragile. And made it without being arrested, no matter how naked I'd been.

Several road trips and developmental stages later, we're all much better at this. By now, we know what we're doing. Charlie, two and a half, scrambles willingly into his car seat, lured by the promise of unlimited all-you-can-eat snacking, and buckles his own harness "until it makes a sssssnap!" He still resents being confined, but I'm less readily moved to guilt by his complaints; his *"pleeeeeease"* still works my nerves, but it no longer plucks my heartstrings.

Paul rides in the passenger seat and navigates, selflessly protecting us all from the poisonous influence of MapQuest. I control the radio, taking requests from the back seat, which come as often for classic rock as for children's music.

Charlie sings along, making ingenious mash-ups out of Steely Dan's "Do It Again" and "The Wheels on the Bus": "And you go back, Jack, do it again, wheel turnin' round and round, alllll through the towwwwn!"

And I drive, my remaining dignity inviolable, my shirt securely buttoned. And a nation of long-haul truckers breathes a silent sigh of relief, a heartfelt prayer of thanks.

From Absinthe to Zeitgeist

Adrienne St. John-Delacroix

L ike most teenagers, mine had never heard of traveling light. She had packed two suitcases and a huge carry-on that weighed almost as much as she did. She had arrived that morning at the San Francisco Airport carrying a long, vintage wool coat her father had given her for her first trip abroad. I groaned, imagining the prospect of lugging the thing halfway around the world in April and May. I learned that she had packed absolutely all of her clothes and shoes, an astonishing display that included half a dozen pairs of black boots and platforms, and the crucial one hundred and fifty or so CDs she felt she could not live without for eight whole weeks.

My original plan was to spend two months on my own in the beautiful city of Brussels, which I'd been exploring online and in books. It looked peaceful and grand. As the departure date neared, Natasha begged to join me. She was seventeen years old, and I knew that all too soon she would fly away on her own. This trip might be my last hurrah as a mother, and probably her last chance to travel on my bank account, albeit with limited funds. I had done my best to prepare her, warning her that she would be confronted with stairs everywhere we went, that Europe just didn't have the escalators and elevators that we are spoiled with. My words were meaningless, however, without a realistic point of reference.

When we arrived at London's Gatwick Airport, it dawned on me that I had raised a child who would never, in her lifetime, be able to live outside of Northern California. Frocked, in two fluffy black petticoats and net stockings, she had been stopped at every single security checkpoint along the way and asked to remove the knee-high black platform boots laced by hook-and-eye that decorated her tiny feet. Terrorist alerts were very high, we had been warned, but we did not know that Goth teens from Sonoma County were deemed particularly suspicious. There was no time to alter this pattern before continuing our journey, and even if there had been, this was in fact her only wardrobe. I focused instead on getting us to Victoria Station, where we would begin passage to Brussels.

Victoria Station is one of the great crossroads of the world, like the Atlanta airport. Still, Natasha's platinum blonde hair and bone-china white skin made her stand out among all the other cultural representatives, perhaps because of the chains of rhinestones that hung around her neck and wrists, sparkling brightly from the high, overhead light. I chose to anchor Natasha and her hundred pounds of luggage in one spot while I went to buy train tickets for Brussels before night fell. By the time I had completed this task, Natasha had demonstrated a shocking knack for adapting to the new environs; she had already purchased her first pack of foreign cigarettes from a nearby vending machine and was sitting on her rolling bag smoking. If there had been any time to spare I would've said something to her about smoking but we were rushed, so the maternal shock and nagging had to wait. And by the time we got through the next security point, boots off, boots on, again, and onto the train, I was the only one not smoking.

From my daughter's perspective, she had already spotted some unforeseen perks to this travel. She could buy alcohol without being carded, and she could get away with behaviors like smoking, against which there was no legal argument. She had brought along a copy of Camus's *The Stranger* for her reading pleasure, although in general she hated all things French, including the language. She preferred German, the native tongue of Kafka and Nietzsche, who had set the gold standard for Gothic Gloom. I knew just enough French to get us around, provided nothing too interesting came up.

We did make it to Brussels in daylight, though the walk to our new lodgings was about an hour longer than it looked on the map. Of course, we were also dragging along the hundred pounds of CDs and inappropriate clothes, clomping them up twelve-inch curbstones, clacking them down the other side. Natasha's feet hurt. We were encountering as many stares as stairs.

Checking in to our apartment, I had my first encounter with what was supposed to be an obscure dialect called Bruxelloise. This is a nifty way to pronounce and restructure French in a manner that no one outside of Brussels could possibly understand. I gathered that they brought it out like Sunday china to help tourists feel less at home. The French sounded tweaked just enough that I wasn't clear whether they were saying to each other that they did not have our rooms ready, that the rooms would not be readied, or that the rooms were ready but not for us. I smiled, pretending to understand, but insecurity had already begun its gradual intrusion upon my fortitude; I felt like a hot-air balloon that had just gained a small but inevitably fatal hole.

The apartment itself was gorgeous—very modern, in that peculiarly Belgian way, a fusion of ultra-mod colors like bright orange in geometric prints, juxtaposed against a wall of windows overlooking the sepia-toned rooftops of the elegant old city. There was a small table before this grand window, where I could easily imagine myself writing or painting with my watercolors, and a long, stone balcony outside it. Our amenities included a small kitchen where I pictured us cooking every day, and a tiny little television set that played three channels, all French. The telephone was yellow plastic, weighed less than one CD, and appeared to have been stolen from someone's preschool toy bin. We were given a book of local maps sealed in plastic to help us locate essentials like restaurants and grocery stores.

Our first mission was to find a grocer, to make the most of our shoestring budget. In fact, we spent three days on the mission. Even with the maps, finding anything at all in Brussels requires a compass. The streets have grown up from centuries past, with odd curvatures and angles that repeat unpredictably. There was also a certain conformity of design, not unlike in an American subdivision, just a lot more picturesque. The only stores we had located were the peculiar, triangular ones perched on small, pointed corners selling candy, cigarettes, and mostly alcohol.

We were living off chocolate bars and tap water, and while it was April everywhere else in the world, in Brussels it was still January. Dining out was out of the question, and besides, the idea was to experience "living" in Europe, not touring in it. Cold winds left our faces feeling slapped as we gradually reduced our efforts to find things, resigned instead to staying indoors staring at the television set playing MTV-Europe. The most popular song on the charts was "Cheeky, Cheeky Boys," sung by a twin-sister Romanian duo. Seriously. It's just one more of those inexplicably European things. It had a catchy tune—"You are the cheeky boys, we are the cheeky girls, it's alright to touch my bum," and so on.

My daughter spent many hours locked into her CD player's headset, and made hundreds of efforts to reach her boyfriend, but the crappy little phone would cut her off after every three or four words. She spoke to him as though she were a prisoner, often whispering, and perhaps because of her desperate tone, it seemed that he was saying he would be flying to Paris the next week to be with her (us), but we couldn't be sure since he kept getting cut off. We considered asking the building's staff if we could use their office computer to email the boyfriend and determine his plans, but the well-dressed and polite office workers, although they tried to be discreet about it, quite clearly disdained us because with Natasha's rhinestones and fluff, we appeared to be some kind of circus spectacle in their otherwise staid environs. I found myself lying to them that my daughter was a singer in a band by way of explanation—though in truth she was just a typical Northern California teen who would not have stood out in a crowd at the coffee bar at home where the kids began their school morning rituals with chai lattes and wheat grass smoothies. The end result of that ploy was that now we heard occasional mutterings about Christina Aguilera and Shakira. Ironically, we soon discovered that the apartment building's ground floor served as an all-night discothèque. I am certain it wasn't by employee choice.

The first weekend arrived. Of course, we had no clue until Sunday was upon us that stores in Brussels do not open on Sundays. Not a thing was open. The chocolate bars would have to last us. Natasha scowled at me with contempt; I was ruining her life. I missed her youthful days of easy laughter and once innate sense of fun.

Monday morning we set out early, starved, crazed from sugar consumption, this time layered in scarves and sweaters and colorful ensembles of dresses over jeans over tights for warmth. I was jealous of Natasha's long wool coat at this point, even though its oversized black and white checks stood out like a crosswalk on the street. We were determined to find a supermarket if it killed us. At one point we were so lost we could not even remember which direction we had come from. Having discarded the futile numbering system, we had resorted to trying to establish our whereabouts based on the shapes of the curiously configured "blocks." Unfortunately there was just enough repetition among them to make this impossible, too.

Natasha insisted I stop holding up the map every three or four steps to perform a visual check because it underlined our tourist status. As we meandered along, pausing repeatedly to consult the map, residents battered us with their five-hundred-euro Gucci bags, refusing us space on the narrow sidewalks. They probably thought we were gypsies; we may as well have been. But better to be gypsies than Americans!

My daughter refused to speak English outside of the apartment. This was April of 2003, and it had been only two weeks since our country had declared its infamous "Shock and Awe" campaign against Iraq, and Europe was outraged by American arrogance. There were anti-American protests forming in most European cities. Natasha was speaking to me exclusively in German then, a language I have no understanding of at all. I retorted by speaking to her in French, which she did not understand, and in fractured Dutch, which probably neither of us understood but was the only alternative to French on the signage and maps we saw. Our toes and fingers were crying from the cold, and we were no longer speaking at all to each other when a mean rain began to snap at our exposed inches of skin. We ducked into a restaurant. My budget had to be let go.

This remains my favorite memory of our trip to Brussels; we took a small table in the center of the crummy diner because it was the only one available. The waitress refused to listen to our awkward French, so we had to point at items on the menu, but it was warm there, the windows steamy, the world outside as beautiful as any fairy tale, and old as stone. By this time I was also chain-smoking, and we spent over two hours sitting there watching the passersby, drinking warm red wine with lemon, and eating the best food we'd ever had in our lives. Belgians, it struck us, have an exquisite existence; perhaps that is why they were so protective of it. Where other European cities embraced Westernization, Brussels wasn't host to that trend, remaining true to its architecture both physically and culturally. It was in this magical moment, while we remained silent, that it felt as if we did not live anywhere, as if we might claim any place as our home.

I felt a little chagrined about my strict American values regarding a small amount of wine with dinner in light of our prevailing laws about underage drinking, because the quiet glass with dinner that so many generations of Europeans enjoyed had not caused any damage that I could perceive. Nevertheless, I made it clear to my daughter that this new clearance was a temporary privilege, one we would not be taking home like a souvenir; this would have to remain on European soil. That and the cigarettes. Later, in 2004, Belgium passed a smoking prohibition for those under 17.

We left feeling lightheaded and toasty, and as if predestined, stumbled into the long-sought grocery store. It was an unmarked building that back home might've been a garage. No windows, no brand name; just a small sign stating SUPERMARCHÉ. Inside, the aisles were lined with treasures. Our hunger had abated, but we wanted to stock up, knowing that we might never find this place again.

When we returned to our apartment many hours later, it was like the luggage scene all over again, only this time we were hauling more groceries than we could manage with grace. The elevator always automatically stopped in front of the office complex, giving the staff a chance at each entry and exit to gaze at us through their narrowed eyes. This day, there was an evil tilt to their smiles, which frightened me, and to which there could be no reply. We kept our eyes focused on our scruffy, tired feet and let ourselves into our apartment with relief.

We unpacked our bounty, tasting everything with abandoned delight. Soon, like Christmas morning, there were wrappings strewn everywhere, much as Natasha's belongings had gradually exploded over every surface in the tiny apartment, lace and black fabric and rhinestones everywhere. At last, we thought, we were saved. We ate so much our tummies hurt. We had begun to smile again, and giggle, just a little, at our predicament. It was a split second, small in comparison to the hours behind and what was sure to lie ahead.

A piece of paper was slipped under the door. Natasha retrieved it, hoping for a mail notification or other communication from the Real World (home). It was a phone bill for our first week there.

Turns out that each time the stupid yellow phone was picked up, we were charged five euros for making the connection to our calling card. Five euros times about two thousand efforts, and suddenly we owed more than the two months' rent paid in advance. I didn't have enough money in the bank to cover it. Being the parent, I felt responsible for solving the problem—even though it wasn't my boyfriend who'd been at the other end. But I knew that if I trudged down to the office to try and negotiate, there was no chance that I would win.

Natasha and I stared silently at the bill. That small hole in confidence was now torn straight through.

There were still a few more daylight hours.

Without a word, our parent-child boundary required immediate erasure, and at once we knew what we had to do: run. We became instant accomplices. We had committed a crime in a country that despised us and the only way out was out the door. With astonishing dexterity, the suitcases were reassembled. We flipped a coin for the coat; she won. We concocted a story about needing to visit an aunt in France, which I relayed to the front desk, as I tried to return the apartment key to them. "For safety's sake," I had said. They had responded that it would be much safer for me to keep the key. "No, no," I had said, with passion. "It is best for you to hold. It might get stolen in the station." I had to promise that we would return during business hours to retrieve it, to which I easily agreed. We knew we would never return. And we didn't.

We connected with Natasha's boyfriend a few days later in Paris, after a complicated series of emails from various Internet cafés along the way. We spent the next seven weeks touring Europe as a trio, staying in odd youth hostels, drinking absinthe, and living day by day. There were wonders to be discovered in free museums and corner markets, and watching street performers. My budget was discarded, my bank account nearly emptied. We had hardly had enough to eat, and Natasha and I had shrunk to just over a hundred pounds each, now officially weighing less than her cumbersome CD collection, which I had, on numerous occasions, considered losing somewhere. All those cobbled streets we walked down, clunking the darned CDs along behind us like the remnants of a former citizenship that we just couldn't shake off.

By the time we returned to America, customs almost refused to let me pass. I was shocked to learn that my passport was suspect. There was no chance that I was the age stated, and certainly my assertion that I was someone's mother was preposterous.

Natasha, at this point, had taken to wearing a lavender wig shaped in a Roaring Twenties bob we'd picked up in a costume store in London. My worn Converse sneakers we had taped together with packing tape slyly stolen from a postal office in Köln, and my jeans had new holes I'd sewn closed with red thread that had come in a tiny sewing kit purchased in a convenience store in Paris.

It was impossible not to smile.

We had left with one relationship and returned with another, and though no one else got the joke, we couldn't stop our laughter. It was the perfect cherry to top off this banana split of a trip. Tears rolled down our cheeks, with words in three languages, well, four if you count English, splicing our sentences.

This did nothing to improve my credibility, but I wasn't hurt by the accusations. I knew it would be sorted out, eventually. I grinned and shrugged at the stern young man tending the customs desk in Philadelphia. We had shed our American poundage, returned with nothing more than memories—I'd not even brought a camera, had written less than four pages—but we had recovered our laughter, an insightful and humbled joy; we had somehow become citizens of anywhere. We had assimilated. Or transcended.

And finding that the country we called home didn't want us back was the most delightful bit of all.

⇒ Shosholoza ⇐

Liesl Jobson

It was the first Christmas we drove to Cape Town—one thousand miles in a tiny Mazda Soho. We were trying to be a family: Stuart, my new partner, and my children Grace, age seven, and Kyle, five, who lived with their father and had come to me for their school holidays. Stuart wrung his hands, sighing, while I packed every last cuddly toy into the trunk. He said, "A lot can go wrong." It was the first time that Grace and Kyle would be spending more than alternate weekends with Stuart. They were all trying to figure each other out. We were going to visit my parents, who were eager to meet my new man for the first time. Before we could even get in the car it was a big mission, a three-day camel ride. It started with the birds.

The cockatiels with their rosy cheeks went to Oupa (Grandfather), who struggled to stick his great gnarled hand in through the tiny cage door to change the seed. The canary, named Egg for its color, went to Cousin, who was no relative at all. But where was I to send our moody beauties, the parrots? You can't foist parrots onto just anybody. They're not everybody's cup of tea.

Our birds are highly strung, so I asked our neighbors to take in our Senegal and our Pionus. Bob and Verity know parrots. They themselves own an Amazon called Spark and a Conure named Hagar, who makes a truly horrible noise. Bob and Verity also have a neurotic cat that cringes when Spark cries "Mouse!", and they run a print shop with temperamental clients, so I figured they could cope with Karma and Parnassus.

Feathered friends sorted, it was time to turn our attention to the needs of the smaller mammals coming with us. The day before we left we visited the library, then bought a stash of coloring books, new crayons, and playing cards at the stationer. At the grocer I purchased fresh rolls, fruit juices, *biltong* (African jerky), and hard candy. Kyle said he wanted chocolate.

"No chocolate," I said. "It messes up the car."

That night, the children removed their schoolbooks from their backpacks and replaced them with the activities we'd chosen for the trip. Before we were outside Johannesburg, not ten minutes into our trip, Grace started singing "Shosholoza." She couldn't remember the rest of the song, so she just repeated that line, over and over.

"Do you have to sing that so often?" Stuart asked, tentatively, after approximately the seventeenth rendition.

"We learned this song at school. Miss Botha said work songs helped workers get through their long and boring day."

"How interesting. Do you know any of the other songs they sang?"

She didn't.

I rather like the open desert punctuated by the occasional windmill and sleepy sheep. The children do not. When we stopped, six hours into the journey, at the Orange River to stare at the water below, Kyle stepped into an ant nest beside the road. Great black ants with sharp pincers ran up his legs and down into his socks.

"Oh, quit the hysterics. It's only ants," I said as I went round to help him. Then I got bitten myself and tried not to howl as the stinging pincers sank in. Back in the car and heading out from Bloemfontein, I handed around butterscotch lozenges, cranked up "Bananas in Pajamas" on the car's CD player, and finally dozed off. Grace took the opportunity to finish her lunch from the day before. Stuart nudged me awake, asking for "more chicken."

"No chicken on car trips, Stu; it goes bad too easily."

"But Kyle wants chicken too."

What did he mean, "too"? I hadn't packed any. I was sleepy. I closed my eyes and rubbed my nose. There was a distinct chicken smell in the air.

"Mom," said Kyle, prodding me in the shoulder, "Grace ate her chicken and I want some as well."

"Where did you get chicken, Grace?" I ask, trying to think clearly.

"From my lunchbox," she said, waving the greasy Tupperware at me. "I packed it, just in case."

Oh, heaven spare us, I thought, rolling my eyes. There was no way that chicken could be okay. I counted the hours on my fingers. I figured that in six hours' time, about four hours away from Cape Town, it would hit. Four hours away from good plumbing and a functional washing machine. Four hours away from my mother and her unflappable calm. I hoped it wouldn't be too severe.

Sure enough, as we approached the historic town of Beaufort West, Grace vomited all over the library's copy of *Where the Wild Things Are*. Two seconds later, the diarrhea started. Stuart screeched to a halt in the middle of the veld. I pulled her out of the car seat, trying to help her squat before her bowels opened. At least it wasn't in the car, but it was all over Grace. I washed her down with sparkling mineral water and threw her soiled knickers into a thorn bush. Stuart scraped the worst of it off the back of his seat and attempted to rinse the library book with the last bottle of mineral water.

I unpacked the entire trunk to find fresh panties. The heat coming off the tar at 6:00 PM was enough to make a soldier faint. If only my child's undergarments were not at the bottom of the bottommost suitcase. I wished there was something other than warm Coke to drink. As we drove away, Grace sobbed for those knickers, her favorites, covered in glitter butterflies. I wished I could console her and, in a vain attempt to do so, gave her the remaining flat Coca-Cola. Kyle kicked up a fuss insisting that he, too, wanted Coke.

We pulled in to a motel with synthetic everything: sheets, bath mat, curtains, mats. In the dining room, a waiter with fake gold caps on his teeth and violent garlic breath served us cold canned vegetables and hamburger patties so full of preservatives I feared we'd all live to be one hundred and twenty.

In the hot bedroom, the four of us sardined into two narrow beds. Everything was sticky and I wished I might lie on the concrete floor naked, but cockroaches and worse lurked in the imagined dark.

When I finally fell asleep, I dreamed of Verity's parrot escaping from its cage, which had been moved closer to the curtains to make space for our birds' cage. He strutted across the carpet and chewed through a cable connected to a printer that was spewing out a last-minute wedding menu for a cabinet minister's pregnant daughter as she prepared to go to the church. When the photocopier seized in the middle of the print run, her eyes widened and her waters ruptured. Verity phoned an ambulance, using as the phone dial the breast of the still-twitching parrot, and the cabinet minister's daughter gave birth to the Savior in her long white gown. The infant was a black Kewpie doll that needed neither nursing nor nappies. It was the Second Coming.

Grace was tugging me awake, crying because she was thirsty and her stomach ached. I gave her Buscopan for the cramps and a drink of water, settling her again by lying on the synthetic sheets against her clammy little body. Awake in the hot insomniac dark, I knew it would be the longest fortnight before I made it back to my therapist.

On our return, Egg had quit singing. Probably from the trauma of being boarded beside Cousin's rat, Cheddar.

The cockatiels had learned to unhook and upend their seed bowl, throwing their food onto the bottom of the cage, and the parrots had plucked themselves naked. They shrieked incessantly, copying Hagar's high-pitched screech. They no longer woke us with the sound of the kettle whistle or the back-door squeak emanating from under the bird blanket. Instead we'd hear a curious clanking: lickety-shick-lickety-shick—sounding just like Bill's photocopier.

Three months later I bought tickets at Johannesburg train station, but only three. The children and I took the train to Cape Town that Easter to visit their grandparents. Stuart stayed behind to mind the birds.

Have Bay, Will Travel

Katherine Ozment

I t was only 7:00 AM but already humid at Boston's Logan Airport, the sticky heat made even more unbearable by the sound of taxis honking and the smell of exhaust swirling around us as we waited at curbside check-in. Three months pregnant, with a toddler in tow, and moving all our belongings across the country to California, I was nudging our two cat carrier bags forward with my foot and pushing the stroller as the line crawled along. My husband, Michael, was on the other side of our outcropping of black suitcases—six in all—checking his watch and scanning the mass of people in front of us as if he could move things along with his eyes.

It was as I gazed down at William, our two-and-a-half-year-old son, happily ensconced in his stroller, that I realized something was missing. Even in ninety-degree heat, William would normally be holding his faded blue blanket, an old, nubby thing he'd had since birth, called Bay. As I looked at his little hands on his lap and his feet swaying idly, the image of Bay floated peacefully in the upper reaches of my brain for a moment and then crashed through to my consciousness like a piano falling through a ceiling. "Bay," I thought, little red lights flashing in my head. "Where's Bay?"

I rifled furiously through my backpack and his, the chaos of the airport falling away as I dug past snacks, DVDs, toys, and books. I already knew that Bay hadn't made it to the airport, but I couldn't yet handle the truth.

Not only is Bay William's most prized possession, which he's pawed and gnawed and loved nearly to shreds since he was born, it's his security blanket, his transitional object—it's what he turns to for comfort when I leave the room. There was, quite simply, no way we could make the six-hour, cross-country flight without it—let alone start a new life. Not only were we uprooting William from his home, we'd forgotten to bring the one thing that would bring him comfort. It made me question why were even going in the first place.

The stated reason was simple enough: Michael is a professor of economics, and we were moving to Berkeley, California, for a year-long sabbatical. In all likelihood, the university would offer him a job, meaning we might never return East. I'd quit my job as a magazine editor, said good-bye to our families and close friends and packed up our house. We were trading everything familiar for the promise of sunshine and stunning vistas, for bougainvillea-draped gardens and a more laid-back way of life.

A California sojourn had sounded like a good idea at the time, but now that we were en route, it seemed crazy. Since Michael and I had met eight years before, we'd lived in D.C., New Jersey, Chicago, and, briefly, before marriage and kids, Berkeley. When we finally got to Boston, we fell in love with the place and started to make a home for ourselves. We'd moved to the city when William was still a mewling baby. He'd learned to crawl in our brick townhouse in Central Square, to walk, talk, and blow kisses over the bow of his crib as we closed the door to his room each night. And we'd learned to be parents. Would we ever live there again?

I gave Michael an urgent look and waved him over.

"I think we left Bay," I whispered, nodding toward the stroller.

He pulled back slowly, his eyes widening. My husband is not given to panic. He moves through the world as if he owns the place, acting on the assumption that, given enough deliberation, any problem can be fixed. I live with the belief that all hell might break loose at any minute. I have to smile whenever Michael says, "What's the worst that could happen?" because I can always think of a few things.

Bay is crucial. Without Bay, William doesn't sleep. When that happens, the thin tendril of control we pretend to have over our lives is utterly lost. Six months before—when Michael picked William up from school and forgot to take Bay from his cubby—I made him go back to the daycare center to get it. When he called to say that the doors were already locked, I shouted, without a shred of irony, "Then call the police!"

He didn't, and William barely slept that night, having rejected the inferior "Blanket," an exact replica I'd naively bought for just such an emergency. Unfortunately, our boy could tell the difference between Bay and Blanket blindfolded. That night without Bay was a nightmare, William crying and throwing Blanket out of his crib, whining for Bay like a child who'd lost his mother. Somehow his transitional object had morphed into the real thing—the tatty rag of a blanket had become more solace to him than even I could be.

"Are you sure Bay's not in your backpack?" Michael asked, knitting his eyebrows in a way I interpreted as accusation. We were already well into our preflight hating mode, which meant any question, comment, or facial expression was to be interpreted as hostile. Normally we get along just fine, but travel brings out the worst in us. We'd already been up for two hours, and every minor decision—when to call the cab, how to fit the suitcases in the trunk, how to get the cats into their carriers—had prompted a disagreement, which inevitably led back to some still-open wound from the past and heated commentary on a range of seemingly unchangeable character flaws. By the time we got in line, our main forms of communication were intermittent glares, curt comments, and peevish harrumphing. The tension usually comes to a head when we get to the security checkpoint and one of us hisses to the other, "Just stop talking!" By the time we're belted in and jetting down the runway, we've made amends.

"I told you it's not here!" I said. "We have to go back!"

"Absolutely not," Michael said. "We'll miss our plane."

I was starting to hyperventilate. In situations like this, my body remains still, but my inner core becomes frantic, like a moth caught in a jar. There had to be time.

"Amanda!" I said.

"What about her?" he asked, thrown by the non sequitur.

"I think she's still at our house."

"You'll never wake her."

Amanda is my twenty-three-year-old half-sister, a journalism grad student who sometimes doesn't go to her first class of the day—at 9:00 AM—because it's too early. She'd been staying with us for our last week in Boston, helping take care of William while we shoved plates and bedding into boxes. There was no way she would answer her phone at this hour.

Just then, William's head turned toward us like a small bird looking for food. "Mama," he said, with big, tired eyes, "I'm hungry."

Hunger with William precedes sleep, as day precedes night. Except sleep without Bay equals disaster.

I looked at Michael. "We have to do *something*."

"You're right. Get her on the phone. Tell her we'll pay her cab fare here and back. Throw in an extra twenty."

The only question was if I could I roust her. *Please, God,* I thought, *let her cell phone be turned on and lying somewhere near her head.*

And then I heard it, the most terrifying thing I could have heard at that moment. "Mama," William said in his small, pleading voice. "Where's Bay?"

Shit!

I fished some goldfish out of the backpack.

"When you finish these, you can have Bay," I said in my best "everything's fine (even when it isn't)" voice. "I don't want you to get Bay dirty with food."

I dialed Amanda's number, saying, mantra-like beneath my breath, "God, let her answer the phone, God, let her answer the phone, God, let her answer the phone . . ." It rang once, twice, three times. My heart was pounding in my chest as I waited for that seventh and final ring and the usual transfer into her already-full voice mailbox.

Then, a miracle.

"Hello," Amanda mumbled, half-asleep.

"We left Bay!" I screamed, abandoning all niceties. "Go upstairs and find it! Hurry!"

"Okay," she said. The rustle of sheets and blankets seemed to go on forever. She walked upstairs at the pace of an eighty-year-old, each step creaking for what seemed like minutes at a time.

"It's here," she said, completely nonchalant. "On the couch."

I could picture Bay there by the front window, our busy street beyond just coming to life, and I felt my first real pang of homesickness.

"Get in a cab and bring it to the airport," I said. "We'll pay you!"

"Alright," she said, surprisingly agreeable given the hour. "Calm down."

My hands were shaking as I gave my ID to the man at curbside check-in. I wouldn't feel OK until I could see and touch Bay.

Michael calmly pushed William's stroller into the airport while I waited at the curb. The cats were meowing in their carrier bags. We had a mere thirty minutes before our plane took off: What were we doing? Why were we leaving? This is our home. When we'd moved here two years ago, we promised ourselves we'd put down roots. And we had. But then the opportunity had come to leave, and we jumped at it without really thinking. Moving wasn't the same as when we were young and childless and could pack a few suitcases and boxes of books and jet off. This time, we had William, who'd had to leave his school, his friends, his uncle, aunts, and grandparents. And now we had another baby on the way—a little girl whose birth certificate would forever read, oddly, like a kink in the program: "Berkeley, California."

Who was going to rescue us out in California, where we had no family or close friends? Who would be there for us when we forgot Bay?

Twenty minutes before take-off, a yellow taxi approached, and I saw a long, slender arm moving in a languid arc out the window. The taxi screeched to a stop, and I punched a fist full of cash at Amanda, who handed over Bay.

"You saved me," I said.

"No problem, Kath," she said, yawning. "Have a good trip."

As the cab drove off, Amanda waving, I felt relief and gratitude, along with shame for not always being the big sister I should have been, and guilt for leaving her and everyone else behind. But I couldn't dwell on such things. We had a plane to catch.

I turned toward the entrance, threw Bay over my shoulder, lifted the two cat bags, and felt the cool, processed air of the airport slap my face as the doors parted and I passed over the threshold from one life to another.

Good-bye, Boston, I thought, leaning my chin toward my shoulder to keep Bay from falling off. I scanned the airport for Michael and William, and when I saw them walking toward the security line, I picked up the pace, my chin moving back and forth over Bay's soft, nubby surface. I breathed it in—the smell of our old house, of our baby boy, of the life we were about to leave—nuzzling Bay as I walked, then ran, to catch up with them.

King Henry and the Field of Frogs

Anita Feng

Any textbook will tell you that stability and predictability are qualities that children thrive on. I would have to say that I've given my kids another kind of upbringing altogether. From an early age, they tagged along as we traveled the craft-fair circuit. There they learned essential life skills—such as demonstrating how to play ocarinas, drums, and horns, the musical instruments their mother made out of stoneware clay. They learned how to survive on trail mix and cubes of tofu dabbed with ketchup. They learned the intricacies of setting up temporary living quarters in a variety of venues—from the watch-your-back city streets of New York to the more pastoral surroundings of a backwater hick town in Ohio. I'm convinced that all this specialized childrearing helped them develop the necessary flexibility to get through anything that normal life would throw at them.

Let me explain, first of all, how it was for us craftspeople. There was no territory to which we had exclusive rights. Business could, quite literally, go south because of a sudden rain storm or blossom inexplicably in Peoria, Illinois. One year we'd get accepted into New York's Lincoln Center Fourth of July show. The next year we might not. As spring approached, we'd be perennially primed for something new and warm, like success and reward. We imagined getting accepted to that one sellout, high-class best show. We hoped to pay off all our debt, finally. We'd get it right the next time around and make that one thing of indescribable beauty.

My children, however, had developed their own aspirations. After a few years' experience, their criteria for a prime craft fair event depended largely on those venues where they could wander freely, have newsworthy adventures, and buy awesome things for themselves.

All of these dreams combined when we heard about Renaissance fairs. Matty, at twelve, imagined a ringside seat at the jousting tournament. Ten-year-old Katrina stockpiled her spending money.

I had been told that the "Rennie" people were wonderful, and the Renaissance fairs made big money. All that one needed was period garb, a "primitive" booth and a fake Olde Englande accent.

Well enough, m'lords and ladies!

I looked into the matter of Renaissance wear. Purple was not allowed. No gold or jewelry or lace suited the plain peasant merchant. However, a knife strung to the belt was very, very period. This fired up Matty's imagination at once and he had very specific feedback for me on the way I made his belt so that it could carry a good-sized knife. He didn't own one, but he saw the pictures in the library books we poured over together. He saw that boys were dressed as men, only smaller sized. Katrina, who loved books, had already read her share of knights appearing in shining armor. For the opportunity to meet one in person she was willing to put on the voluminous skirts and petticoats that would be necessary to attract one.

Even I was inspired. I rummaged through heaps of fabric, sewing peasant clothes, capes, bonnets, and drawstring purses. I worked late into the evenings building up my arsenal of ocarinas.

Unable to sleep at night, I conjured up personas for myself. I would go as the wandering Jew, fled from Spain to England, wending my way in a wooden cart. I would go as the romantic heroine of an old English song, and play the tune of my love's loss on my ocarinas. I would go as . . . I would go as . . .

Of course I already knew how the dramatic tableau would be played out. I would go as a mother with two children packed into a minivan.

When the day came, we set out early in the morning, and Matty, carsick as soon as we began, groaned as the van rose from the flat, monotonous cornfields of Illinois into the rolling hillsides of Ohio.

Never mind that Katrina had a serious phobia of seeing someone being sick. She threatened to jump out of the van and walk home. Never mind. I played cheerful Renaissance music on the car's tape deck. I promised them, as all mothers promise children, that we would get there soon.

As the sun was going down, we came to the outskirts of the small rural town listed in our directions. We would have missed the sign if it hadn't been for my keen-eyed daughter, who spotted the flimsy banner, RENAISSANCE FAIRE, tacked under the weathered sign for UNCLE ED'S AUTO REPAIR. The fairgrounds, we now saw, took over a large field, newly plowed, with a patchwork of handmade tents set up in the back.

At the entrance two young men slouched against the gate in tight leather pants with black T-shirts cut away at the shoulders. Their hair was half spiked, half shaved. One of them pulled out a walkie-talkie strung to his belt.

"Yeah, we've got another one here wanting to set up. You got any idea where they should go? Yeah, whatever you say, boss. I'll send them over that way."

"Where's the craft vendor representative?" I asked, already wary of this beginning.

At that moment, Matty folded in half, clutched his stomach, and turned white as rice paper. Katrina refused to come near us and walked off toward the middle of the field.

"Who?" the young man asked. "Oh, I get it. You mean, who's in charge of the merchants? King Henry's the boss of everything. He'll be along in a minute. He's the one riding around in the golf cart; can't miss him, in or out of costume."

Matty and I drove over the bumpy, plowed-up field. From the rearview mirror I kept an eye on Katrina, trailing us slowly in her long peasant skirt. It was clear that the vendor spaces hadn't been marked off. I noticed lots of small creatures jumping in front of the van. Then I realized what they were— millions of frogs leaping under the wheels of the van, overeager to turn into Renaissance princes.

Matty yelled for me to stop before we squashed one. We stopped.

Just then the golf cart appeared. We looked over to see a middle-aged man, baseball cap on backwards, beer belly hung over frontwards, well-groomed beard in place. He stepped out of his golf cart with all the presumed authority of a king and pointed to where we stood by the side of the van and said, "There. That's your spot. You'll be right in front of the jousting."

"Wonderful," I said.

The King disappeared. I looked at Matty.

Matty threw up in the center of our booth-to-be. Katrina ran away to the woods.

Early the next morning we crawled out of our sleeping bags in the back of the van and scrambled into our costumes, cranky and cold. We were all hungry and snacked on authentic Renaissance-era bread bought from a nearby booth while setting up our booth. It tasted suspiciously like store-bought day-old bread with an extra ingredient of ash thrown in for good measure. Gradually the field of frogs transformed into a festival of costumed Rennies strolling in elaborate dress up and down the aisles. Wandering minstrels burst into song. Everywhere we looked there was an ancient event being re-created with loving detail.

Perhaps things would turn out fine after all.

Katrina was already the best of us at making change and making sure the customers paid the correct amount. Matty, inspired by the gallantry all around him, took off on a mission to find the booths selling handmade knives. I was so relieved that he wasn't sick, I agreed to let him buy something approximating a pocket knife—with all the stringent, modern-day rules that would apply. He would keep it, at all times, in its sheath. He would be extremely careful not to ever use it, not really. He could wear it on his belt. Matty agreed to all conditions, though I'm sure if he'd been pressed to repeat any of them, he wouldn't have recalled a single one.

As it turned out, I needn't have worried. He did buy a knife, but lost it almost immediately, somewhere in the ten yards between the dangerous weapons booth and his mother's musical instruments booth. Most of the rest of the day he walked back and forth, eyes glued to the ground, oblivious to the jousting, jesting, and other Renaissance charades going on all around him.

"Perhaps," I said, patting him on the head, "it just wasn't meant to be. Never mind. We'll get you another one."

Just then King Henry marched down the aisle leading a morose procession accompanied by weeping ladies-in-waiting. "What's going on?" I asked a passing Rennie. "Oh, that? It's another wife's execution." He shrugged, and straightened his starched velvet doublet. "Must be two hours since the last one."

That first day we had a lot to learn. Business was abysmal. Several craftspeople took up a collection to put the King in the stockade to pay for his poor advertising

While Katrina manned the booth, Matty and I shopped for daggers.

One knife-maker complained, jerking his head at the sword-maker across the way. "When people like that make things out of junk and undersell us, the ones making authentic, hand-forged knives, our name is tarnished. People don't appreciate our craft and the knowledge behind what we do. Better not go near that man's booth."

Matty picked up a six-inch curved dagger and looked to me for approval.

"Well, we're just looking for a—" I hesitated to say "souvenir" in fear of my life. "We're looking for something small. Very small—for a little boy."

Matty frowned and dug his shoe in the dirt.

I wanted to add that a blunt, rubber knife would be best. But in Renaissance times, rubber hadn't been invented yet, had it? So we struck a deal—a 3 ¾" knife, purchased at twice the cost of the first one.

The next day I gave up on saying "m'Lord" and "m'Lady." It just wasn't in me anymore. I watched the wandering Rennies. I scanned the horizon for the buying public, and wished I had a period spy glass to see them coming in from afar.

Around noon, Katrina ran up to me, breathless and beautiful in her peasant dress and smock. "Have you met Death yet? You've got to see him," she said. "He squirted me with a water pistol!"

A moment later Death appeared at our booth wearing a thin black robe, a hood covering his face, and sleeves and skirts that covered his hands and feet. I watched him tuck the water pistol inside the folds of his sleeve. Silently, he withdrew his business card from his other sleeve. Katrina snatched the black-edged card and showed it to me. "Isn't this cool?"

It said:

> DEATH
>
> No Phone   No Address
>
> You Have Survived a
>
> Near DEATH Experience

I introduced myself to Death and said, "Hi, nice to meet you. Thanks for the reprieve."

"You're welcome," he said.

"You know, I could never go around, clowning with people like that—I'd much rather stay home, quiet, working in my studio by myself."

Death threw back his hood to reveal a young man with great dimples in his cheeks, full of vigor and charm. "I'm not really the type either. Just an introvert like you who'd as soon stay at home listening to CDs and eating tortilla chips."

Katrina was charmed. She had no fear and followed Death around for the better part of the day. I think she thought he was cute.

After Death left, the King stopped by to see how we were doing. He was irritated, because he hadn't appreciated being put in the stockade for an hour. He said it wasn't authentic.

"What kind of advertising did you do for the fair?" I asked, almost politely.

He ignored the question and asked, "That thing there, is that a horn?" He pointed at one of my horns.

I thought about the extravagant claims that had been made about this show, about how we poor peddlers had come such a distance and paid such a horrific fee to be a part of the festival. I bit my tongue because he was still the man in charge. I said, "Yes. It's a horn."

"Mind?" The king reached for the horn and blew into the mouthpiece. Air came out, minus the sound of music.

That satisfied me; I felt disinclined to help him further.

The embarrassed king put it back. "So. How are your sales today?"

When I told him that it was fairly slow, he nodded his head gravely and then disappeared.

At the tail end of the last day, as the last few Mundanes left the show, we weary artisans made our last few sales. Matty lost his second knife and spent the latter part of that day crisscrossing the field again. Frogs ogled him from the sidelines but none gave away the secret of where his knife had gone. Katrina had long since tired of Death, and I accompanied her as she scoped out trinkets on sale. At an old jeweler's booth, she found a little silver bracelet. I was ready to buy something nice for her after all her hard work. We examined it together and it appeared as if some of the links were a little crooked, so of course she immediately wanted the piece. She asked the jeweler how much it cost, and he told her that the fair had been going so badly, he'd sell it for a nickel. Katrina looked in her little hand-sewn coin purse and told him she only had a dime. He laughed and said, "Show's so bad, can't sell anything, even for a nickel! Tell you what—it's yours. For free!"

After the van was loaded up and ready to go, Matty, Katrina, and I walked out to the gate behind the jugglers. We watched as goblets, balls, and masks went flying between them. "Whoa! Catch that," one of them shouted to Matty.

A beautiful leather mask fell at his feet. Matty picked it up by the silken ties and held it back out to them.

"Hey! You drop it, it's yours," the man shouted back.

Matty held it out at arm's length, smiling, as the jugglers cavorted away. At last, he'd found something. One of the jugglers turned and called to me, "Hey, ocarina lady! Enjoyed listening to you play all weekend, really cheered us up. Enjoy the mask, young man. Cheers!" He raised the goblet that happened to be in his hand at that moment, and then sprang off with his companions.

And we three wended our way homeward—with a truckload of unsold stock, a dashing mask, a lovely trinket, and countless tall-but-true tales to tell.

Laos with Lucien

Willow King

Traveling with a child is like having the common cold. Everyone offers advice. "Bring a stroller" and "Whatever you do, don't use the stroller." "Don't go in December, too hot." "Only go in December; otherwise it is far too cold for children!" Everyone has a tip, even if they have not been to the place you will be traveling, even if they don't have kids themselves.

Laos, like most other Southeast Asian countries, still holds a strong association of war for many Americans. It is not exactly a typical holiday to take with a two-year-old in tow, but after living in Vietnam for several months we were looking forward to further explorations and had met many families who had raved about traveling in the region.

I packed with enthusiasm. I made a checklist. Sunglasses, camera, sandals that slip on and off easily at temple entrances, tunics to cover toddler knees in holy places and then of course diapers (*you never know when you will find them again*), sunscreen (*how could I ever protect my fair-skinned son from the intense sun of Southeast Asia? SPF 75?*), snacks for the plane, snacks for the train, snacks for the bus. The backpack expanding . . . good walking shoes, sippy cup, and—oh heck, why not?—the stroller.

We arrived in the capital of Vientiane in April on the evening of the water festival—a raucous Laotian holiday that involves boat races, beer drinking, and lots of firecrackers. Unfortunately, we arrived too late to see the races and instead arrived for the polar opposite: a traffic jam leaving the river that took the old Russian Lada that was serving as our taxi two hours instead of the expected thirty-minute skip to the hotel (*snacks for the taxi!*).

We had selected what sounded like a child-friendly hotel that was nice, but not too nice and, most importantly from Luc's perspective, it had a pool. After a day of transit a nice swim seemed like the answer to our prayers.

Le Parasol Blanc, it turned out, had seen better days. The pool was murky from leaves and flowers that had fallen in from the "garden," er, jungle that surrounded the squat little strip of rooms. The taxi had already pulled away, so my husband and I shouldered our bags (they were so heavy! What had I put in there?) and tried to be optimistic. The room was paneled with dark wood and the beds sagged in the center from humidity and heavy use. We pulled on our swimsuits and headed outside. Luc, in typical toddler fashion, undeterred by the flotsam in "his pool," swam in the cool water, naked; there was nobody around to tell us not to (in fact, was there anyone else staying at Le Parasol?). From Luc's grin, you would have thought we were staying at the Ritz.

There was a little restaurant where we ordered some basic fare: rice noodle soup, bamboo shoots, and chicken in a dubious spicy sauce. Bellies full, we retired to Room 3F to peruse the guidebook and decide what to do next. Luc soon decided for us, collapsing into the saggy family bed. My husband abandoned his travelers' map and marveled A) at the fact that we could also fall asleep with him, even though it was only 7:00 PM and B) at how much the thing we call "traveling" had changed since having a child.

In the days before Luc we would have ventured out into the night, found a corner in which to sit and perhaps drink some of the local brew, maybe throw a few firecrackers. Now I found myself avoiding big drunken crowds (*they are unpredictable! So noisy! They will wake up the baby!*). We consoled each other with a favorite Asian maxim, "Same, same but different," and curled up to sleep. There was no mosquito net. I knew I should have tried to squeeze one into the backpack.

Sometime around 3:00 AM I found myself awake, fanning my hands over my child's sleeping body to discourage mosquitoes from landing on him while making a catalog of all the blood-borne tropical diseases I had read about. I started to think maybe this trip was a mistake. Luc peacefully slept on.

Morning brought renewed enthusiasm, and after a strong cup of coffee we were ready to see Laos by day. We had hired a driver who was to take us north, first to Vang Veing and then to Luang Prabang, where we would stay for a couple of days. We were particularly looking forward to the latter, of which our trusty copy of the *Lonely Planet* said, "the city's mix of gleaming temple roofs, crumbling French provincial architecture and multiethnic inhabitants tends to enthrall even the most jaded travelers." Not that we were jaded as such. We were just in a new paradigm. Although we had been living in Vietnam for many months, we were still within the confines of a home, padded by our toys, our books, our habits. This was that glorious floating experience we loved . . . or was it? My husband would look longingly at the modern nomads zinging by on rented motorcycles, wind in their hair. I looked fondly (*enviously*) on the women absorbed in a book for hours in sidewalk cafés, glancing up occasionally to ponder the world from behind their sunglasses.

Luc was not into sitting for hours at cafes. He wanted to keep moving, climb on things, examine the mud puddles, chase the chickens (*bird flu!*), and pet the local dogs.

The drive up the country's one working highway took many arduous hours, but it was also very beautiful. The countryside was so green. Life in the villages seemed to be carrying on as it must have done for hundred of years. The women weaving baskets from bamboo, men tending the fields, children running around barefoot, and (*surprise!*) elephants hanging out on the edges of the forest. Luc gleefully pointed out the window chanting, "Efalent, efalent!"

Luang Prabang is indeed an enchanted place. We were also getting into the traveling groove and starting to feel the benefits of traveling together as a family. For one, we were up before all the tourists who stayed up late drinking cheap cocktails and falling in and out of love at the hostels. We saw pristine waterfalls at dawn, and without the constant company of camera flashes, could imagine ourselves prehistoric and pure. Luc was an instant celebrity wherever he went. Everyone from old women to teenage boys came up to pinch his pink cheeks, rub his curly blond hair, and offer him sweets and fruit. Through Luc, we were able to connect with people who would otherwise never have given us the time of day. We received the benefits of being in his golden ambit. Men offered their seats on the bus; other children shared their toys (*sticks, plastic spoons, masticated sugar cane*). There was a newfound sweetness to traveling with our boy that reached far beyond the sugar cane—we were part of the universal equation of family, something that transcends the vast gaps of language and culture.

We cruised the streets pushing the little red stroller that had come all the way across the globe, although it was usually Luc pushing his doll in it rather than sitting in it himself. Yes, it was nice to have an extra diaper or two in our backpack, but the truth was, we really didn't need anything extra. There was no secret to traveling with a child. The basic needs of food and shelter were all that were really necessary; the rest was merely a matter of convenience or preference.

We explored caves, took a boat down the wide Mekong River, watched the Hmong women weave their rainbow-silk tapestries at the night markets. We drank tamarind juice, ate river algae and toasted locust. Luc liked eating bugs.

The gift of traveling with our little one was in the way he greeted each experience with openness and grace, the way he noticed small details that I would not have noticed without him. On our fourth morning, spotting a few pieces of rice left on the sidewalk after morning alms, Luc looked at the grains, and then at us, and said quietly, "Monk food."

Things have changed, that is true. My husband and I still pine sometimes for the carefree travel that collaged our youth, but the new poetry of exploring the world with Lucien is both humbling and beautiful—after all, our desire to travel is a desire to open our minds and our hearts to strange, unknown realities. Nothing like a child to lead the way.

Traveling Songs

Elrena Evans

O ver the span of a four-hour car trip, my husband can sing the so-called "ABCB Spider" song exactly four hundred and eighty-eight times. Figuring it takes twenty-three seconds to sing one round of the Spider, approximately one and a half seconds for a two-year-old to say, "ABCB Spider again?", and four seconds for my husband to sigh, roll his eyes, and resume singing, that works out to four hundred and eighty-eight times over the span of two hundred and forty minutes. I should know. I did the math. I also took the trip.

To be fair, though, we didn't sing the "ABCB Spider" song the entire way. We also sang the more traditionally known ABC song, both to the original tune and to the snazzy, jazzed-up version made popular by LeapFrog. We sang "I'm a Little Teapot." We sang "Twinkle, Twinkle, Little Star." We sang "Old MacDonald's Farm," complete with a full complement of entities on said farm that neither God nor nature ever intended.

"Had a farm E-I-E-I-O again?" the songmistress trills from the backseat, interrupting the train of thought steaming through my mind, full speed ahead toward the academic conference at which I'm going to present on a panel tomorrow. My husband sighs and rolls his eyes, catching mine. "Old MacDonald had a farm," we obediently sing out. "E-I-E-I-O!" I wonder what's going to land on Old MacDonald's farm this time—we've already exhausted all the normal farm animals, zoo animals, and every single animal featured on "Baby Noah," including the wombat. (For the record, the wombat makes a ticka-ticka sound, here, there, and everywhere.) We've also had a princess, a dragon, and a bellybutton on the farm, the bellybutton making an uhn-uh sound here, there, and everywhere, thanks to "The Bellybutton Song" from VeggieTales. I arch an eyebrow toward the back seat and wait to see what Old Macdonald will be welcoming next.

"And on that farm he had a . . . " My husband pauses expectantly.

"Go-gie!" the songmistress calls out, and I muffle a snort. Go-gie, for the uninitiated, is the toddler's word for nursing. It rhymes with "bogie," like in golf, and I have absolutely no idea how she came up with that one.

"O-kay!" My husband responds, gamely. "And on that farm he had a go-gie! E-I-E-I-O. With a . . . " He takes his eyes off the road for a second to glance over at the toddler, sitting merrily in her car seat like a queen on her throne, two hands stuffed full of crumbling Goldfish crackers.

"What does go-gie say?" he asks.

I'm interested to hear this one, too.

"Yum *yum!*" calls the songmistress, popping a fish in her mouth, and the song continues on. "With a yum yum here and a yum yum there, here a yum, there a yum, everywhere a yum yum . . ." (For the record, I no longer believe in Child-Led Weaning. That line, along with Your Milk Will Dry Up When You're Pregnant, has been filed away in a mental drawer marked, "Apparently not.")

Old MacDonald had a farm, E-I-E-I-O.

I glance at the clock. It's 6:30 PM, almost an hour into this trip. The baby whose pregnancy didn't dry up my milk is chewing slurpily on his hands, contented, leaving husband and me free to play Toddler Jukebox whether we want to or not.

I had kind of hoped the little ones would fall asleep on the trip, leaving husband and me with four lovely hours of open road and adult conversation (complete with some nice prep work for my panel), and I mentally file Your Kids Will Sleep in the Car in the same drawer as before: "Apparently not."

The song draws to a close, my husband glances over the seat. But the toddler is quiet, munching her fish. "Free Bird!" I yell out, jumping the gun on another round of E-I-E-I-O. My husband grins. "If I leave here tomorrow," he choruses in his best Lynyrd Skynyrd voice, "will you still remember me . . . "

"*Had a farm, E-I-E-I-O!*" This loud request is punctuated by a vicious kick to the back of the driver's seat.

We sigh. We sing. Only three more hours to go.

The lights of the used-car dealership are glaringly bright, but we've pulled over to nurse here because the only other choice on this middle-of-nowhere stretch of the trip was a seedy-looking bar. I remember the days when this trip to our old college town was made in one fell swoop; now we're lucky if we only stop twice. I fumble with the catch on my nursing bra and glance over my shoulder to look at the songmistress. She isn't too happy, strapped into her car seat for the fourth and final hour of this trip, watching her little brother nurse while none is offered to her.

"Round and round again," she sulks, kicking the seat in front of her.

I leave my husband to sing "The Wheels on the Bus" (complete with the same complement of animals, princesses, dragons, and bellybuttons recently found on Old MacDonald's farm) while I stroke my son's head and attempt to rearrange my cramped limbs. We're packed into our tiny car like proverbial sardines, the Volkswagen Golf a purchase made back when we thought the babies were years away, as we held hands in another used-car lot, blue with cold and warm with newlywed laughter. Oh, let's get this one, we said as we strolled along. It's little, it's cute, and we're not going to have children for ages!

I got pregnant about six weeks later. Now two adults, two kids, two car seats, all our luggage, a thousand goldfish, and a stroller the size of a Lincoln Continental are all crammed into our newlywed car. The makers of Tetris would be proud.

"The mommy on the bus says . . . " my husband sings, pausing for the toddler to fill in the line.

"Go-gie," she replies promptly, glaring at her brother.

"Cookie?" I ask brightly, and my husband hands her one, which she manages to grab without dropping any of her fish. I notice a man in a truck peering through the car window at me, and I pause to thank God that this is not my first child, that I'm past the days of self-conscious nursing, jumping at every little sound and paranoid that someone will see me. I attempt a friendly wave, but we are too jammed in for me to free up a hand.

The wheels on the bus go round and round, all through the town. My son finishes nursing, we strap him back into his seat.

"Had a farm E-I-E-I-O again?" the toddler calls as we signal to exit the used-car lot, and pivot our overstuffed Golf back out on the open road. I grin at her mollified expression now that baby brother is no longer blatantly nursing in front of her, and begin to sing.

We arrive at our friends' house way past bedtime, but the toddler can't fall asleep. We're staying in a bedroom the family's two young daughters share, and it is little-girl heaven: dolls, books, tea sets, and a real live window seat with plush pillows and a battalion of stuffed animals. The toddler is beside herself with joy, and as the clock slips into single digits she is squirming in my arms, wide awake, while I valiantly sing lullabies in counterpoint against her rendition of the theme song from "LarryBoy."

"Sleep, my child, and peace attend thee, all through the night . . ." I stroke her hair.

"Lean and mean, green machine, LarryBoy!" she bellows back. It's going to be a long night.

Soon I am on my fifty-seventh round of "Hush, Little Baby," deliriously tired, and envious of husband and son obliviously snoring away in rhythm.

"And if that mockingbird don't sing, mama's gonna buy you a diamond ring . . ." I stare at the clock, willing it to stop, and struggle in vain to remember what I'm supposed to be presenting mere hours later. I sing on.

"And if that diamond ring don't shine, mama's gonna buy you a porcupine." That can't be right, I think, but I am too tired to care. The songmistress has ceased her rendition of "Larryboy," and her breathing grows slower and heavier until finally she slumps against my chest and begins to snore. I carefully peel her arms from around my neck and lay her down before sinking my head into the bliss that is my ruffled pillow. I take one last look at the clock and close my eyes.

"Kum-ba-yah, my Lord," a tiny voice drifts out into the stillness, and I bury my head into the pillow to muffle my cries of laughter and frustration. I don't even *like* that song.

T he conference goes off without a hitch, and we spend the rest of the weekend visiting all our old haunts, reliving graduate school days. My son has his first "solids" at the University Creamery, where his eyes widen in delight at Butter Pecan ice cream; I buy my daughter a new pink umbrella and matching boots at a favorite college shop and send her out on the campus, splashing in the rain, to the adoring coos of several undergrad girls. I do my impersonation of Gene Kelly as she stomps through puddles, and for once, she doesn't object to the deviation from kid songs.

When the weekend is over, we pack up the car, an even tighter fit now to accommodate our new purchases. I nurse the baby and strap him into his seat, where his head rests against the padded side and his eyes drift close. I buckle in the toddler and hand her the cell phone as a momentary distraction.

"Ah, yes. Pizza," I hear her say into the phone as we fasten our seat belts. "And chicken, and, um . . . cheese fries, and soda." I hope the phone isn't actually on; the number for the college pizza joint is still programmed in there somewhere, but I leave her be. Maybe she'll entertain herself until she falls asleep, I think, allowing myself a tiny peek into that closed mental drawer where Your Kids Will Sleep in the Car is still glistening at me, tempting as a polished jewel.

My husband signals, turns out onto the road, and reaches for my hand. "I love our little family," he says, his fingers laced through mine.

I smile at him, and as if on cue, the songmistress hurls the phone to the floor.

"Had a farm E-I-E-I-O again?" she calls.

And our trip has begun.

Flashdance Snow White

Mary Jane Beaufrand

It is four in the afternoon Dallas time. My husband, Juan, our two children, Sofia and Ricky, and I are in the DFW International Airport. We have come from Seattle and now need to catch a connecting flight to Miami. Our final destination, eleven hours south, is Maracaibo, Venezuela, where Juan's family lives.

We make this trip every other Christmas. And, just like every other time, Juan's scare stories started two weeks before we left. "Nobody can get anything there," he said as he shuffled around our house. Juan is slow but graceful—a tall, athletic guy who is never in a hurry. As he walks he casually kicks his legs as though performing a soft-shoe dance. Step-shuffle-step-shuffle.

"What about gas?" I said. It hadn't been that long since a failed coup had shut down half of Venezuela, taking out the gas supply, along with all international flights.

He shrugged and rummaged through the fridge. "All right, you can get gas. But don't expect much more. Don't expect our plane to arrive on time. Don't expect our luggage to arrive at all. There is no mail, no ambulances, and you have to stand in line forever to get hardware."

I didn't see what the hardware thing had to do with me, but I let it slide. Juan's message was clear: *Don't be a spoiled American.* I told myself it was okay, that I was ready for Venezuelan privation. I'd made the trip at least five times before and, if my movements were restricted because I was a gringa, at least there was plenty of rum and avocados the size of footballs.

I had no way of knowing that this time, while the Venezuelan portion of our trip would be festive and almost hassle-free, the American part would not.

We are at our departure gate in Dallas and taking up a whole row of seats with our junk five carry-ons containing juice, Fruit Roll-Ups, Goldfish crackers, boxes of puzzles, coloring books and crayons, satin-edged blankets, two changes of clothes for Sofia and Ricky, one laptop, and two of Sofia's favorite Barbie dolls: Ariel the mermaid and Snow White. Sofia is four years old and a princess fiend. Ricky, who is almost two, is corralled in his stroller (not the deluxe kind with raincover, the "umbrella" kind that can fold into practically nothing) and he's arching. He's been imprisoned in an airplane seat since Seattle, he's got eight hours still to go, and right now he's in prime escape mode. Usually in airports and restaurants Juan is in charge of Ricky and I'm in charge of Sofia. But Juan is looking frazzled, as though the last four hours of thrashing and decompression screams have been enough and he'd rather have a turn watching the easy child.

I look up at the monitor. Our next plane leaves at 5:30 PM; we have another half hour until we start boarding. "Stay here, honey," I tell Juan. "I'll run around with Ricky."

As soon as I unbuckle my son he zooms off. The terminal is crowded and he dodges this way and that, every so often checking back with me, smiling his smug smile. It is his job to escape, mine to keep up. I call, "Please don't bonk into that guy," more than once. After about twenty feet he makes a sudden left turn into a hallway that isn't so heavily trafficked. I am relieved. Here is someplace he can run without knocking into anyone. He runs to the end of the hall and I follow two paces behind. He pushes open a door.

Suddenly red lights go off and there is a security guard behind us at the entrance of the untrafficked hallway waving his arms. I scoop Ricky up and ask the guard what's happened.

"Once you go down this hallway you can't come back," says the man, without explanation. I don't understand. There were no signs marking the hallway; just no one in it. How was I to know, let alone a zooming toddler?

I should probably mention that I think heightened airport security is a fine thing. I was a nervous flyer even before 9/11. I know that all the extra screenings at airports can be a pain, but because of them I no longer need Lorazepam. The extra harassment is a small price to pay for keeping me and my precious bundles safe.

So I put on my most reasonable face, but I've got a good grip on Ricky, who squirms in my arms. "What now? My son just ran out. We need to catch a flight."

"You'll have to show your boarding pass and go through security again."

I feel the blood drain from my face. "We don't have a boarding pass. They're with my husband at Gate 26. If you can't let us in, can you have someone get him at the gate?"

The guard scratches his head. "Let me get my supervisor."

While he's gone I take another look at our surroundings. Spanning the length of the hall is a plexiglass window. Through the Plexiglas is a security checkpoint. A thin stream of passengers trickles through three security stations—taking off their shoes, their watches. They all have the dull look of people who can't wait to plunk themselves down and read a *People* magazine.

I see the guard talk to a man with thinning hair that is way over-moussed. I see the over-moussed guy shake his head, the hair barely shifting, then the two come back and talk to me.

Ricky rocks in my arms. He wants to be let down. I grip him tighter. I look at my watch. 4:45. Fifteen minutes until boarding.

"I can't help you," says the supervisor. "I can't justify pulling any of my guards away from their stations. We're just too busy."

I look again at the security stations. There are five passengers for six agents. I still don't feel resentful. You just do your job, I think; I'll figure something out.

"So what now?"

"Either talk to a ticket agent or have your husband paged. If you want to page him the red phone is down that way." He points out the door and to the left. I nod and thank him and look at my watch again. 4:50.

I let Ricky down and direct him toward the phone. He is more than happy to take the lead and have me follow after him. We pick up the red phone and give our information to the operator. Juan Beaufrand. Gate 26. Flight to Miami. Come to security and bring boarding passes.

I go back to the security station where I hear the information repeated over the intercom. I hoist Ricky on my shoulders. 4:55. We start boarding in five minutes. On the other side of the plexiglass, the guards are studiously *not* looking at us.

More time passes. 5:00. 5:05. I go back to the red phone and ask them to repeat the page. I won't let Ricky down off my shoulders so he's whacking my head now. We go back to the security station. 5:10. And then I see something that tips my mood from frantic yet reasonable to all-out mad. The supervisor, the one who uses too much hair product, walks past me carrying a Styrofoam container of spring rolls. I say nothing aloud, but think: You're too busy help me but not too busy to go on your break? This, I realize, is no longer about security. It's about Chinese food.

With Ricky on my shoulders, still raining whacks on my head, I go for the ticket counter. I've given up on getting any help from security or the red phone. Behind the ticket counter are four agents helping no one, talking about what they're doing once their shifts are over. I am not optimistic. I am about to cry. Ricky's already crying. The agents break up their conversation and look at a spot above my head. Each of the four juts out her lower lip, imitating Ricky's pout.

"Excuse me . . ." I begin.

I'm cut off by an immaculately groomed blonde in red, white, and blue. "The baby ran out. You ran after him," she guesses.

I nod. Each agent is quickly mobilized. "What's your name? What flight are you on?" They fire questions at me, even more rapidly after they find out that my plane is already boarding.

"I don't have any ID," I apologize in between responses. "I don't have anything."

But they don't ask for it. They print me new tickets and lead me to the front of line of the evil security gate. Ricky and I take off our shoes. I don't bother putting them back on when we're on the other side. I just grab them from the gray plastic basin and sprint.

Juan is halfway down the hall, dragging Sofia by the arm. It's beyond time to board. He looks mad enough to spit. What right, I think, does he have to be mad at me? Where was he during the two red phone pages that he clearly didn't hear? I hand him Ricky and snap: "Don't start. You don't know how close I am to flipping you off right now."

The four of us race onto the plane and situate ourselves just as we pull out of the gate. Juan and Ricky sit across the aisle from Sofia and me. It's Juan's turn to deal with the squirmy child. On the girl's side of the aisle, I ask the attendant for an apple juice for Sofia, an extra large chardonnay for me.

The plane takes off; there are no more incidents—at least not on this flight. We will arrive in Miami on time, and then in Maracaibo five hours late and sans luggage, just as Juan predicted. He was right: time to steel myself for a different way of life.

But somehow none of that—the delayed flight, the lost luggage—will seem as dramatic as the sight of a man in a uniform walking away from us with a carton of spring rolls in his hand.

For the moment I'm all right. Sofia has pulled Ariel and Snow White out of her backpack and is now imagining stories that involve makeup and pretty dresses and glass coffins. I can't help but notice that her Snow White doll looks more frazzled than she did in Seattle. Her thick doll hair looks like a bad weave; the red hair ribbon is garroted around her neck. Her gown is halfway off her shoulders. She now looks like Flashdance Snow White.

"I didn't hear the page. Well, I heard it but they mangled my name. I thought they were talking about somebody else. I thought you were just browsing in a bookstore. I was so mad," Juan says once I've calmed down and we've got the incident sorted out. He shakes his head and pats my hand across the aisle. Then he pulls out the food carry-on and feeds Goldfish crackers to Ricky one by one. As long as there's food in front of my son, he usually doesn't feel like escaping. Besides, there's nowhere to go. We can all relax.

I help Sofia arrange her Snow White doll. As we retie her red ribbon, arrange her gown, and brush her hair, I begin to let go. I don't feel like flipping anyone off anymore. On balance, we came out all right. One unhelpful person to four supremely helpful pouty-lipped ticket agents—five helpful souls if you count the flight attendant who took one look at my face and made my white wine double tall.

As it is, I am beginning to think this episode is like Juan's scare stories in which bad things happen but no one gets hurt. "Things are bad in Dallas–Fort Worth," I say to no one in particular. But I don't really believe it. As soon as the words are out of my mouth the feeling is gone.

I kiss my daughter and blow an air-kiss to my son. "Mwah!" he lobs an air-kiss back. Then I settle into my seat, ready for the next bad time.

Senseless in Seattle

Ivy Eisenberg

There we were at Seattle Center's International Fountain, drooping in different directions like a quartet of wilted flowers. It was the last afternoon of a nine-day Pacific Northwest family vacation—the kind of forced togetherness that makes a mother realize that her cute little ones are neither cute nor little anymore.

This was the trip my husband, David, had been planning since our courtship days, a sort of prenuptial agreement attached to the decision that we were firmly planting ourselves on *my* home turf, the Northeast, and not his (the Midwest), for the forseeable future. "When we have children, I want to take them to the beautiful Pacific Northwest, where my dad took us when we were kids," David had said many times.

Our two little ones grew up hearing tales about port towns, ferries, natural parks, and mountain vistas. I woke up one day years later to realize that my daughter's feet were the same size as mine, and I knew that I was almost out of time to get all four of us across the country together. So, the kids and I bought four round-trip plane tickets to Seattle, purchased some guidebooks, attached a simple note that said "Okay, show us," and presented this to Daddy on his birthday.

All that week, in true family-vacation tradition, each of us had had a turn where the other three had ganged up on them. Today, it seemed, was to be my day to be the outcast.

Simon, my eleven-year-old whiny brat of a son, wanted to go on the Space Needle. My infuriatingly sullen teen daughter, Margot, preferred to go to the Experience Music Project instead—a rock music museum that was legendary for, among other things, the Jimi Hendrix room.

"I want to go with Daddy, not with *you*," Margot announced.

"Well, tough—Daddy has to take Simon on the Space Needle," I retorted. As loathe as I was to be within 520 feet of my iPod-obsessed, earphone-plugged, hormone-fueled daughter by this point of our trip, there was no way I was going 520 feet above ground, locked in a chamber with a group of effusive tourists, wetting my pants and white-knuckling the railing for an hour.

"Oh, come on, Mom, I won't try to scare you," Simon pleaded. He had that smirk of glee on his face.

"But Daddy's cooler for this sort of music," my daughter mumbled. (*What are you talking about?* I wanted to say but didn't. *I thought you don't like Daddy. Who's cool, if not me? Okay, I'm wearing my dork shorts, but look at the dangling earrings I have on today.*)

I had never cursed in front of my children. This afternoon, though, I was a split-second away from screaming "F—you all, I'm going shopping and then I'm going back to New York alone." Just as I opened my mouth, however, Margot unplugged her iPod and said, "Okay, let's go, Mom."

"Fine," I conceded. "I won't stand near you."

The admission price was $19.95 for me and $14.95 for my daughter. "Wow, why is this so expensive?" I bellowed to no one as I waited in line. My daughter furrowed her brows, gave me the black stare of evil, and then edged away from me.

"I'm sorry," I whispered.

The museum, though very dimly lit, had many interactive, child-friendly exhibits. There were drums to investigate, guitars to jam on, and a huge, odd, computer-animated guitar sculpture from which electronic sounds emanated.

Margot immediately ascended the stairs to the second floor. I followed closely enough so that I could locate her at all times, though not so closely that it would appear as though we were unquestionably together. This took a lot of concentration, as the place was almost pitch black and my night vision is terrible. I could feel that she could feel my eyes on her. Every time she stopped to look at something, she turned around and sneered at me. And if she saw me looking back, she would quicken her pace and not even stop to look at whatever exhibit was in front of her.

We both became captivated by the Jimi Hendrix room, however. "He was the greatest electric guitarist ever. I was your age when he died," I pined. Okay, that was a dreadful "when I was your age" remark, but no little snot was going to tell me that this sexy-fringed, guitar-smashing music icon was not cool. She knew it was cool, there was no denying. She was especially impressed by such relics as the broken guitar fragments and the album covers.

"I feel like there should be a head shop around the corner," I said. Bingo, that must have been a hip thing to say; I got a smile out of her, though hauling out a drug reference was a low thing for a mother to do.

As luck would have it, there was a disco exhibit down the hall, complete with a lighted dance floor, mirrored ball, and pulsing '70s music screaming from the sound system.

I pretended to be disinterested in the hallway as my daughter went—alone—into the disco room. "Lady Marmalade" blared from the speakers, and Margot began dancing, entranced by the colored reflections swirling across the room. Her back was to me, and I inched closer, gingerly taking a step into the room, my hips involuntarily swaying to the music.

Margot spotted me, but kept dancing. That was a good sign. "Do you mind if I dance?" I gestured. I took her nonanswer as acquiescence.

Next, "Turn the Beat Around" came on the speakers and I began to cut loose a little more. This was too good a moment for me to miss, and I strutted in syncopated rhythm to the opposite corner of the room. Dork shorts notwithstanding, I twirled, twisted, shimmied, bumped, and ground my way back thirty years, the joy of youth pervading my every limb. I owned that disco floor.

Four minutes later, totally pumped and glowing, I turned around to see that my daughter had left the room. She must have gone into hiding somewhere, as she had done years ago at the Natural History Museum, eventually discovered on all fours in front of the brown bear diorama. I knew that if I called out to her she'd only go further into hiding. Instead, I race-walked through the entire second floor, checking every room, exhibit, corner, and rest room. I ran to the first floor and looked everywhere. I looked in the gift shop. I ran back upstairs, and did another race-walk. Nothing.

I didn't want to alert security just yet. What would I say? That my daughter ran away because I embarrassed her at the disco? Plus, I was drenched in sweat and one of my dangly earrings had fallen out—so it was questionable whether they would have returned her to me if they had found her. I had attracted the attention of the museum personnel nonetheless. Several uniformed men watched as I traversed the halls of the museum yet again, squinting in each direction. They all watched, relieved to see me go, as I got my hand stamped to go outside and call my husband.

As I fumbled for my cell phone, I noticed that there on the stone wall sat my daughter, together with my husband and son, the three of them, normal human beings, eating ice cream cones.

"How was it?" my husband asked.

"Fine. I lost an earring," I replied.

My daughter had plugged in again. She was looking down and calmly playing footsie with my son. They both looked so cute and little I couldn't stand it.

Saving Grace

Amy Bustraan

"Are you crazy?" The ranger looked at us incredulously. "You want to canoe the Pine River, the fastest in Michigan, with a six-month-old?" Before we began our journey, we had stopped at the Department of Natural Resources station to buy a pass for our boat.

"We have a life jacket and booster seat for her," answered my husband, Chad.

"Well, 99 percent of the people who go down the Pine tip over. The last two miles are level-one white-water rapids, after all."

I looked at Chad, panic-stricken. "I don't want to tip over with Gracie."

"We're not going to tip over," Chad tried to reassure me.

"Also," the ranger added, with no regard whatsoever to reassurance, "the water level is down due to the lack of rain. Watch out for rocks and branches that are normally covered by water."

As we left the ranger station, I was still nervous about the white-water rapids. As an experienced boater, I knew that if we got into the rapids, it wouldn't be easy to get out. However, my mom's old adage rang through my head: "Amy, 90 percent of what we worry about never happens." Yeah, right;

I don't remember my mom ever contemplating traveling down fast-moving water with a six-month-old!

My husband, Chad, and I love the great outdoors. Residents of Grand Rapids, Michigan, we love to explore every river, trail, hill, and valley by hiking and backpacking. When our daughter, Gracie, entered our family six months ago, we aspired to include her in our travels. As a first-time mom, I bought everything I could to help merge her life with ours as easily as possible. Our little camper has an umbrella to protect her from the sun, and happily rides atop a Kelty Kids Pathfinder Backpack when we hike. When she tried on her little life jacket for the first time, she never fussed despite its confining embrace. A true Michigan girl, she was baptized into the realms of the wild outdoors with several small camping excursions, all of which went off without a hitch. We were ready for a bigger adventure now, and were excited to tackle the mighty Pine River, followed by two nights' camping.

Despite the ranger's dire warnings, we arrived at the tributary and prepared to embark on our six-hour journey. Seeing the Pine brought me comfort; it looked like any other river that Chad and I had conquered. A little fast, but nothing we couldn't handle. We put the life jacket on Gracie, lathered sunblock on her skin, and buckled her into her booster seat. As we had been packing for the trip, we had realized Gracie needed a chair; she couldn't just lie on the bottom of the canoe with an umbrella over her as if in a row boat in Hyde Park. We had decided, therefore, to bring the booster seat she used at meals. We took off the tray, and with a padded back and straps to buckle her safely inside, the seat fit nicely in the bottom of the boat. Chad arranged an umbrella in order to protect Gracie from the sun.

We finally pushed our aluminum canoe into the water and began our journey. My fears dissipated, as everything seemed to be going perfectly. The weather was ideal for a canoe ride. Mid-July in Michigan is the best time to go camping because it's sunny and not yet too hot. Under the shade of a lofty maple tree, the warm sunrays pouring down aren't even noticeable. A gentle breeze blew across the water and kept us cool. The sky was a beautiful blue speckled with light, cotton clouds. July has sporadic rain showers, but we have always been lucky and stayed dry on our excursions. The strong current provided a sense of urgency, making us keen to begin traveling down the waterway, yet the soaring birds overhead reminded us of the freedom that nature provided. Gracie was enjoying the ride even though she couldn't move her arms. With her arms stuck out to the side like a scarecrow, her only entertainment was the beautiful scenery and the back of my head as I paddled with Chad. She had complete confidence in us.

After a while, we took a break for Gracie's sake. My maternal instinct told me that she needed to stretch and eat, as well as have a diaper change.

This waterway lacked the grassy or sandy shorelines prevalent on other river excursions, where we were able to easily tie up and relax. The tributary's borders consisted of craggy trees, sharp rocks, and daunting cliffs. Instead, we settled for an inlet of shallow water and pulled ashore.

The sun climbed higher in the sky and we grew anxious to continue our voyage while Gracie was in good spirits and before it got too hot. I knew that we would have to make more rest stops later, depending on her mood.

So far, the trip was going smoothly. Just as I prepared to dismiss the ranger's cautions, I spotted something that made me change my mind. "Rock!" I yelled. We quickly paddled on the left side to avoid a huge rock. In order to maneuver efficiently down the river, the person in the back steers while the paddler up-front guides the craft and looks out for obstacles. To turn left, we paddle to the right side, and vice versa to move the opposite direction. We narrowly missed the part of the rock sticking out of the water, but this was a "glacier rock": there was much more under the water that we weren't able to see. We were stuck fast on the huge underwater structure. Chad jumped out in to the rushing, cold water and heaved us off the boulder.

Moments later, I yelled again, "Rock!" This time we successfully avoided it. As the current carried us faster, we braced ourselves and prepared for the challenge of our lives. Chad and I have canoed down obstacle-strewn waters before, but never with cargo like Gracie. Having her along was even more motivation not to capsize, when before we wouldn't care if we tipped over and were soaked for the rest of the ride. But now we were concerned about the safety of our child.

"Rock!" We paddled hard to the left. Another near miss. Straight ahead, a large fallen tree blocked our path and we paddled hard to the right. Too late, we saw a granite precipice jutting upwards directly behind the tree. This time it was my turn to jump out and free our wedged watercraft. As the frigid water swooshed around my legs, a sliver of fear entered my body. Was I crazy to have planned this trip? Unfortunately, no matter what, we were heading downstream, committed to completing our journey since the surrounding terrain would be impossible to walk through with Gracie and the canoe.

I jumped back into the canoe nervously and began paddling hard on the left to avoid another downed tree. This continued for only ten minutes, but it felt like an hour, and we weren't even near the white water rapids yet. I checked on Gracie, who looked back at me with a blank expression. She wasn't afraid, but she wasn't happy either. The ranger was right; this was not a "baby friendly" adventure.

Exhausted, we decided to take another break. We found a sandy spot ahead in the shade, pulled the boat into the sand, and stretched our legs, thankful to find a sliver of land. I noticed uneasily that my discharged flip-flops were floating in the bottom of the canoe. Chad dismissed my concern, saying that water probably splashed in while we were jumping in and out.

Gracie was once again relieved to remove her life jacket. Her back was getting sweaty, and she was tired of sitting. I prepared a snack while Chad scooped out some of the water from the canoe.

After fifteen minutes, we got ready to push off again. This time, Gracie was not very happy about wearing her life jacket and struggled against the confinement. Chad turned her seat around to face him. A daddy's girl, she calmed down a bit.

While we were not dodging boulders and trees, the scenery was breathtaking. I love the feeling of being alone on the river; the solitude helps me pray and put things in perspective. Like many people, we live in a city where urbanization constantly encroaches upon the natural environment. Strip malls and parking lots now take the place of many parks in my once verdant city. But the giant trees, full of green leaves that rustle like whispers in the wind, still line the banks, guarding the water from civilization. The grandeur of the trees is something that stays with you long after a trip to the outdoors. I fully understand how nature distracts Gracie. Chad was in the back pointing out a blue heron and various fish to her as we rode along. I had a feeling that she understood everything he was saying to her and she kicked her legs in excitement.

Suddenly, the river became more turbulent and shook us from our peaceful thoughts and ornithological delights. We put our game faces back on and braced ourselves for the worst. And I mean worst.

"Rock!" I screamed to Chad. Not fast enough, the canoe jammed and the fast current spun us around. I panicked as water rushed up and around the watercraft—almost pouring in! The park ranger's prediction swam through my head. I didn't want my baby to bob in the water because we tipped over! Emotionally, I was finished. I hated that river. I started crying hysterically, but Chad remained calm. A police officer, he can suppress panic and instead act instantly. Our hero leapt out and dislodged us from the boulder in seconds.

"Chad, I want off of this river!" I demanded. Before having Gracie, I never acted like this in precarious situations. But motherly instincts kicked in and I could only think of my daughter's safety.

"Just a couple more miles to the campground. Just hang on!"

I pulled myself together and glanced back at Gracie to make sure she was okay. She wore a look that seemed to say, "Come on, Mom; can we get going again?"

The last couple of miles were the longest. Gracie enjoyed the ride, but she was tired of her life jacket. We were stopping every thirty minutes to stretch, but now our stops were every fifteen minutes. But stretch where? Once again, we had to stop by a shallow area, and Chad simply held the canoe while I fed Gracie and balanced the umbrella. As I played "Hit the Moving Target" with Gracie's mouth, I noticed that our vessel had even more water in it. All of our bags were floating in the bottom.

"Chad, I think we have a leak."

We jumped back into the boat, our urgency to reach the campground even more desperate. The faster we rowed, the louder Gracie giggled. This was exciting for her; this was an adventure! She was able to see mommy panic because of big boulders and a leaky boat.

The bright, blue sky turned an ominous gray. The light, cotton clouds morphed into rain clouds.

"Chad, we better get going, and fast. I think we're going to get rain."

"Nah, it's just gray clouds."

With less than a mile to the campsite, I began to feel a sprinkle of rain. I just wanted to get Gracie into the tent where it would be dry. I covered her with a blanket and thanked God we brought the umbrella. Finally, the campground loomed ahead and we made a beeline for the shore. I grabbed Gracie, the umbrella, and my raincoat and sat down at the picnic table while Chad set up the tent. The two middle poles went in and the center of the domed tent popped up. Chad looked for the rain-fly to cover the tent from the impending heavy rain. Without the rain-fly, our tent is like a convertible caught in the rain with the top down.

"Amy, where's the rain-fly?"

"Isn't it in the tent bag?"

"No."

I felt my throat clench and my heart stopped. This had turned into the trip from hell.

"What do you mean it's not in the tent bag? We always roll everything up and put it in the bag."

Chad paused for a moment. "The last time we used it was two weeks ago at your aunt's house in Traverse City. I remember taking it off so the tent could air out . . . " He stopped and looked at me. "We never rolled it up. It's still at your aunt's house!"

That was the last straw. I wanted to get out of the wilderness then and there. City life suddenly looked incredibly appealing again.

We decided to call the trip quits. At a neighboring campsite, a man agreed to drive Chad to our truck. Meanwhile, Gracie and I hunkered down in the tent. I wrapped Gracie tightly in the blanket and then enveloped her in my rain jacket.

I felt like the worst mom ever. But suddenly, I realized that I shouldn't panic anymore. Gracie didn't seem bothered, so why let it bother me? I needed to use her as a role model for flexibility and simply roll like the river. She didn't care about the water rushing around the boat; that was an adventure. And it didn't upset her that we had to sit in the tent; it was finally an opportunity to stretch and play with some toys. Although young, she understood that we have to make the best of whatever situation we found ourselves in.

Finally, Chad returned and loaded up the canoe. That's when he noticed that one of the rivets was missing, which explained why we were taking on water.

When it was time to take down the tent, Gracie and I sat on the picnic table under the umbrella and played peek-a-boo. Just hearing Gracie's giggle reassured me that everything was going to be okay.

By the time everything was loaded, it was almost ten o'clock at night and Gracie had fallen asleep. Exhausted, we opted to camp instead at a local motel. In place of a campfire, we prepared our hardy fare of freeze-dried macaroni and cheese using the warm water from the in-room coffee machine. Afterwards, we gave Gracie a bath and she fell asleep again.

We fell into each other's arms laughing about the whole adventure. At moments it was terrifying, yet we managed to take our daughter down the rapids safely. The new rule in our family is that we do *not* take Gracie on a river we haven't been down before. Despite everything, we may not have conquered the mighty Pine River, but we have instilled in our daughter the love for nature. Look out, world: Here we come.

Mouse Ears and Monster Faces: Adventures of the Medicated

Leesa Gehman

Imagine, if you will: One averaged-sized hotel room. One five-year-old boy. Two fifty-five-year-old people. Me, the (single) mother to the five-year-old boy and the daughter to the fifty-five-year-olds. Walt Disney World. Saturday to Saturday. And a wedding.

It took until Wednesday, but we eventually reached the breaking point.

My mom's a neat freak. I'm not. Tommy's asthma medication had just been changed to a steroid inhaler, and his mood change made me think of Cinderella morphing into her evil stepsister. In other words, I thought he'd gone batshit insane. My lovely dad is not renowned for his patience, even under the best of circumstances, and Tommy's current mood could not be described as the best of circumstances.

So was it really any surprise that I felt like I should be the one on some sort of medication? Just not Tommy's. Something slightly less likely to induce violence or hyperactivity, like Prozac or Valium.

Why, you might ask, did we take the trip at all? Well, Erin, one of my closest friends, was getting married there. I was a bridesmaid and my terror of a son was the ring bearer. Everything, from the bachelor/ette parties through to the ceremony, was taking place at Disney World, so we thought we'd make a vacation out of it. My parents had also been invited, which seemed just perfect. Famous last words.

It had started off like any other trip. We flew from Allentown, Pennsylvania, to Atlanta, Georgia, on a forty-passenger commuter plane. There were high-wind warnings that day, and the plane bounced and shook like a 1985 Datsun with bad shocks on a dirt road. Twenty minutes into the flight, Tommy was clinging to me, terrified and begging to get off. By the time we got to Atlanta to catch our connection to Orlando, Tommy didn't want to look at the new plane, let alone get on it.

It was probably a sign.

By Wednesday, the four of us had gone everywhere together. We'd been to MGM Studios on Sunday, Animal Kingdom on Monday, the Magic Kingdom on Tuesday, and Epcot on Wednesday. At night we were asleep by eleven and awake the next morning by seven or eight. We were worn out and tired a few days into the trip, but like any good vacationers we pressed on.

So was it any wonder that the day before the wedding I was walking around Epcot at 11 AM slightly looped? A food and wine festival was in full swing and the four of us were eating and drinking our way through the worlds. Actually, my dad wasn't drinking but he was enjoying most of the appetizer-size foods for sale, my mom was doing a little of both, and I was doing most of the wine-tasting. Of course, Tommy refused to eat anything but the Durban Spiced Chicken from South Africa.

We were about a third of the way through the World Showcase when my mom turned and looked at me, her brow furrowed and her mouth set in a tight line. It had been drizzling all morning and her short hair was frizzy and glistening from the rainwater. She squinted at me from behind rain-smeared glasses. "Your cheeks are bright red."

"That would be the wine, mom." I'd had an excellent Riesling in "Germany," a great green-tea-plum wine cooler in "China," and another Riesling in "Australia," rationalizing that they were all only "dessert-sized portions" of an ounce or two.

"Maybe you should slow down."

"I'm not stumbling yet," I said. She rolled her eyes and sighed, so I continued, "I won't drink much more. But how often do you get to do this? Look, there's Morocco."

By the time we got to "England," which was about three-quarters of the way through the World Showcase, I still wasn't stumbling. However, being twenty-seven years old and sharing not just a vacation but also a hotel room with my mom, dad, and son was becoming much more bearable.

My father was sidetracked by a sign for fish and chips so we stopped while he got food. Tommy spotted a traditional English red phone booth and ran over to it.

"Look!" he yelled, and waved his arms. He did a little dance that involved arm flailing and some butt shaking for flavor. "It's Jimmy Neutron's time machine!"

"It's actually a phone booth, honey. That's what they have in England," I said. I had been trying to point out interesting things to him in each country, to counteract the effects of his missing kindergarten for a week.

"IT'S A TIME MACHINE! FROM JIMMY!" He screamed and pummeled me with fists the size of eggs. His eyes were so narrowed in anger I could barely see the cornflower-blue iris. Before he started his new inhaler, my son would hug me for no reason. Once the steroids took hold, he could barely stand to touch me and when he did it was usually with his fists. He had started the meds two weeks ago, but it had taken me until the start of our vacation to realize that my son's transformation from calm, laid-back kid to demented changeling was because of the steroids. And of course I was 1,700 miles from his doctor.

I got down on my knees so that we were eye to eye and held his wrists in my hands. "Jimmy Neutron made a phone booth like this into a time machine. It's not a big deal. Why are you so mad?"

He ignored further attempts to placate him and, with his fists effectively out of commission, started to kick me. At least he wasn't attempting to bite me this time.

Like storm clouds arriving for the wedding ceremony, my father reappeared with his steaming basket of fish and chips. Unfortunately, the last few days with my unusually violent son had taken their toll.

"Now what the hell is his problem?"

"I've got it under control, Dad. Leave us alone for a minute."

"I've had it with this. If this is how he's going to be all day, we can go back to the hotel room and he can sit there."

"That won't make things any better," I said. I stood up, preparing for an argument, but Tommy wrenched free of my grip and bolted for the phone booth that had so innocently started it all. He pulled open the door and tried to lock himself inside.

I left him to Dad and went off in search of "Russia" and some vodka. Maybe a fifth would do it. So, I was self-medicating. Hey, it was just one day.

By the time we'd finished walking around the worlds of Epcot, we were tired and cranky. I was more than slightly looped by that point. After the "England" debacle, I finished up with a mead from "Ireland," an ice wine from "Canada," and some pierogies and raspberry wine from "Poland." And still not a stumble in sight.

We made it over the bridge and back into Future World before Tommy's next breakdown.

"I WANT SOMEONE TO CARRY ME!"

"Sweetie, we're almost to the rides," my mom said and attempted to smile at him. She looked like she was headed to the gallows rather than to The Seas with Nemo and Friends. We'd exited the walkway and were almost into the main plaza so I pulled him aside to a black iron fence and knelt down. Tommy, repeating the monster face he'd refined in "England", was radiating anger the way he radiates heat when he has a fever.

"I WANT SOMEONE TO CARRY ME!"

"No one is carrying you. If you can't walk, we're not going on any rides. We're going back to the hotel room and you can stay there all night," my father interjected.

"That's not going to work, Dad," I said.

"He's being a brat and should go back to the room."

"In case you've forgotten, Tommy and I have the rehearsal dinner tonight in 'Canada'. You two go back to the hotel. The groomsmen are bringing Tommy back later anyway." My father opened his mouth to say something, but I shook my head. "You know what? Why don't you and Mom find a bench and let me deal with him. We'll talk about this after I'm done."

My dad grumbled something unintelligible but he and my mom walked a good distance away and sat down. I found a shady bench for me and Tommy and drew him into my lap. I tried to talk to him.

"Honey, you're getting too big. I can't carry you all day."

"I DON'T WANT TO WALK!"

"And you threw a fit about the stroller. You said they were for babies." The memory of that battle loomed in my mind and I opted for distraction. "Look, Soarin' is right over there. We can ride on it and you can sit down for awhile. It's supposed to be really cool and you feel like you're flying."

"I DON'T WANT TO WALK!"

"Babe. Do you want to take a nap? How 'bout you rest your head on my shoulder and we'll sit here for a few minutes?"

"NO!"

Eventually Tommy relented and lay his head on my shoulder. I tried to rock him in the middle of the busy plaza, but he was long past the infant days of being able to sleep anywhere and anytime.

But for a while he allowed me to hold him. It was the first time in almost two weeks, I realized, that I'd done so. I felt for a moment a vice in my chest, which squeezed my heart into a million little pieces and shattered it into a million more on the asphalt beneath me.

I buried my face into his sweaty head and let my hair fall around us like a cloak. All I could think of were the moments I'd wasted before, all that I had taken for granted. Spontaneous kisses and hugs, his small hand clutched in mine, the sound of his laughter. I wondered if I had squandered it all and if those moments were just memories. I loved him more than life even in those violent periods, but I missed him, too.

I closed my eyes tightly and tried not to cry.

I spoke to him in low, hushed tones. He cried and told me he didn't know why he was so mad. He was sorry. I told him I thought it was his new inhaler and that we were going to the doctor as soon as we got home. I told him no matter what, I loved him. I love him always.

I'd like to say that after our talk things turned out okay but it was only a momentary calm to the storm, like the eye of a hurricane. As soon as I stood up to walk, the monster came back. He wasn't moving unless someone carried him.

And I'd really like to say that the rest of the week was easier with Tommy, but in fact only one day was easier. Fortunately it was the day of the wedding. Unfortunately, between a nervous bride, multiple wedding coordinators, and the requisite evil sister-in-law-to-be, I still had more stress than a lunar landing.

That lovely Wednesday in Epcot, my parents left Tommy and me and went back to the hotel. The two of us went to the rehearsal dinner, and afterwards some of the groomsmen who were staying on the same floor of our hotel took Tommy back to my parents.

With Tommy passed off, I went out with the bride and some friends for a last-minute bachelorette party, in reality just barhopping through Pleasure Island. Sometime around three in the morning, all four girls in the bridal party ended up at the Grand Floridian. We had booked a suite there because we had to be up early the next morning for hair and makeup and all the other girly stuff that's required before a wedding. By sheer luck we had been complimentarily upgraded to the Walter E. Disney Suite, one of the nicest rooms in Walt Disney World. Two bedrooms, two-and-a-half bathrooms, Jacuzzi tub, marble columns in the foyer, and plasma TV. I felt a little like royalty. Drunk royalty, but royalty nonetheless.

The next morning, after I had been transformed by the hair-and-makeup lady from bride of Frankenstein to bridesmaid, I met up with my son in the lobby. He was waiting with the groom's parents next to the Grand Staircase, watching a cartoon on one of the TVs that were scattered throughout the lobby. His tuxedo fit perfectly, black with white vest, white tie and red rose boutonnière. He looked up as I walked to him.

"Hi, Mommy!" He jumped from his chair and ran over to me. I knelt down and hugged him.

"I missed you," I said. "You look so handsome."

"You look beautiful," he whispered and fingered my bouquet of white and red roses. He flashed a smile at me and ran back to the TV.

"He's been an angel," the groom's mother told me.

I was struck dumb. "Tommy?"

"Oh yes. And you'll see the boys have taught him a few things," the groom's father said and laughed. I raised an eyebrow, but was distracted by the photographer before I could ask exactly what my son had been taught.

I didn't need to wait long, however, before Tommy displayed his newfound knowledge. A passing groomsman ruffled his hair and asked him, "What's a cheap beer, Tommy?" Without hesitation, my son gazed up adoringly at his new pal and replied, "Coors. And Natty Ice."

That wasn't all. If you asked, "What does the Captain say?" you'd be met with a shouted "ARGHH!", as Tommy put his hands on his hips and lifted his left foot as if propping it up on something, just like Captain Morgan does on the label of Captain Morgan's Spiced Rum. As far as I'm concerned, Tommy thought he was imitating Captain Jack Sparrow, or Captain Hook, which was fine by me.

Tommy made it through the ceremony with some yawning, but with nary a temper tantrum. He was remarkably well-behaved through the reception, too. For this I thank the groomsmen, bless them. They passed him around from one guy to the next, keeping him occupied. By the end of the night, four groomsmen offered to adopt my son.

The nervous bride . . . well, that's another story. After vomiting all day, not drinking or eating (which we put down to nerves and the pleasures of Pleasure

Island), she barely managed to stand during the ceremony. She missed most of her reception, save for the dance with her husband, who seemed to be holding her up through most of it. That evening, she went to the emergency room and then spent almost a week in the hospital after they removed her gallbladder.

Friday was spent lounging by the pool and went by in a blink. Saturday we flew home. The flight was uneventful, although the airline did lose our luggage. It seemed only fitting.

And my son? It was a rough road for a while, but we weaned him off the medications and onto something that worked without making him crazy.

I needn't have worried about missing my sweet boy once the drug was flushed out of his system. A few short months after Florida, as we snuggled on the sofa watching *Star Wars: A New Hope* for the 915th time, Tommy put his head on my shoulder and sighed. "Mommy, when I'm not with you, I feel weird."

"What do you mean?"

Tommy pulled away from me and furrowed his brow. When he can't think of a word, he makes a particular motion like he's trying to pluck the words from the air in front of him. He puts his fingers to his thumb and makes a pinching action with both hands, like a crab on the beach. He stopped, and the words came to him, as they usually do. "My head, Mommy. My head feels unbalanced when I'm not with you."

Sometimes, I thought, as R2-D2 clicked and squeaked in the background and Tommy snuggled against me, the best vacations are the ones at home, with a bowl of popcorn, a boy, and a movie.

I hugged him to me and kissed the top of his head. I whispered back, "My head feels unbalanced when I'm not with you, too."

Friendly Fire

Sarah Shey

In the old, pre-child days, vacations used to be about escaping what we knew rather than seeking out more of the same. In foreign lands, my husband and I prized routine-free days. We let the movements of a particular locale, whether city calm or country cacophony, direct us instead of needing to take charge. We craved novel foods: white Bordeaux, unidentifiable cheeses, shots of dubious sugar concoctions at cafés. We reveled in our ignorance, only too happy to let the day unfold however it may. The only mainstay from our country of origin we refused to snub was a good night's sleep.

Then, four years ago, I gave birth to our son Henry and for a time our adventures took place at home in Brooklyn, New York. Every day was more of the same. Spotting airplanes, fire engines, and buses over and over again became vital to our new itinerary, as did his midday siesta, which we had never before allowed ourselves. I had entered the child-beloved sphere of repetition and routine. For some reason, all this at-home training with a child did not prepare me for trips abroad.

So the St. Barts incident was a shocker (and I'm not talking about the runway, the world's second-shortest). It was a trip in which my husband, my son and I ended up looking like we had perms (the humidity) and the chicken pox (the mosquitoes). Only our family could visit a glamorous island and resemble campers in the Boundary Waters. But even worse than looking like we should be quarantined was the habit Henry, our two-year-old son, picked up and wouldn't let go of. Soon I wanted to take a vacation from our vacation.

It started our second evening on St. Barts—innocently enough, of course. Dusk had crept into our son's bedroom and my husband clicked off the lights and began, "Once upon a time." Henry was transfixed by the story his father made up involving Henry's best-liked objects—my parents' farm in Iowa, a propeller airplane, Fire Engines 101 and 202 from Brooklyn. The narrative was such a success that my husband told another story the next day at naptime. I told one at suppertime and again at bedtime. A ritual had been started. It didn't take long to hook a child.

After the first few stories, my husband and I congratulated each other. Telling stories could be used anywhere—particularly in outposts that lacked electricity, libraries, and running water. Tibet, anyone? Finally our carry-ons would be lighter, emptied of books. We seemed to have emerged from the bulky realm of nursery-inspired travel. Move over, Dr. Spock.

But then, after the seventeeth time (we counted), storytelling began to weigh on us like an Ultrasaucer. What had once been adult downtime—walking along the beach, eating supper as a family—became opportunities for our son to demand stories that came from our heads rather than Dr. Seuss's. Breakfast, lunch, supper, two snacks, two naptimes, in the car, in the stroller: eight prime times for stories. The three-word command—"Tell a story"—could strike at any time.

Our patience got shorter—as did the stories. We decided that it was not fun to participate in story on demand; it was not cute, and it was not clever. To sum up storytelling in one word: exhausting. My husband and I began to run out of ideas so we borrowed storylines from famous authors (Richard Scarry and Rosemary Wells), which put their work and our hubris into perspective.

As if it wasn't bad enough that we had to use our brains on vacation, Henry developed exacting opinions about our narratives. I was digging a hole on Flamands Beach, a gentle stretch popular with families on the northwest part of the island. My husband was scooping up water with a bucket from the ocean.

"Tell a story," said Henry.

"Once upon a time there were two ducks," I said.

"No, ten ducks," Henry said. He did not look up from pummeling a sand mountain with his shovel.

"Okay, ten ducks and they decided to ride a fire engine."

"Not a fire engine."

"Okay, a taxi."

"Not a taxi."

"A street sweeper."

"Not a street sweeper."

Frankly, what did we expect? Henry came from storytelling stock. My father and his side of the family loved yarns. They'd gather in their southern Iowa town after Sunday mass and narrate tales for hours, tossing out dramatic gasps, bemused lip-twitches, and thigh-slapping punchlines. My relatives were participating in the oldest form of storytelling—the oral tradition—which was as much a part of our landscape as glaciers. Even in the modest narratives that we told our son about heroes (a little boy escapes his bedroom with his stuffed black cat to fight fires) or about magical realism (a toast town in Germany becomes soggy after a rainstorm), he was transported elsewhere and participating in the most streamlined kind of travel: the imagination.

But we didn't yet have the perspective or the patience or eight hours of sleep to see it that way. I was an old-fashioned parent who wanted her son to savor the vacation's scenery not only because I said so but because such scenery was one of the reasons we went on the trip in the first place. By being constantly entertained, Henry was not living in the moment or allowing us to do the same.

My husband and I were being attacked from within, ambushed by friendly fire, the peace of our vacation disrupted by a bug of our own making. Improv, we decided, should be left to the professionals. I later realized, of course, that requesting things that comfort was how toddlers traveled. Every day in this great big world of sensory overload, no matter the dialing code, was a trip for Henry—not just the ones to the Caribbean. In fact Henry could have been anywhere: Dubuque, Branson, or Duluth. A story trumped any locale—as long as his parents were there with him.

But first things first: we needed to get through this vacation.

"I'm checking into a hotel," I said to my husband after several days of Storyteller's Corner. I waved my hands as if to make myself disappear in a poof and land underneath a royal-blue umbrella with a glass of chilled Brouilly, personal waiter at the ready.

My husband's eyes did not leave my face. In fact, he looked horrified. If I left who would provide backup? Who would tell the other forty-five stories remaining? We glanced at our son, his hazel eyes, superlative eyelashes, and cheeks the color of Braeburn apples, such a portrait of sweetness.

I didn't desert the troops but implemented what seemed a brazen strategy. Being eighteen times older than my son, I was going to be bamboozled no more—all for parental sanity (one of the world's worthiest causes.) In retrospect, my idea was not only simple but obvious. A more experienced parent (like my mother) would have known to lather on storytelling sunscreen long before getting charred.

At lunch time, the next meal, Henry said, "Tell a story."

I picked up a spoon of oatmeal and offered it to him.

"I'm on holiday," I said. It was true.

"No, no, not on holiday," he said. He shook his head back and forth.

I presented another spoonful. "Yep, on holiday."

Henry studied my face. I smiled at him but stayed firm.

I scooped up more oatmeal.

It worked, despite Henry's protestations. Even so, for several weeks after our trip, I was taken aback. I thought about where danger lurked in a foreign country. It wasn't necessarily the water or the pickpockets or the hurricane or the propeller plane or the tsetse fly or the lions in a game park but in something we harbored ourselves, created ourselves, and, which on St. Barts, had a beginning, a middle, and, thankfully, an end.

Rock Me like a Hurricane

Donna Collins Tinsley

"**A**re we in China? There's the Great Wall!"

On recent trip to Tennessee, I realized my grandson Isaiah had been watching too much *Dora the Explorer*. Driving along the Georgia interstate on our way to the Georgia Aquarium in Atlanta, we passed the many sound-barrier walls that keep the noise factor down for home-dwellers. We couldn't convince three-year-old Isaiah that we weren't in China. He thought his Abba (Granddad) had taken him on a worldwide excursion.

"We're in Georgia, Isaiah."

"Uh-uh, no, we're in China." No amount of talking would convince him otherwise.

To the mind of a child some trips must seem endless. Actually, to parents they can seem endless too.

Making long trips with a toddler was something I dreaded, to say the least, and avoided at all costs. Our first long trip with Isaiah was when he was less than a year old. To call it unscheduled would be an understatement—Hurricane Frances was on its way and being here for it wasn't a priority on my to-do list.

Think.

1. Buy formula
2. Arrange playdate for Isaiah
3. Endure rocking of the house from the hurricane

I don't think so! Living in a high-risk hurricane zone, I thought I had figured out everything I needed to know about getting ready for a hurricane. But the next hurricane is upon us before I can ever expect it; or at least it was in 2004, when Hurricane Jeanne followed Hurricanes Charley and Frances, which hit the Florida Peninsula, and Ivan pounded the Panhandle, as Governor Bush urged Floridians to take hurricanes seriously. When Hurricane Charley had roared through I didn't sleep at all, and I remembered even promising God after that hurricane, "I am going to clean out the garage." I knew I would be totally embarrassed if all the stuff in there somehow blew out and into the neighborhood. Loving your neighbors as yourself means not putting them in mortal danger of your junk flying through their windows. And then, as I lay awake the winds rattling every window, I also made many promises to myself about things I would do if we survived this one. Top on my to-do list was evacuation. Even my husband had said, "We're getting out of here if another one comes."

Those words are from a man who doesn't even like to make the ten-minute trip across the river to Red Lobster with a toddler. When I'd imagined being fifty-five, my plans had never included surrogate-parenting a three-year-old. If we make it out the door to a restaurant with him we consider it a victory. After we have let him sit there stuffing his face with crackers so he won't disturb other diners, little Isaiah is too full to eat his pricey kid's meal. My husband swears that on the rare occasions we venture out alone, we always end up eating near someone with either a crying baby or a noisy unruly, toddler. "I don't want to be the person inflicting this experience on someone else who may not get out too often," he has said, as we try to pretend we don't hear the commotion at the next table.

At least living in a hurricane-prone area has one advantage: You get to check out all the good places to flee to. When outrunning Hurricane Isabel the previous year, a hurricane which had thoughtfully arrived, gift-wrapped, on my husband's birthday, I had discovered Macon, Georgia. Bill, electing to stay home with our dogs, had forfeited any chance of birthday kisses or cake and sent me off with our daughters at 5:00 AM.

He didn't realize how smart he was to get me off early. Hundreds of families spent the day stuck on the interstate eating Twinkies, with no way to get off for food. I managed to drive the three hundred or so miles to Macon right before the traffic became bumper-to-bumper. But I was so stressed by the game I called "Mama can drive faster than a hurricane" that by the time we stopped for lunch five hours later at Shoney's in Macon, I didn't even eat. Who goes to the South's most famous food bar at Shoney's and doesn't eat? Fried chicken, gravy and biscuits, clam chowder, salad bar, and strawberry shortcake; it's an all-you-can-eat deal.

"What are you ordering, Mom?" my daughter, Shiloh, asked.

"Y'all go ahead and order," I said as the waitress poured my long-awaited coffee. "I don't think I'm hungry." That's when the girls knew that things were tense. They had never seen me go to Shoney's and not just eat, but also go back for more. Smart kids that they were (we had many times before been through the lesson, *If Mama ain't happy then no one's happy*), they just ordered their food and ate quietly.

As I sat there checking road maps and looking around I saw that Macon had everything we needed as hurricane refugees. Just far enough away from Florida, packed with restaurants, fast food, movie theaters, museums, it would be great! But when I checked for vacancies at the adjoining hotels there were none.

Note number one: Always make your hurricane reservation before you leave home. My Macon brainwave thwarted, I headed a couple of hours further north to Marietta. We were safe and comfortable, while my husband was home with the dogs and no electricity for five days.

So when Hurricane Frances came, Macon it was. I made reservations at the La Quinta Suites before we left the state and thought we could pretend we were on a vacation. That is, if you would normally vacation with two vehicles, three teenagers, three dogs, a cat and a grandbaby, trying to outrun a category-two hurricane with maximum sustained winds near 105 mph and hurricane-force winds extending outward 85 miles (140 kilometers) from the storm's center.

The La Quinta Suites, three hundred and seventy-one miles away exactly (but who's counting when you are entertaining a little one for each excruciating mile of that journey?) were indeed very nice, and vacation-worthy. However, their hospitality didn't extend to our three big dogs, Brandy the Springer Spaniel, Cocoa the Chocolate Lab, and Stardust the Golden Retriever, who had to be boarded twenty miles away in the country. To accommodate the rest of us we rented a suite and a double room. The suite held my then-thirteen-year-old daughter, Shiloh, my husband, Bill, and me. Much to my chagrin, Isaiah stayed in the other room with Ashley, nineteen, and my ever-so-independent sixteen-year-old, Amber. This was their first time to assert their independence staying in a hotel room alone; they promised would take good care of Isaiah and the cat. Since Bill is such a light sleeper and not used to having Isaiah in our room at night, he quickly agreed to the plan. (Clearly it was too much to expect the rooms to be adjoining or even next door.) A supervisory check on the snoozing Isaiah entailed a fifteen-minute walk through the maze of the hotel, then back again. Hoping to spare Ashley having to get up early while we were "vacationing," I kept a spare key to sneak in early and get Isaiah out for breakfast downstairs, as I took the "day shift," which included feeding him instant oatmeal and telling him it was porridge like the three bears ate.

Just packing for our impromptu vacation, I had broken out in a cold sweat: Did I pack enough bibs, diapers, baby food, formula, snacks? I had to take Isaiah's portable crib in case the hotel didn't have one available; besides, he needed something familiar from home, didn't he? Even with a van and a truck, we were jammed. And to add an extra-scented frisson to the whole experience, the cat decided to get sick in the van, and my husband's new truck didn't smell new anymore after taking the dogs with him. One of my daughters got sick while we were out of state, and guess what? The Florida insurance didn't cross state lines! We hadn't really planned for our annual vacation this year to be running from hurricanes. However, driving past the many hotels and motels along the way with No Vacancy signs out as we drove up, and hearing of the many people who had to go to shelters, we were finding things to be grateful about.

Just as we were feeling good about our decision to evacuate, we learned that even if lightning never strikes twice, natural disasters certainly can. We were traveling around looking at the beautiful countryside when my daughter Shiloh screamed, "Mom, is that a tornado coming?" We made it back to the room before storm winds tried to sweep the van off the road. So I guess if we try to outrun a hurricane again, we will also factor in a tornado-safe zone, too.

After four days in Georgia, it was time for the trip home, a journey that consisted of every nursery rhyme, every possible story involving three bears, and buying eighty-five orders of french fries. By the time we arrived at the (fortunately still intact) front door, we had made up a song consisting of a few words: "We're nearly home, We're nearly home, We're nearly home," and then "We're home, We're home, We're really, really home."

We tried traveling with a toddler to get out of the way of a hurricane and it was so stressful that we decided to stay home for the next one. And the next and the next.

When Mommy Met Sally

Melissa Balmain

"We're back!" I crowed. "We're home!" Five years after leaving California for the East Coast, five minutes after returning for vacation, my husband and I stood on a bluff above Laguna Beach. The Pacific was growing yolky in the sunset. Drummers were thumping their congas along the boardwalk. And Bill and I were busy planning to do every California thing we loved: We would wade in the cove where we always used to wade, eat at our favorite restaurants, hike our favorite trails. Bill would play chess by the ocean. I would shop for exotic beads.

"I've missed this so much," Bill said between gulps of salt air. "Were we nuts to leave?"

The answer he got was a world-class whine from our two-year-old. Davey hadn't been conceived the last time Bill and I stood on this bluff. Now he squirmed in Bill's arms, reminding us that not only did he exist, he was ready for bed. Bill and I tried to perk him up ("Wow, Davey, do you hear the sea lions barking?"). Davey did an impression of a sea lion having its toenails removed.

So long, sunset. Hello, motel.

The message was clear: We hadn't been nuts to leave the West Coast—we'd been nuts to think we could return with a toddler and pick up where we had left off. Further proof came the next day when we realized that, instead of hanging out in our beloved, distant cove, we'd better stick to the puny beach behind the motel so Davey could be near a bathroom.

Bill and I spread our towels and sighed, missing the cove. Davey—not sighing—clawed the sand: "What's *that*?" He was pointing to a clump of seaweed strung with slimy-looking, mustard-colored bladder pods. I tried to see the disgusting wad through his eyes. It probably seemed full of potential—like a roll of weird Bubble Wrap. "Hey," I said, "should we pop some of these?" The pods weren't slimy, just rubbery; when juice ran out, I found myself whooping right along with him.

As Davey moved on to rubbing sand all over my legs, I decided that maybe this trip would be good for me. Maybe it would make me more low maintenance, more willing to settle for minor pleasures. So what if touching seaweed wasn't my very favorite activity, compared with, say, touching beautiful anemones in the cove's tide pools? It was still sort of fun. Dirty sand on my legs? I would try to think of it as an exfoliating spa treatment.

For years, Bill had teased me for acting like Sally in *When Harry Met Sally*, ordering stuff on the side and insisting that everything be "the way I want it." Now I had the feeling I was ready to kiss Sally goodbye. In just a few hours of vacation, after all, I had put a happy face on a number of disappointments. Seaweed Beach was only the latest.

For starters was our motel, not to mention the fact it was a motel at all. Bill and I had seldom set foot in one, pre-kids. Instead we had splurged on bed-and-breakfasts—the kind where you could lounge in your frilly room while snarfing down an almond croissant. I had called B&Bs to make reservations before our trip with Davey, but learned that none of the owners wanted Bill and me around anymore, now that we had reproduced. I assured them Davey was a great kid. They said they looked forward to meeting him in a few years. Since my family's arrival in Laguna, I had tried to see the upside of this rejection: We were lugging a lot of stuff here (Davey's Pack 'n Play, his stroller and sun canopy, his gargantuan diaper bag, his even more gargantuan suitcase, his three thousand must-have books, puzzles, and stuffed animals, and a couple of toothbrushes for Bill and me). So really, I should feel *lucky* not to have a frilly room three flights up a Victorian staircase—and grateful for what we did have: a no-frills room three steps from our rental car.

Then there was breakfast. I had pined for the aforementioned croissants our first morning in Laguna, it's true. But I just couldn't see schlepping to a bakery, Davey howling with hunger, when there were shrink-wrapped Danishes in the lobby of our motel. With a little nuking, the Supreme Caramel Swirl didn't taste as bad as I had feared. Especially before I read the ingredient list.

And last but not least, snorkeling: Way back when, Bill and I had loved to swim with schools of silver and blue fish. Now, thanks to a lack of equipment and babysitters, this was impossible. Big deal, I told myself. After a morning spent chasing Davey, and sunblocking Davey, and urging Davey to use the potty, the only fish I had energy for was stuffed in a tortilla.

See? I was becoming less Sally-like by the minute. On day two, when my bead-shopping plans got preempted (Davey was too cranky from teething to drag into stores), I made do with window shopping. On day three, when we ate with friends at a beloved Italian restaurant, I even started to feel a little superior. Davey had been antsy after we ordered, so Bill had taken him outside to run around. By the time they got back, the *timballino* on Bill's plate was stone cold. He moped. He had waited five years to taste this dish again. Selflessly, I told him he was welcome to both our second slices, still piping in their iron pan. What mother needed hot food when she had the warmth of her toddler's hand in hers? What kind of loser longed for creamy sauce when she had the rich joy of two-year-old laughter?

Me, that's who. A few evenings later, in a café up the coast in Cambria, I was served a slightly scorched potpie. Not just any potpie, mind you, but my favorite chicken potpie on the planet, one that (truth be told) was my main reason for making the ten-hour round-trip to Cambria. I choked down a bite. Tears, I am embarrassed to say, sprang to my eyes.

"I want another one," I hissed to Bill.

"We don't have time," he hissed back. "It'll take half an hour for them to cook a new pie. Davey's got to go to bed."

I knew he was right. But that didn't stop me from sulking all the way to our motel. *Go away, Sally,* I thought.

She was back later in the week, though, when we visited friends in Rossmoor—friends with a toddler of their own. Years before, we had loved to spend hours yakking with these people. Now we couldn't have a five-minute conversation that wasn't interrupted by a diaper crisis, a Fruity Booty crisis, or an invisible boo-boo crisis. Okay, I figured, we'll stay up late and talk instead. But the moment our kids turned in, we grownups started yawning too. I drifted off, sulking again. *Sally, begone.*

And then, just a couple days after that, I realized she might as well stay.

The idea first hit me in Huntington Beach, while I stood in a friend's shower feeling the pure, voluptuous high that comes only when you rid your scalp of potato salad. Davey had slathered it there at a barbecue. I had made a sleepy effort to scrape it off before bed. Now, eight hours later, I was quite sure I had never enjoyed a shampoo more in my life. Minor pleasure? No way. My happiest moments on this trip had had nothing to do with being a low-maintenance martyr, settling for less than my vacation ideals. Instead, they were about finding new ideals—more attainable than most of the old ones, maybe, but just as thrilling.

Potato-salad showers, say.

Or—better still—fast-track toddler learning. For some reason (the sea air? the smiles of strangers?) vacation was proving quite the galvanizer for Davey. While Bill and I gained nothing more impressive than a few pounds, our firstborn was gaining skills: carrying a tune; climbing stairs without wobbling; puckering up and giving us a real good-night kiss instead of the soggy lip-smoosh he used to bestow. Perhaps his finest hour had come at the Los Angeles Zoo. The three of us were sitting outdoors, eating limp French fries within sniffing distance of the gorillas, when ecstasy struck. Davey, my own amazing son, was actually, for the first time in his life, drinking milk through a straw. At home I had urged him to try this for months. No dice. Now here he was, sucking down the 2-percent like a pro. My heart thudded with pride.

Whenever I focused on Davey's vacation triumphs, it dawned on me, I didn't long for the old days—just enjoyed the new ones. Same thing with another fresh travel ideal: watching friends make fools of themselves. Thanks to Davey, Bill and I got to see the goofy side of one woman who had always intimidated us. (Who knew she could make faces like that? Or that she had such energy for blowing raspberries on a kid's neck?) We saw other friends act thirty years younger as they taught Davey to fly a kite, pranced in his Mickey Mouse ears, and chased him around while puffing air from a turkey baster. Several people let their guard down in other ways, too—like an elderly friend who had always been quick to discuss her professional life and hide her personal one. "He's at such a wonderful age," she said, lunching with Davey and me. Then she bent her head near mine and told stories about her own children when they were young, followed by tidbits about her current boyfriend. I talked more freely than usual, too. (Once someone has heard you imitate a basket of kittens for your son, you don't have much to lose.)

Yet another new ideal, I decided, was noticing stuff I'd normally overlook—and not just seaweed pods. At the Getty Museum, while Davey played on grass out back, I studied the building's dramatic angles and considered that before, I had rushed inside museums without appreciating their outsides. At Disneyland, where Davey chose to spend long minutes buckling and unbuckling the straps of lined-up strollers, I had time for a semiscientific study: How often did a certain cute janitor come by to sweep up Popsicle wrappers? (Every ninety seconds. Wow.) The Davey effect even worked in "It's a Small World." He was so thrilled by the animatronic dolls that I started spotting new ones myself—plus, for the first time ever, I was distracted enough from the awful music that I didn't long to strangle the nearest singing mermaid. All this bracing discovery, I assured myself, was enough to replace any of my outdated, pre-parental, California cravings.

Almost enough.

Towards the end of our trip, Bill, Davey, and I went hiking with friends at Montaña de Oro State Park. Bill and I had often done this hike, marching along the ocean path to work up a virtuous sweat. But Davey and our friends' toddler didn't cooperate with that plan: Instead of riding on our backs, they insisted on walking. As they zigzagged and dawdled, I admit, Bill and I noticed things we surely would have overlooked on a power hike: Day-Glo bugs. Dainty wildflowers. Scrub that smelled like mincemeat pie. At the same time, though, we were burning almost no calories from the actual pastry we had eaten at lunch.

"That was beautiful," Bill said afterwards.

"Yeah," I said. "But I did kind of miss the exercise part."

"Me too."

"Someday, we really have to come back here again—without the kid." And, of course, with Sally.

Ocean City, New Jersey

Elizabeth Roca

'm the one who packs. It makes sense: My husband is at work full-time, ten hours a day, while I'm the one at home with the children, able to throw in emergency loads of laundry and search out the number-fifty sunblock (removed and rearranged, as is everything in our house, by tiny, industrious hands). I like packing. I like folding little T-shirts and tucking them into a duffel bag. I like planning just the right snacks for the children to eat in the car: nothing too dull or too sugary.

Yet in the days leading up to our planned week at the beach, I also feel the occasional twinge of resentment. I didn't remember preparing for our earlier vacations—that is, vacations taken in the years before my husband and I became parents—as being so *hard*.

My husband and I haven't traveled much in the past few years. When you acquire three babies in a space of twenty-one months—twins and a bonus baby, conceived on her siblings' first birthday—something must give, either your budget or your nerve. In our case it was a bit of both. Out were the flights to England to visit my husband's family; out were the more modest five-to-eight-hour car drives from our home in Maryland to the Roanoke Valley or Vermont, now unimaginable in scale and the sheer volume of preparation required for a journey that would last less than a week. Going to the grocery store, where the bright lights made the baby cry and the twins amused themselves by running up the aisles and swiping at anything glass-bottled or easily bruised, was trip enough for me.

But this summer we are taking the plunge. My parents have rented a house in Ocean City, New Jersey, and have invited us to spend a week with them. They're involved, energetic grandparents, happy to play with the little ones. They've promised me and my husband a night to ourselves while they babysit. Surely, with four adults among the three children (plus my younger brother, who is planning to drive up from his home in Baltimore and can move effortlessly between the two camps, wrestling with the children while discussing home renovation), we should be able to have a lovely, relaxing family vacation.

I'm looking forward to this trip. Ocean City is the vacation spot of my childhood and my memories of it are fond and vivid: bodysurfing in the ocean with my brothers and cousins; building elaborate, moated sand castles; lying drowsily on a beach towel, squinting at my book as the hot sun toasted my back and legs. Best of all is the boardwalk at night, with its crowds of people, its glowing arcades, and its thrilling smell of roasting peanuts and authentic New Jersey pizza. Kohr Brothers frozen custard! The Bookateria! The log flume at Wonderland! Oh yes, I'm looking forward to all of it.

The twins are three-and-a-half years old, our younger daughter twenty months, so naturally they won't be able to partake of all this entertainment. Bodysurfing, for instance, is out. But they'll love the sand and the gulls, I predict. They'll love the boardwalk's bright lights and neverending flow of people.

After a leg-cramping but uneventful three-hour car ride we reach my parents' rental house. We admire its spaciousness and its view of the ocean.

Then we dump our things and hustle after the kids, who are ready for some exercise.

A s it happens, the children do love Ocean City. They love splashing in the surf and digging in the sand. They love the seashell museum and the pizzeria. They love the kite my husband flies for them in the evenings, after the beach is cleared of people. But they always—and herein lies the rub—love these things at different times.

We all work to please them. My father takes the children every morning for a walk to buy the newspaper, with a stop at the doughnut shop on the way. My mother, armed with tiny seashells, wooden picture frames, and copious amounts of glue, does crafts with them in the afternoons. My husband builds a network of sandy tunnels for Jonah's trains. I read and reread the picture books I checked out of the library before we left Maryland. The adults' efforts always earn the enthusiastic approval of one, often two, children. At the same time, there's always at least one child who is cranky, or hungry, or falling apart for unknowable reasons.

My brother, thirty years old and unmarried (and forever childless, he claims), spends a couple of days in our company, then sets off on several solo day trips up and down the New Jersey coast, muttering, "Pretty noisy for a *vacation.*"

Weep for the irrefutable truth! Our offspring are no shrinking violets; rather, they are lusty-lunged, full-tilt-boogie toddlers, as apt to run into the oncoming ocean as they are to sit constructing a docile sand castle. No activity lasts for longer than ten minutes before they stampede on to the next. In this houseful of quiet adults, the noise is deafening.

My husband and I lie in bed in the mornings, each willing the other to stand up and go to the children, who are already rattling the sliding glass doors in their eagerness to go out to the beach. At home we have a routine, but here it has dissolved. There is no vacation etiquette to guide us. We both want to sleep in. Don't we deserve to sleep in? But there are children to care for, and their needs will not be suspended until post-vacation the way our office work always was on past vacations. I hadn't realized how much time I expected to spend sitting down on this trip until it became apparent that I would spend most of my time carrying, fetching, wiping faces, and rinsing sand down the bathtub drain.

The house, however, is large and luxurious. While the children watch a video and my mother browns ground beef for dinner, my husband and I sneak into our room, with its plushy carpet and big, inviting bed. We stretch out and put our arms around each other. Then there is a noise at the door. It's the baby, Camille, rubbing her eyes and stumbling with tiredness. My husband gives a small sigh, but recovers quickly, lifting her onto the bed and offering to read stories until she falls asleep. Camille screams and thrashes away from him, yanking at my shirtfront. My husband grimaces. When Camille is sleepy, she refuses any friendly arms but Mommy's.

There's a screech from the living room—one of the twins smacking the other one, I predict—and my husband groans and leaves the room. I'm left with Camille clinging octopus-like to my chest. Our vacations used to be so harmonious, I reflect. In the nine years before our children were born, my husband and I traveled to various locations in the United States and Europe without exchanging a harsh word, even when we rode the train from New Jersey to California, a three-day trip during which we slept, sitting up, in our seats.

We're not exchanging harsh words now, but there's tension in the air. As I finish nursing and soothe the baby to sleep, I'm aware of feeling self-righteously irritable. I'm tired, and I'm looking for someone to blame. I stalk into the living room without offering to help with dinner. My husband puts the older children to bed after we eat, but instead of joining in the game of Trival Pursuit we start up afterwards he opts to read a book on the porch. I feel ridiculously wounded, as if his desire to relax by himself for an hour means that we will never have another happy vacation. Ever.

Our little family seems irrevocably separate in our desires and our efforts to achieve them. Jonah wants to drive wooden trains through the sand. Lily wants to fly the kite herself, tangling the string beyond repair. Camille wants to nurse. My husband wants to be alone with me. I want to sleep, which is the one thing no one has called on me to do in the past four days.

Camille wakes me numerous times during the night, and my mood does not improve. The next morning my husband and I barely exchange words over our cornflakes and toast. We take the children to the beach and then, on impulse, to the very end of the boardwalk, to the amusement park called Wonderland. Wonderland has big rides, like the log flume and the Ferris wheel, but it also has tot-sized rides, the likes of which our kids have never seen before.

We buy tickets and scramble after the twins as they bolt different directions, the baby still corralled in the stroller. Miraculously, they choose the same attraction first, the boat ride. It's the simplest ride in the park, a little circular tub of water with tiny boats that travel in a circle. They ride it once, twice—cheering and waving at us, ringing their bells—and then ask for the fire-engine ride. More of the same: miniature fire vehicles that stay static while traveling in circles. Then the vintage-car ride. The baby falls asleep in her stroller and my husband and I lean against the railing, waving at our preschoolers as they travel past. My husband sighs. Everything I feel— exhaustion and gratitude for this moment of peace—is in his sigh. "All I want is for them to be *happy*," he says.

"Yes," I say. "To understand what makes them happy, and for it to work for all of them at the same time."

"Yes," he says, and we fall silent, but it is a companionable silence. My husband takes my hand in his and squeezes. I squeeze back. I'm no less tired, but I feel soothed. I've clung to that broad palm through the streets of London, on a choppy ferry ride to France, and in a hot tub in San Diego. I'm happy to cling to it here, on a boardwalk in New Jersey, as we watch the beautiful products of our love burn through their two-dollar ride tickets like fire through newsprint.

The children clamber off the car ride and indicate they want to try something different. No more traveling in circles for them. They point out a ride we haven't seen before, one with little pastel-colored bucket seats connected by spokes to a central wheel. We haven't seen this ride operate, and it doesn't occur to us to watch it in action. It's in the kiddie section, it's got the animal cutout at its entrance indicating its height restriction; surely it's as tame as the other rides the kids have tried.

The attendant accepts our tickets and straps in the children, side by side in a butterfly-yellow bucket. They wave, grinning. We wave back and blow kisses. The ride begins to move. The little buckets travel in circles, just as I thought they would. Then they begin to rise into the air. They rise to a height of perhaps four feet. It's nothing like the Scrambler, nothing like the Octopus, both of which jolted and thrilled me during adolescence, but it's more than Lily can manage. Looking at her little face as it cycles past, I see the warning signs: the redness, the crumple. Her mouth opens wide and she bawls.

"Oh!" My husband and I drop hands and look at each other. This is an unfamiliar parenting challenge. Do we demand the ride to be stopped? We are not the demanding sort. But what if Lily tries to get off? We begin walking around the barrier toward the ride attendant.

Jonah's face is a study in the battle for self-control. His forehead creases. The corners of his mouth turn down, then up, then down again. He puts his arm around Lily's shoulders and draws her close, an unexpectedly adult gesture. Then the bucket begins to spin, and Jonah loses his struggle. His face crumples, his mouth opens wide, and he bawls.

My husband and I run, matching each other stride for stride, jostling the baby in her stroller. The twins are howling loudly enough to drown out the ride's bright Calliope music. The ride's bright pastels and formerly benign machinery now appear sinister. All I can think of is how easily little bodies can be broken. Here we've been desperate to gain space apart from the children, and now we're desperate to get our hands back on them.

The attendant, who must be experienced in dealing with toddler panic, has already begun to slow the ride. By the time we reach his station the twirling has stopped. Pneumatic air hisses, and the steel arms sag. The attendant unbuckles the children's harnesses and they step out of their bucket with the unsteady gait of the elderly, weeping.

We hug them, squeezing their warm little bodies. We praise their bravery, praise their ability to remain in their seats.

Our ride tickets are gone. We buy Italian ices and, restored, travel down the boardwalk in the baking sun, red and blue sugar water melting down everyone's chins and wrists.

Toddler crises pass quickly. We go back to the rental house and the children describe the rides for my parents, focusing mainly on the boats. They seem not to remember being scared. They're relaxed, so I relax.

One image remains with me: that of Jonah putting his arm around Lily's shoulder as she cried. After the children are in bed, during that night's Trivial Pursuit game we've all joined in—I catch my husband's eye and say, "Jonah. When Lily was crying."

He breaks into gentle laughter. "He was brave," he says.

"Yes," I say. We are united through our pride, our amusement, our easily banished fear. It's not the kind of vacation we're used to, but it's not such a bad one, after all.

My mother reads out a question. It's one of the dratted orange questions, the sports-themed ones I can never answer, but I turn to listen with good will. I see how it can be, how it will be, when our small family's desires are brought into sync. Because all each of us wants is for the others to be happy.

The Rules of Germany

J. Anderson Coats

He's worried.

We've cleared customs at the Dallas airport and my son, Owen, is chewing the strap of his backpack, staring hard through ghostly skiffs of fog at our plane, the 777 that will take us to Nürnberg, Germany, an imperial city with a link to the medieval spice trade five hundred years in vintage.

He's not sure we should fly in winter. We'll miss Thanksgiving at Grandma's. The cat will be lonely without us. We probably shouldn't go. He'll tell me on the trip home that he thought Germany would be dirt roads, horse-drawn carts, thatched houses, and Nazis.

He brightens a little upon hearing that Germany is a lot like America and not lacking familiar things like pavement, bubble gum, and indoor plumbing.

"I will ask everyone what they think of Hitler!"

He will, too. At age three he asked a group of World War II veterans if they had shot any Germans. He was disappointed to learn they'd fought in the Pacific, but he perked up when one said he'd been a pilot. Owen asked him, "Fighter, or bomber?"

The first rule of Germany: no random references to the Führer.

"It's not polite," I explain.

Once we're settled on the plane, Owen forgets his anxiety and becomes downright cheerful upon discovering a tiny TV screen embedded in the seatback in front of him. This personal technological marvel can be tuned to twelve different channels of prerecorded cable fluff. It's an eight-year-old's pipe dream.

"I can't wait to tell Mitch about the TV stuck *right in the seat,*" he raves. He pulls out his little Instamatic and snaps a picture.

Two weeks we'll spend in the Old World, where kings and emperors once ruled, where we will witness medieval pageantry at least as old as Martin Luther, and the features of the 777 are what are receiving full-court press.

"Save some pictures for the Kristkindlesmarkt," my husband suggests.

"Okay," says Owen, and he snaps two more pictures of the smeary screen before stowing the camera.

Yes, Kristkindlesmarkt. The market of the Christ Child. It's what we've based our trip around, what's gotten me on a plane in the ramp-up to winter when all I can think of are the stock-in-trade fiery wrecks and cannibalism of plane-crash movies. Christmas markets occur throughout Germany during winter, but the Kristkindlesmarkt in Nürnberg is the biggest, oldest, and grandest. News crews worldwide come to film the crowning of the Christ Child that takes place on the first Sunday in Advent at the opening of the market, in a ritual almost five hundred years old.

I wanted a two-week cruise on the Mediterranean. Maybe a stopover in Marseilles or coffee in Istanbul. In May.

"You'll love Kristkindlesmarkt," my husband promises. He remembers it as a child does, high counters and cold fingers and stout *Hausfrauen* with armloads of fragrant evergreen. He was an army brat who grew up in a lot of places, but Nürnberg is the one that draws him back. "In the market they'll have *Liebkuchen* and *Glühwein*. Gingerbread and hot spiced wine."

Any place you can buy wine on the street is a winner with me. Crammed in the 777, Owen complaining that there is no *Mythbusters* on his miracle TV, I fantasize about liberal European alcohol consumption. This allows me to tune out the sound of trucks de-icing the wings of the plane. I'd sure like some *Glühwein* right now.

We land in Frankfurt twelve hours later, but through the miracle of time zones, our bodies are pretty sure we've spent a whole day in the air. We're greasy, sore, surly, and jet-lagged. Owen has been awake more than twenty-four hours and he crashes hard on the two-hour bullet-train journey through the beautiful German countryside to Nürnberg. It's just after seven in the morning, and all the impeccable German businessmen lift their elegant eyebrows at the rumpled little gradeschooler with his face pressed against my shoulder hard enough to leave a woolen pattern.

We emerge from the Hauptbahnhof in the Altstadt of Nürnberg, blinking in the gray morning light and stumbling up a cobbled ramp under our mountainous luggage. Rising at our left is a massive stone tower, and beyond this stretches the old city wall, cutting notches against the plaster sky. Fifty yards ahead is a Pizza Hut. There is city chatter all around, but it could be in Klingon for all I can understand it.

We decide to walk to the hotel. My husband is pretty sure he knows the way. Pizza Hut can come and go, but Kaiserstrasse is still Kaiserstrasse even after almost thirty years. We're each carrying a suitcase and a carry-on, Owen too, exhausted and fueled on two hours' bumpy transit sleep as he is.

I brace for a sit-down strike and a litany of whining, but to his credit Owen does neither. His eyes are glassy and he drags his feet, but he rattles his suitcase over the cobbles, uphill, step after tedious step, as we wind through midmorning shoppers and three-piece suits toward Josephsplatz and the Hotel Romantik.

"Just a little longer," we coax Owen as he lags, as the small wheels of his backpack slow their rhythmic cadence. "Just a few more streets. Then you can sleep. Promise."

We find the hotel, a charming five-story brickwork tucked between a bakery and a peep show, overlooking an open space where pigeons gather. The landlady is a graceful woman of middle years wearing a well-cut caramel-colored suit.

"Check-in isn't until three this afternoon," she says with a rolling, deep accent that reminds me of a ship at sea.

Aaaaand my child will be sleeping on your tasteful pink and green lobby carpet until then, right between the radiator and the cigarette machine.

But already the landlady is taking in Owen's vacant eyes and tiny frame slumping beneath the backpack full of plastic spiders, stuffed marine life, watercolor paints, two broken watches, and Legos in a sandwich bag.

"But I think perhaps your room might be ready now," she amends, like she's seen this before.

She sorts through some paperwork, makes a quick call, then hands over the key and winks at me. I want to hug her, but I strongly suspect that the second rule of Germany is not to freak out the locals with excessive American displays of emotion.

We trudge up two sets of sharply curving stairs, hauling and dragging and strong-arming our luggage. We crash, Owen in a fold-out wing chair surrounded by two stuffed fish and a twin-sized mint-green acrylic blanket crammed bulbously into his school backpack. It isn't yet ten in the morning.

Kristkindlesmarkt won't open for another week. The stalls are only beginning to appear in the Marktplatz, red and white striped tents with their fronts covered, while glints of light wink mysteriously between folds of canvas.

Owen glances suspiciously between my husband and me. "This isn't very interesting. Where's Martin Luther? Isn't he supposed to get crowned?"

Even I'm not sure we can find enough to do in a week, but my husband is bluff and confident. "It's better this way. We have a week to explore before all the tourists show up."

"Aren't we tourists?"

My husband considers. "Well . . . maybe a little."

We start with churches. Owen has been to church exactly twice in his life, once at Easter with his Presbyterian grandparents and once at his cousin's Lutheran baptism, where he loudly admired the green shag carpet in the same breath he complained about wearing a suit. He takes in Lorenzkirche wide-eyed, its soaring Gothic arches and reconstructed stained glass, its statuary and frescoes, its cold candlelit grandeur.

"This is *church*?" he breathes.

There's a donation box at the entrance. I drop in a few euro. Owen's eyes bug out. "You have to *pay* to get into church here?" His voice echoes around the stark stone nave, and church ladies lean out of the souvenir bookstall and candle-lighting niches, brows like thunderclouds.

The third rule of Germany: There will be no drawing attention to our English-speaking selves with excessive volume, especially since our German is *sehr schlecht.*

Owen darts cheerfully from painting to fresco, zipping through bored British teenagers annoyed that they must switch off their mobiles in a house of God while forced to absorb culture.

"Why doesn't Baby Jesus wear a diaper?" Stage whisper this time. "Isn't Mary afraid he's going to pee all over her?"

Across the river Pegnitz is Sebalduskirche. More reconstructed stained glass, rows and rows of statuary, walls full of frescoes, and pillars of stone, all dark and cold, candlelit.

"Can we *go* now?" Owen demands, sulking beneath a four-hundred-year-old relic niche and whirling his camera by the strap.

"Why don't you take a picture?" I suggest.

"Because it's *boring.*"

It's no TV in a seatback, that's for sure.

"They used to put bits of dead saints in there," I coax.

"Oh, all right. Just *one.* I don't want to waste my film."

Outside, Owen squints up at Sebalduskirche's mismatched spires and wonders aloud why they're different.

"Well . . . " I hedge, but just for a moment. "Because Americans bombed the heck out of Nürnberg during the war. It was where the Nazis held their rallies. They had to rebuild the whole city, including Sebalduskirche."

Owen glances up again, more speculatively. "We bombed this place?"

"Pretty badly."

"That's why everything says 'reconstructed'?"

"Yep."

He considers. "That's why I can't ask people about Hitler?"

"Yeah. That's why."

Owen digs through his pocket. "I have some euro. Can I go put them in the donating box?"

"I think they'd appreciate that."

Owen comes back 1.87 euro lighter and announces, "I have to go to the bathroom."

"But we're on our way to Albrecht Dürer's house."

"I have to go now."

"C'mon; he made really gory engravings of Hell back in the sixteenth century. Can't you wait till lunch?"

"I really have to go *now*."

Owen and I set off to find a bathroom while my husband detours through the Marktplatz to take some pictures. There's a restroom sign at the Rathaus (town hall) and we duck in gratefully. An amiable black-haired German sits on a stool near a turnstile and a coin slot.

A coin slot. It's a bloody pay toilet.

Owen begins to do the Toilet Dance.

"Crap," I mutter, and I paw through my purse for change while resisting the urge to hum "America the Beautiful" under my breath in honor of the undeniably civilized American tradition of public toilets.

The German guy says something to me and points at the turnstile. I understand German when it's spoken slowly and in words suited to a slow-witted toddler. I shrug at him and smile and keep searching for change while Owen's dancing gets dangerously animated.

"Kinderfry," he says, and holds the turnstile up and points at Owen, then the men's room.

Then it occurs to me. *Kinder frei*. Kids can use the bathroom for free.

"Go ahead," I tell Owen, and he ducks under the upraised turnstile and dashes into the men's room.

Kinder frei. More than civilized. Just when I thought the parents of the average three-year-old would have to take out a second mortgage just to get through a morning in the Aldstadt of Nürnberg.

I *vielen Dank* the Nice German Toilet Warden and wonder fleetingly how one puts such job experience on a résumé.

When Owen comes out of the bathroom, he pulls out his camera and snaps a picture of the coin slot. "I can't wait to tell Mitch that you have to *pay* to use *the toilet!*"

At the national museum, Owen wanders impatiently among original Rembrandts and one-of-a-kind Dürer etchings, putting his nose inches from the priceless works of art and drawing fiery looks from burly uniformed security personnel.

The fourth rule of Germany: Do not, under any circumstances, touch anything at all in the national museum, no matter how bumpy and inviting it looks. Do not even touch the fixtures in the bathroom. We will spray your hands with Lysol back at the hotel. Mama's limited language skills are not up to handling an international incident and we're a long way away from Miranda Rights and habeas corpus.

The national museum redeems itself for Owen with sculptures of saints martyred for the faith in creatively violent ways. By the time we leave, Owen, whose prior religious knowledge consisted of a computer game where cannibals eat missionaries, can identify Saint John the Baptist by the lamb on his book and Saint Sebastian by his torsoful of arrows.

At dinner, we eat the best schnitzel ever at a six-table hole-in-the-wall where the proprietor wins Owen's everlasting devotion with the addition of a tinselly straw in his glass of Mezzo Mix. Across from us is a young German couple trying to eat pasta while their two-year-old squeals and scampers from table to floor to radiator. There is a scatter of books and toys and crayons around an empty booster seat. They have that tired, strung-out look of parents who've chased a baby all day and just need ten minutes to eat food in peace, goddamnit.

Some things don't require translation.

Owen gets up to use the bathroom. It's downstairs, and the toddler tries to follow him down. He grabs her hand and waits at the top of the stairs while her father hurries over and leads her away, addressing Owen in a stream of German so rapid I only catch *danke*. Owen smiles and tromps downstairs.

When Owen gets back upstairs, the toddler is waiting for him by the cigarette machine. She smiles and pushes a button. Owen pauses a moment, looks at her parents, then pushes the same button.

"Twenty," he says, pointing to the number next to it.

She just looks at him.

Owen thinks for a moment, then says, "*Zwanzig.*"

Her face lights up and she points to the button again. He repeats the number in German, then says it again in English.

"Ten-tee," says the toddler.

They go through the numbers one by one. In German, then English. The toddler's parents finish their pasta and drink their wine. Then they sit quietly, one eye on the cultural exchange at the cigarette machine while leaning back in their chairs most peacefully.

As we leave, the toddler stumps over to our table and gives Owen a hug. Her parents look like they're ready to do the same.

It's Saturday night, dark and starless, without any of the sickly orange glow thrown up by American cities of similar size. The Marktplatz is crammed so tight there is literally no room to turn around. We're all facing Frauenkirche, thousands of us from dozens of places worldwide. Our eyes are turned up toward a dark balcony.

We are waiting for the Christ Child.

Children perch on their fathers' shoulders. My husband has heaved and hoisted Owen painfully onto his own shoulders. At eight, Owen will probably never be able to have that view again, and not just because of his weight.

Everyone is smiling. No one is jabbing and elbowing for position. No one is complaining they can't see. People are chatting, but there is nothing of anger in their tone, no annoyance or frustration. Of everything I have experienced here, cold cuts for breakfast and toilet wardens, timely public transit and kids allowed in bars, this cordial gathering of complete strangers in a painfully packed space is the most foreign.

The lights on the Marktplatz abruptly go out. There is a great indrawn breath all around, and then the balcony of Frauenkirche explodes in brilliant white light. A girl appears, all in white with honey-colored hair, standing like a queen on the balcony, holding some kind of wand. She lifts her arms and the crowd explodes with cheers and whistles.

I glance up at Owen, high on his father's shoulders. His eyes catch glints of the Christ Child's blinding klieg-light aura. His little camera is in his hand but forgotten. He will not need a picture to remember this.

It's five hundred years ago. It's right now. Cold burns my ears and all around is the sizzly smell of Nürnberger sausage and crisp evergreens, bright and glittery light, the shuffle of wool and leather. Every soul on this Platz holds their breath while the Christ Child recites something rolling and cadenced, something I don't catch a word of, but I don't need to because it's in the whiff of ginger and the winter-cold stillness drawing us in, taking us back, suspending all the rules.

We've had our *Glühwein*. We've bought ornate hand-blown ornaments and crossed our fingers for their survival en route home. We've descended to a damp chamber where witches were tortured and looked over where a synagogue once stood. We've wandered the house where Albrecht Dürer fretted, etched, and questioned his genius. We've peered down a well that plunges three hundred feet into bedrock and was guarded as a state secret.

Now we're packing up. It's time to go home.

Owen is subdued. His eyes are a little red. Later he'll tell me he wants to keep the ratty sneakers he's wearing forever because they walked on Germany.

He solemnly thanks the hostesses in the breakfast room who always remembered he liked hot chocolate. When we check out, he ducks behind the desk and gives the landlady a hug, which she warmly returns.

Perhaps there are some rules that I have misjudged.

For souvenirs, Owen has a stuffed ladybug, a Garfield book in German, and four rolls of film, which will later prove to be a series of churches with their spires cut off and people severed at the knees with landmarks erupting improbably from their shoulders, the ultimate child's-eye view of Christmas in the Old World.

Maybe he will bring his own children here much like my husband did, and it will still be the same, red and white striped tents, *Glühwein*, and the spectral wonder of the Christ Child. It will be five hundred years ago. It will be right now.

As he rattles his suitcase expertly over the cobbles toward the Hauptbahnhof one last time, Owen takes in the bronze fountain, the cobbles, Weisser Turm sliding its tower-shaped shadow over us and he laughs aloud. "I can't wait to get home. I will tell everyone about our trip!"

Two weeks in the Old World, where kings and emperors once ruled, where we can orient ourselves by the spires of churches and tell time by their bells, where we can navigate the underground transit maze like locals and walk past priceless art on the way to dinner, an old imperial city in all its glory and richness, and he can't wait to bring it alive.

"Yeah. I can't wait to tell Mitch how *weirdly* a German *toilet* flushes!"

About the Contributors

C. Lill Ahrens (cclill@comcast.net) is an editor for *Calyx Journal* and leads writing workshops on the Oregon coast. Award-winning excerpts from her upcoming memoir, *Seoul Survivor* (from which "Shock and Paw" is excerpted), appear in literary journals and anthologies, including *The Risks of Sunbathing Topless* (Seal Press, 2005). A shorter version of her essay also appears in the anthology *More Sand in My Bra* (Travelers Tales, 2007).

Elena Aitken is a freelance writer and the social coordinator for her very busy five-year-old twins. Since the family's first adventure on the high seas, they have returned for a repeat visit and are planning another adventure in 2008. Elena can be reached at www.inkblotcommunications.ca.

J. Anderson Coats has been given the curse of Cromwell on a backroad in Connemara. She has also been a mile underground, dug for crystals, and held Lewis and Clark's original hand-written journal. Her essays have appeared in *off our backs*, *MotherVerse*, and *Mamaphonic: Balancing Motherhood and Other Creative Acts*. She lives near Puget Sound in Washington State.

Melissa Balmain's essays and articles have appeared in *The New Yorker, The New York Times, Details,* and elsewhere. She's currently a contributing editor and humorist for *Parenting* and *Babytalk.* Five years after their California trip with Davey, she and her husband still haven't managed a grownups-only visit. Instead, they returned recently with Davey and his new little sister, Lily—and discovered how smoothly things can go when your ideals no longer reach higher than restaurants that offer crayons and balloons.

Julie Barton lives, writes, and drives in Vermont. She writes a popular blog about infertility, pregnancy, and parenting at www.alittlepregnant.com, which has been featured in newspapers, magazines, and radio programs worldwide, and contributes regularly to *Redbook*'s Infertility Diaries at www.redbookmag.com.

Mary Jane Beaufrand lives in Seattle with her husband (who thankfully is not overmoussed), two kids, and slobbery Saint Bernard. She is the author of *Primavera,* a novel for young adults, published in March 2008 by Little, Brown.

Sally Bjornsen is the author of the nonfiction book *The Single Girl's Guide to Marrying a Man, His Kids, and His Ex-Wife* (Penguin, 2005). When Bjornsen, a marketing veteran, bio mom and stepmother, is not thinking and writing about women and motherhood she is busily marketing commercial photographers to clients and advertising agencies. Bjornsen has a degree in liberal arts from Oregon State University and has completed the writing certificate program at the University of Washington. She writes both nonfiction and fiction pieces and has been published in various business trade journals. Along with writing about stepmotherhood, Bjornsen has also been a stepmother guest-expert on the ABC Radio Network's national radio show "Satellite Sisters."

Born and raised in Grand Rapids, Michigan, **Amy Bustraan** has always been eager to get out of the city and explore nature. As a married twenty-eight-year-old mother of a young child, she says, life in and out of the city is always an adventure. As a youth minister, Amy has introduced the love of the outdoors to many students from her church through camping and canoe trips. This is her first published piece.

Veronica Chater has narrated her stories on Ira Glass's "This American Life," and published in such venues as the *Los Angeles Times Magazine*, the *San Francisco Examiner on Sunday*, the London *Guardian*, and *Herstory: What I Learned in My Bathtub . . . and More True Stories on Life, Love, And Other Inconveniences*. More recently, her unpublished novel, *The Sowers*, was nominated for the 2007 Pushcart Editors' Book Award, and her memoir about her eccentric Catholic family of thirteen, entitled *Waiting for the Apocalypse*, is slated for publication in winter 2008 by W. W. Norton & Company.

Sabra Ciancanelli received her MFA from Goddard College. She is a stay-at-home mom and writer for an inspirational website. Her work has appeared in *Brain, Child, Watchword, Daily Guideposts*, and *Angels on Earth*.

Donna Collins Tinsley is a procrastinating, hormonally challenged stay-at-home mom of four daughters (ages sixteen to forty) who aspires to write while homeschooling one daughter, dealing with stress, and chasing after a three-year-old grandson she has custody of. Her subjects range from handling hormones to healing from sexual abuse, and she just finished writing a book called *Somebody's Daughter*. She has been recently published in several compilations and is working on her first novel, *Daytona Streets*.

Sarah Davies is a graduate of Smith College and Yale Law School. Her checkered professional past includes stints as an Air France flight attendant, a flight instructor, and professional pilot. She currently is engaged in her most challenging career: mom to three little landlubbers who always prefer a Happy Meal to foie gras. Sarah and her family live over a mile high in the White Mountains of Arizona. This is her first published piece.

Ivy Eisenberg, a resident of Westchester, New York, writes and performs humorous essays, poems, songs, and children's picture books. She is at work on *Fat, Forty, and Pregnant Again?*, a collection of humorous writing on the childbearing challenges of aging mothers. She is also writing a memoir, *Adventures in Cooking,* which includes recipes as well as vignettes of some of her infamous cooking disasters. She has been seen on the small stage throughout New York and Connecticut. Ms. Eisenberg won Honorable Mention in HumorPress.com's "America's Funniest Humor" contest in 2007.

Elrena Evans holds an MFA from the Pennsylvania State University and is coeditor of *Mama, PhD: Women Write about Motherhood and Academic Life* (Rutgers, 2008). She writes the monthly column "Me and My House" for *Literary Mama,* and her work has also appeared in various mother-centric literary magazines as well as in the anthology *Twentysomething Essays by Twentysomething Writers* (Random House, 2006). Her website is www. elrenaevans.com. She lives in Pennsylvania with her family, and spends an inordinate amount of time singing.

Anita Feng's previous publications include two books of poetry, *Internal Strategies* and *Sadie & Mendel*. Currently she is completing a novel, a coming-of-age story about a woman who makes musical instruments out of clay, titled *The Fifth Revision of Estonia Divine*. Anita's ocarinas can be found at www.anitasocarinas.com.

Tiffany Fitch was dragged kicking and screaming to small-town Mississippi from Dallas, Texas in 2001. When not chasing her munchkins around exotic locations, she writes about the state she has come to love. Her stories can be heard on Mississippi Public Broadcasting or read on her blog at www.xanga.com/neuroticfitchmom.

Sarah Franklin (sarahefranklin@gmail.com) is a writer, editor, and publishing professional. Her personal essays have appeared in anthologies published by Seal Press (*The Risks of Sunbathing Topless*) and Adams Media (*HerStory*) as well as in the *Seattle Times* and on NPR affiliates. Sarah has also contributed regular features for www.red-tricycle.com, a website/gathering space for clued-in Seattle parents. Aside from writing, Sarah has been working on "the other side" of book publishing for the better part of a decade, in Europe and the U.S. She now lives with her family in Dublin, Ireland (no first-class flights to the U.K., but far less jetlag).

Leesa Gehman has lived in northeastern Pennsylvania her whole life, except for a brief stint in central Pennsylvania. For the moment, she's living vicariously through her friends but she does find the humor in the not-so-vicarious. She lives with her son, Tommy, who isn't batshit insane, a spastic dog named Betsy, and boring cat named Spaz. She's had nonfiction essays published in several parenting magazines and short stories published under a pseudonym.

Donna Gephart has written essays for *Family Circle*, *Parents*, *Fitness*, and other magazines. She and her husband live in South Florida with their two sons, who are now teenagers. Her humorous middle-grade novel, *As if Being 12 ¾ Isn't Bad Enough—My Mother is Running for President!*, is available from Delacorte Press/Random House. Learn more at www.donnagephart.com.

Jennifer Graf Groneberg lives and writes at the end of a twisty gravel road in the mountains of northwest Montana with her husband of fifteen years and their three young children. She recently completed her first book-length work, called *Roadmap to Holland* (NAL/Penguin, 2008), about mothering Avery, a fraternal twin diagnosed with Down syndrome at five days old. You can read more about her and her family at www.jennifergrafgroneberg.com.

Liesl Jobson is a South African musician and writer. Her writing has appeared in *The Southern Review*, *The Mississippi Review*, *Snow*Vigate*, *3:AM*, *elimae*, *Diner*, *Noö Journal*, *LICHEN*, and in South African journals and anthologies. She won the 2005 POWA Women's Writing Poetry Competition and the 2006 Ernst van Heerden Award from the University of the Witwatersrand. Her anthology of short-short fiction, *100 Papers*, will be published by Botsotso in spring 2008.

Cathy Keir is a trapeze artist turned journalist who ran away from the circus to join the BBC. She then spent thirteen years working as a radio and television journalist in Jersey, Guernsey, and Devon, before leaving the BBC to spend more time with her children and to pursue her dreams. She recently completed an MA in Creative Writing at the University of Plymouth, and has almost completed her first novel. She has contributed articles to *The Guardian*, *The*

Stage and Television Today, Junior Magazine, and to the BBC and Bad Mothers Club websites. She has two children who think women can't be prime ministers. She blames herself.

Willow King holds an MA in English from the University of Colorado, Boulder. Her work has been published in *Passionfruit, Rebellion, Square One, Lineas*; a journal of translation, *26* magazine, *Heritage Fashion, Saigon City Life, AsiaLife,* and *DestinAsia*. She currently lives and works in Ho Chi Minh City.

Holly Korbey is an actress and writer. She has appeared in Broadway National Tours, performed her own material, and her writing has appeared on www.McSweeneys.net. Forever a New Yorker at heart, she has recently moved to Dallas, Texas, with her husband and two sons.

Julia Litton is a devoted daughter and daughter-in-law who should cease complaining and just be grateful that people are willing to spend holidays with her at all. She and her husband are now expecting twins and they swear (SWEAR) they will not be attempting any holiday travel with three children—ever. . . . Her writing has appeared in numerous anthologies and she writes a blog about motherhood for *Redbook* magazine at www.redbookmag.com/home/mom-blog/. She also has a personal blog at http://julia.typepad.com/julia.

Jennifer Margulis held a researching/teaching Fulbright fellowship in Niger (not Nigeria) for the 2006–2007 academic year. She's the editor of *Toddler: Real-Life Stories of Those Fickle, Irrational, Urgent, Tiny People We Love* (Seal Press) and the author *of Why Babies Do That: Baffling Baby Behavior Explained*

(Willow Creek Press). Her latest book, *The Baby Bonding Book for Dads* (Willow Creek Press), cowritten with her husband, was published in March 2008. Margulis's work has been published in *The New York Times, Military History Quarterly, Ms. magazine, Parenting, Wondertime, Parents, Mothering Magazine,* the *Christian Science Monitor,* and dozens of other newspapers and magazines. She and her family have traveled extensively in Europe and West Africa.

Katharine D. Morgan graduated with a Bachelor in Arts in journalism from Northern Illinois University. She and her family reside in the Chicago suburb of Batavia, Ilinois. Kathy's essays have appeared in local newspapers as well as in national magazines such as *Country Sampler's Decorating Ideas* and *Birds and Bloom.* She currently enjoys freelance writing and substitute teaching in her neighborhood's elementary school.

Katherine Ozment is a freelance writer working on a memoir and a collection of essays. Her work has been published in *The New York Times, National Geographic, Salon, Child, The San Francisco Chronicle Magazine, Boston, The Chicago Tribune, Literary Mama, Brain, Child,* and elsewhere.

Elizabeth Roca is staff editor for *Brain, Child: The Magazine for Thinking Mothers.* Her essays have appeared in *Brain, Child, Utne, The Washington Post,* and the anthology *Not What I Expected.* She lives with her family in Silver Spring, Maryland.

Madelyn Rosenberg has worked as a journalist for eighteen years, the best of them covering music and features for *The Roanoke Times,* a daily newspaper in southwest Virginia. In 2000, she moved to Boston, Massachusetts, where she earned a master's in creative writing from Boston University. Her nonfiction has appeared in *Parenting, Blugrass Unlimited, eMusic, The Washington Post, The Rough Guides Book of Playlists,* and more. Her fiction has appeared in *LadyBug* (for kids) and *Other Voices* (not for kids). She and her husband now live in Arlington, Virginia, with their two children, both good travelers— though they have their moments.

When **Sarah Shey** is not spearheading search and rescue missions for Little Black Cat and four-propeller airplanes, she is at work on a nonfiction narrative. Shey has written for *The New York Times, Time Out New York Kids, Time Out New York,* the *Forward,* the *Philadelphia Inquirer, This Old House,* the *Des Moines Register,* and *The Iowan,* among others. She wrote two children's books set in Iowa, *Sky All Around* and *Blue Lake Days.*

Gabrielle Smith-Dluha lives, writes, and teaches English in the Czech Republic with her husband and three children. She loves to hike, ride horses, and travel. Her essays have been published in *It's a Girl* (Seal Press, 2006), *The Sun* magazine, and in the Czech university press. She is currently working on several children's books.

Adrienne St. John-Delacroix has been traveling and writing for as long as she can remember. She has published poetry in *Women's Voices* in Sonoma County and other Sonoma County publications, and recently won the 2007 Duncan Frazier Creative Writing Award. She is currently working on a young-adult novel.

Dana Standish is a freelance writer and the associate editor of *Swivel: The Nexus of Women and Wit* (www.swivelmag.com). She has written for *The Seattle Times*, *Bark* magazine, *Metalsmith*, *American Craft*, and many other publications. She spends several hours a day standing at her kitchen sink in Seattle, Washington, watching water pour from the tap and pretending she is atop the highest waterfall in the Andes. In her spare time, she gives thanks that she has no occasion to travel.

Stephanie Sylverne is a compulsive reader, an unorganized writer, an aspiring academic, a hopeless idealist, and mother of two wildly entertaining daughters. She somehow managed to complete a BA in anthropology and a Master of Arts in secondary education. Stephanie was also published in *You Look Too Young To Be a Mom: Teen Mothers Speak Out on Love, Learning, and Success*. She resides in the Chicagoland area with her partner, two daughters, and two crazy cats.

Susan Wolter Nettell was raised on a farm/ranch in North Dakota where she acquired the ability to chase cattle, an appreciation for the tang of diesel fumes in the morning air, and a place in her heart for the resiliency and beauty of the prairie. Since completing degrees in business administration and accountancy, she has resided in large metropolitan areas, a chameleon life that has taught her to talk traffic, earnings-per-share, wheat, or weather with equal fluency. She married a native son of Los Angeles, California, and they have a twelve-year-old daughter and a nine-year-old son. Her short stories have appeared in *Talking Stick*, volumes 15 & 16, a Minnesota literary journal. She currently lives and writes in the Minneapolis/St. Paul area.

Selected Titles from Seal Press

For more than thirty years, Seal Press has published groundbreaking books.

By women. For women. Visit our website at www.sealpress.com.

Check out the Seal Press blog at www.sealpress.com/blog.

The Unsavvy Traveler: Women's Comic Tales of Catastrophe edited by Rosemary Caperton, Anne Mathews, and Lucie Ocenas. $15.95, 1-58005-142-1. Thirty bitingly funny essays respond to the question: "What happens when trips go wrong?"

Solo: On Her Own Adventure edited by Susan Fox Rogers. $15.95, 1-58005-137-5. An inspiring collection of travel narratives that reveal the complexities of women journeying alone.

No Touch Monkey! And Other Travel Lessons Learned Too Late by Ayun Halliday. $14.95, 1-58005-097-2. A self-admittedly bumbling vacationer, Halliday shares—with razor-sharp wit and to hilarious effect—the travel stories most are too self-conscious to tell.

Zaatar Days, Henna Nights: Adventures, Dreams, and Destinations Across the Middle East by Maliha Masood. $15.95, 1-58005-192-8. One woman finds spiritual rejuvenation on a journey from Cairo to Istanbul with countless unforgettable detours in between.

The Risks of Sunbathing Topless: And Other Funny Stories from the Road edited by Kate Chynoweth. $15.95, 1-58005-141-3. From Kandahar to Baja to Moscow, these wry, amusing essays capture the comic essence of bad travel, and the female experience on the road.

Mexico, A Love Story: Women Write about the Mexican Experience edited by Camille Cusumano. $15.95, 1-58005-156-1. In this thrilling and layered collection, two dozen women describe the country they love and why they have fallen under its spell. Also available, *Italy, A Love Story: Women Write about the Italian Experience*, $15.95, 1-58005-143-X; *France, A Love Story: Women Write about the French Experience*, $15.95, 1-58005-115-4; and *Greece, A Love Story: Women Write about the Greek Experience*, $15.95, 1-58005-197-9.